Clothes Make the Man

THE NEW MIDDLE AGES
VOLUME I
GARLAND REFERENCE LIBRARY OF THE HUMANITIES
VOLUME 1991

THE NEW MIDDLE AGES

BONNIE WHEELER
Series Editor

The New Middle Ages presents transdisciplinary studies of medieval cultures, with particular emphasis on women's history and feminist and gender analyses. The series includes both scholarly monographs and essay collections.

Clothes Make the Man: Female Cross Dressing in Medieval Europe
by Valerie R. Hotchkiss

Medieval Mothering
edited by John Carmi Parsons and Bonnie Wheeler

Fresh Verdicts on Joan of Arc
edited by Bonnie Wheeler and Charles T. Wood

Clothes Make the Man
Female Cross Dressing
in Medieval Europe

VALERIE R. HOTCHKISS

GARLAND PUBLISHING, INC.
NEW YORK AND LONDON
1996

Library of Congress Cataloging-in-Publication Data

Hotchkiss, Valerie R., 1960–
    Clothes make the man : female cross dressing in medieval Europe /
by Valerie R. Hotchkiss.
        p.   cm. — (Garland reference library of the humanities : vol.
1991. The new Middle Ages ; vol. 1)
    Includes bibliographical references and index.
    ISBN 0-8153-2369-7 (alk. paper)
    1. Transvestism—Europe—History—Sources. 2. Costume—History—
Medieval, 500–1500. 3. Women—Europe—History. 4. Men's clothing—
Europe—Psychological aspects. 5. Costume—Europe—Religious aspects.
6. Costume—Europe—Symbolic aspects. 7. Christianity and culture—
Europe. 8. Civilization, Medieval.   I. Title.   II. Series: Garland reference
library of the humanities ; vol. 1991.   III. Series: Garland reference library
of the humanities. New Middle Ages ; vol. 1.
HQ77.H67   1996
305.3—dc20   95-48380
                                                              CIP

Cover Illustration: St. Eugenia baring her breasts to reveal her sex. Detail from a
thirteenth-century antependium by the Master of Soriguerda. Reproduced with
permission from the Musée des Arts Décoratifs, Paris.

Printed on acid-free, 250-year-life paper
Manufactured in the United States of America

For

David Price

CONTENTS

SERIES EDITOR'S FOREWORD

The New Middle Ages is a series dedicated to transdisciplinary studies of medieval cultures, with particular emphasis on women's history and feminist and gender analyses. It includes both scholarly monographs and essay collections. *Clothes Make the Man: Female Cross Dressing in Medieval Europe* inaugurates the series.

In this absorbing study of literary and historical female transvestism, Valerie Hotchkiss details some causes, costs, and consequences of gender inversion in the Middle Ages. Here "woman" is the subject of *disputatio*. Gender is the disputed text. Hotchkiss situates some medieval understandings and perplexities about gender through analyses of specific women and their particular moments in medieval culture. As Hotchkiss argues, women who cross dress both challenge and re-inscribe one traditional view of the feminine as a shattered speculum of the masculine. By donning male garb, these fictional and historical women experience for themselves a new form of expressiveness—a "manly spirit"—and new (often heroic) possibilities of self-realization. This study is thus an important contribution to our knowledge of the Middle Ages and to our understanding of gaps in the sex and gender codes of western culture.

Bonnie Wheeler
Southern Methodist University

ACKNOWLEDGMENTS

I am indebted to several colleagues for their generous assistance and support. Ingeborg Glier and Fred Robinson of Yale University encouraged me with their enthusiasm for this project and for medieval studies in general. To Jaroslav Pelikan I owe a special note of thanks and the promise: was ich ererbt habe, versuche ich zu erwerben, um es zu besitzen!

Although there are many more reasons to thank her, I express my gratitude to Bonnie Wheeler of Southern Methodist University in this case for including my monograph in *The New Middle Ages* series. One could not wish for a more gracious and inspiring editor. I also thank Gary Kuris of Garland Publishing for his expert copyediting and his support of this project and David Lawrence for his assistance with technical matters.

Finally, I owe an enormous debt of gratitude to David Price, who read this study at every stage of its development. I dedicate this work to him because without his encouragement, I might never have known the pleasure of studying medieval literature.

Clothes Make the Man

Chapter One

INTRODUCTION

> A woman shall not wear anything that pertains to a man, nor shall a
> man put on a woman's garment; for whoever does these things is an
> abomination to the Lord your God.
> —Deuteronomy 22:5

Recent studies of women in the Middle Ages privilege the
anomalous over the ordinary. Hrotsvitha von Gandersheim,
Hildegard von Bingen, Christine de Pizan, and other extraordinary
figures have stirred the interest of twentieth-century scholars and
students because they transcended societal biases against women to
succeed and even achieve renown in a male-dominated culture. The
subjects of this study, women who dressed as men, are also anomalies,
although usually fictional ones. One could argue that the portrayal
of disguised women contradicts a gender-based view of female
inferiority more dramatically than do the intellectual accomplishments
of women in the male world of letters. In both instances, however,
these unusual women accede in some way to male hegemony or
social constructs of gender. Whereas female authors often emphasize
femininity by adopting an apologetic stance, the female transvestites,
both in literature and as documented historical cases, conform to
androcentric models by assimilating maleness. To the medieval mind,
it seems, man was indeed the measure of all things: women's activities
in male spheres were invariably judged against the standard of the
male. It follows—although not without inherent paradoxes—that
the transvestite heroine finds enthusiastic approbation when she
performs as a man.

A study of the female transvestite in medieval literature and history
is a study of aberrations, but not a recondite endeavor. In the Middle
Ages, female cross dressing was a common literary device and a
significant, although rarely recorded, historical phenomenon. Female
transvestism occurs so frequently in medieval texts that feminine

stereotypes, women's roles in literature, and the perception of women in the Middle Ages warrant reexamination in light of it. The historical Jeanne d'Arc and the legendary Pope Joan have received their share of attention as exceptional women, but the distinction of male dress links them to such less well known figures as Hildegund von Schönau, who lived among men as a monk, and to scores of literary and hagiographic heroines who cross dress for reasons ranging from escape from sexual abuse to desire for worldly adventure. As alternative paradigms of female heroism, disguised women combine traditional feminine virtues with stereotypical male qualities of daring, strength, and perseverance. Paradoxically, the empowering force of male disguise reveals the limitations in medieval inscriptions of female identity since success—which is often attributed to the "manly spirit" of the heroine[1]—is contingent upon suppression of femaleness.

The general phenomenon of transvestism is the subject of numerous psychological, historical, and literary studies. In the early twentieth century, Magnus Hirschfeld coined the word "transvestite" in his study *Die Transvestiten*, which focused on cross dressing as a sexual variation or "erotischer Verkleidungstrieb," not always related to sexual orientation.[2] Havelock Ellis studied transvestism as a psychosexual phenomenon: reporting scores of case histories of male and female transvestites, he suggested that transvestism arises from extreme admiration of the other sex.[3] The term "transvestism" has been used primarily as a clinical designation for the desire to dress like the opposite sex—but, above all, for men who dress as women. Because of its origins, orientation, and use in the field of psychology, "transvestite" generally connotes something more than gender disguise. Nonetheless, the term has gained acceptance in discussions of literary cross dressing and female disguise. The verb "transvest," has long existed in English, meaning "to clothe in other garments," particularly in the garments of the opposite sex in order to disguise oneself. It is in this broad sense of the word, without the connotations of sexual desire, in most instances, that I use "transvestite" and "transvestism" in this study, although I also use the related terms "gender inversion," "cross dressing," and "disguise."

Given the clinical nature of early research on cross dressing, it is not surprising that the case-study approach also provides the model for more recent studies of cross dressing as a social phenomenon. It is interesting to note, however, that the female transvestite has garnered more attention in historical studies, which tend to glorify female cross dressing as a reaction against male dominance. Male transvestism remains largely in the domain of psychology and social anthropology, where it is still studied as a cultural or psychological variant. Several historians have studied female transvestism by investigating the lives of women disguised as soldiers and sailors in modern history. Rudolf Dekker and Lotte van de Pol have collected and analyzed one hundred nineteen cases of disguised women in northern Europe from the seventeenth through the nineteenth century.[4] They offer two basic explanations for historical female transvestism, arguing "that the pressures which led to the decision of cross dressing could be both material, such as poverty, or emotional, such as patriotic fervour or love for another woman, or a combination of these."[5] Working in the same period and with some of the same personalities, Julie Wheelwright describes the exploits of numerous "amazons" (women who served in military campaigns with or without the cover of male disguise), presenting them as models of female emancipation.[6] Perhaps because medieval records are far rarer and less reliable as evidence, both studies ignore cases of cross dressing in the Middle Ages. Dekker and van de Pol make the unlikely claim that the phenomenon actually begins in the latter part of the sixteenth century and is generally restricted to the Netherlands and England.[7]

In a popular cultural study of transvestism, Marjorie Garber modifies the case-study model, offering an anecdotal survey of the transvestite in western society from Shakespeare to the rock star Madonna.[8] Broadening the scope to include not only literature and history but also film, television, and cultural iconography, she focuses on the power—both political and sexual—inherent in clothing and champions the transvestite as one who disrupts societal norms. This disruption, although it can have different meanings for the groups and individuals practicing cross dressing, confronts, questions, and ultimately enhances culture. Although Garber summarizes the lives of some transvestite saints and mentions the cases of Pope Joan and Jeanne d'Arc in passing, her book is a study of transvestism in modern western culture from the Renaissance to high modernism.

As Garber observed, there is no lack of literary and cultural studies of the post-1500 transvestite.[9] I would add only that the female cross dresser has received the larger share of attention in these studies as well. One might attribute the preference in literary studies for female cross dressing to the overwhelming interest in women's studies over the past fifteen years but it is actually more a function of the predominance of this type of gender inversion than the result of a scholarly bias. In growing numbers, critics have turned their attention to disguised women in Renaissance, baroque, and modern literature, developing feminist, historical, and sociological approaches to a variety of post-medieval texts. Elizabethan and Spanish Golden Age drama has long offered a wealth of material for such studies.[10] Although these studies rarely look to medieval antecedents as anything more than sources or analogues, their interpretative approaches have broken ground for this treatment of earlier disguise literature. Work on cross dressing in later literature covers a variety of topics: Phyllis Rackin's article on the female page in Elizabethan drama examines the androgynous nature of the character;[11] David Price argues that the "manly" woman in sixteenth-century German drama, although a symbol of the inverted world, actually reinforces a strict gender hierarchy;[12] Kristina Straub studies cross-dressed actresses of the eighteenth century as "castrated" figures who challenge male sexuality;[13] Susan Gubar writes about "modern" women, such as Willa Cather, Radclyffe Hall, and Frida Kahlo, who dressed in a masculine style or created transvestite characters;[14] and Estelle Jelinek's study of the autobiographies of female sailors and soldiers in eighteenth- and nineteenth-century England offers some insight into the difficulties of concealing sex from the disguised woman's point of view.[15]

Medieval gender inversion remains a less cultivated field of investigation. There has been some work on individual aspects of cross dressing in the Middle Ages, such as the motives of the men who wrote the lives of transvestite saints,[16] ambiguous language in medieval romances of gender inversion,[17] and the influence of medieval literary cross dressing on modern society's attitudes toward male and female transvestism.[18] Although gender issues have become a primary theme of medieval scholarship,[19] the general phenomenon of medieval women in male disguise has not been studied in detail. This arises not from a lack of examples but rather from the slight attention the texts in which they appear have received. Most of these sources are not represented among the "canonical" texts of medieval studies. Few of the Latin hagiographic texts have been translated, and many are edited only in the massive *Acta Sanctorum*. Likewise, most of the Old French and Middle High German texts have not appeared in modern translations—a fate that unfortunately often consigns a text to the status of literary arcanum. Some of the works, it might be argued, seem to be of secondary importance when compared with the better-known texts of the Middle Ages, but it also appears that the inability to categorize many of these works within traditional frameworks, such as Arthurian romance, heroic epic, or religious literature, has left them without a context, making it more difficult to incorporate them into conventional studies.

This book covers a wide variety of female cross dressing from historical, pseudo-historical, hagiographic, and literary sources.[20] The broad scope documents the medieval fascination with the transvestite, whose ambiguous position provided a basis for constructing, challenging, and reconstructing gender identities. The hagiographic texts, including the accounts of Hildegund von Schönau (which almost certainly have some historical basis) illustrate the problem of differentiating between historical and literary as discrete forms of discourse. Although demonstrably fictionalized, they clearly commanded the same authority as historical texts or, even more prestigiously, the status of authentic texts of salvation. Conversely, Jeanne d'Arc's life, one of the best documented in the Middle Ages, attracted to it a massive body of literary works that cannot be overlooked when assessing how her contemporaries constructed female identity.

In my approach, I follow some of the concerns of new historicism: focusing on issues of authority; recognizing shifting boundaries within hierarchies; and incorporating different types of discourse into the discussion, with the understanding that all cultural expressions—literature, history, art, theology—influence the construction of social conventions. In some cases, however, I tend to invert (fittingly perhaps) the common model of reading the historical in literary texts, often interpreting the constructed qualities of historical texts instead. Authentic documents, such as historical or juridical texts, and overtly fictional texts certainly differ in that audiences were presumed to accept the veracity of the one and the fictionality of the other, yet both groups engage in the same general debate on what to make of the woman who enters the male world. It is not my intention—indeed, it would be impossible—to record a history of cross dressing in the societies of the Middle Ages. Rather,

I will show how medieval documents, both literary and historical, record interpretations of sartorial attempts to overcome gender hierarchy and also illustrate, mainly through the device of inversion, a remarkably sustained desire to examine and reexamine the nature of social gender identities.

To some extent, recent critical approaches to gender and gender inversion in post-1500 western society have established the methods and context for discussing sexual identity. Essentialist and constructivist views of gender have not only become a matter of debate per se but have also colored feminist criticism for some time.[21] Literary portrayals of the woman as "Other" reflect essentialist concepts when they present women as outsiders or archetypes defined by gender. The view that society constructs and determines gender behavior and even sexual distinctions, however, has gained the upper hand in more recent criticism, particularly historical and sociological studies but also in literary studies that recognize such mythic figures as the muse or temptress as significant only in relation to male experience. Thomas Laqueur, in his book on sex and gender, correctly observed that this tension between nature and culture or "'biological sex' and the endless social and political markers of difference" permeates feminist scholarship.[22] Women become the focus of gender studies, because "woman alone seems to have 'gender' since the category itself is defined as that aspect of social relations based on difference between the sexes in which the standard has always been man."[23]

Because defining "gender" has become a topos of recent critical writing and political discourse, I should note that in this study the term is used to describe the societal perceptions and expectations for behavior, familial roles, physical and mental abilities, and even sexual orientation that distinguish, and divide, men and women. To what extent these differences are considered a natural consequence of biological sex or a response to cultural influences is a recurring question within the texts of gender disguise and in my analysis of them.

In the diversity of medieval thought, one finds traditional assumptions about inherent differences between men and women as well as assertions that gender behavior arises from cultural training. Questions of gender identity, cultural inscription, and essentialism— topics that ring quite modern—inform most medieval texts about cross dressing. In Heldris de Cornuälle's *Roman de Silence*, for example, Nature and Nurture debate the origin and formation of sexual identity and cultural roles. Medieval accounts of women in men's clothing rarely fail to address the problem of true and perceived sex/gender, often coming to the conclusion that a woman's sex does not necessarily determine her societal function. This is a radical departure from the common conception of medieval views on male and female as separate and unequal. Notions of male and female difference do inform most of these texts, but portrayals of protagonists who do not conform to the idea of sex as a determining factor in behavior, preferences, and abilities force authors to reconsider the nature of gender difference. This book aims to show that the boundaries between genders blurred long before the "modern" era, if, in fact, they were ever clear.

Whether as a consequence of nature or domination by one sex over the other, there is no doubt that biological distinctions, cultural training, and socially determined roles have separated and categorized men and women in a system that generally values men more highly. Medieval sources that vitiate women are not hard to find. What then can account for the apparent belief in the superiority of most of these women who passed as men? The necessity for them to cross dress points to superficial societal biases, but the popularity of the type betrays a desire to acknowledge or create female heroism. Even in texts that communicate a view of behavior as biologically determined, authors and narrators tend to marvel at women who successfully cross over into male roles since it should be against their very nature to participate in "male" activities. In many cases, as I hope to show, it is precisely the inbred notion of a hierarchy of the sexes that gives rise to a positive view of female transvestism.

Because of the social implications of gender inversion, interpretation often remains ambiguous. Does the empowerment of the woman in disguise empower women in general or is there a residual uneasiness with the phenomenon? Is female cross dressing a liberating and revolutionary act or a repressive and ultimately confirming validation of presupposed gender identity? How is inversion used to define female identities, both sexually and socially? Moreover, what effect do genres, cultural metaphors, and society have on these questions? Recent research on perception of inversion, political or literary, suggests a profound ambiguity in the meaning of the device. Whereas Michel Foucault, like Mikhail Bakhtin before him, and Julia Kristeva after him, considers transgression a liberating act of social or political protest,[24] other cultural critics, most important, Peter Stallybrass and Allon White, recognize the darker side of the "poetics" of transgression that often inverts in order to reaffirm societal and political norms.[25] In some cases, transvestism confirms traditional order; in others, it genuinely overturns order; in yet others, it remains an ambiguous trope. To arrive at an assessment of the "woman's place" in these literary and historical accounts, it is necessary to investigate the rhetoric and structure of inversion, the cultural context, and the degree of auctorial ambiguity and ambivalence toward gender transgression. I will examine the reversal of hierarchies and conventions inherent in inversion, assessing its effect on male authority within cultural narratives and in the context of their implicit audiences.

Disguise has flourished in the literature and folklore of almost every nationality at least since Jacob purloined Esau's inheritance and Achilles attempted to elude his fate at Troy.[26] Identity is concealed for different reasons, although in general the goal is participation in activities from which the disguised individual would otherwise be excluded. This desire to circumvent societal barriers motivates subterfuges that obscure class, education, trade, or—in the cases of the women discussed in this work—physiological gender. Gender inversion is perhaps the most radical form of disguise because it contravenes not only societal rules but also biological fact.

Women in male dress appear with greater frequency in medieval literature but there are some instances of male cross dressing, especially in comic or lewd situations. Such characters sometimes suffer the brunt of cruel tricks, as in Hans Rosenplüt's *Knecht im Garten* (fifteenth century), in which a husband dresses in his wife's clothing, ostensibly to defend her from an annoying suitor, while she enjoys an undisturbed tryst with her lover.[27] According to medieval legend, St. Jerome also was tricked into wearing women's clothing. In an effort to sully his reputation, Jerome's enemies left a woman's dress by his bedside and he inadvertently put it on as he hurried to early mass.[28] In other cases, men cross dress to fulfill masculine desires, as in Guillaume de Blois's *Alda* (twelfth century), where a man uses disguise to infiltrate a restricted area to seduce a woman.[29] In his *Frauendienst* (1255), Ulrich von Liechtenstein claims that he dressed as a woman (the goddess Venus, no less!) and enjoyed a series of adventures, including the organization of an elaborate love tournament and participation in private gatherings of women.[30] More common for male characters, however, is disguise within gender, such as the knight who disguises himself as a pilgrim to enter a hostile court or a king who goes out among his people dressed as a beggar.[31]

As Vern Bullough noted in a ground-breaking article on medieval transvestism, gender disguise diminishes the liberating effect of impersonation for men since femininity constricts freedom and lowers social status.[32] On the other hand, male disguise frees women from the constraints of their sex. Perhaps for this reason, women posing as men appear more often than transvestite males in medieval literature and history.

According to most accounts of medieval cross dressers, the practical difficulties of passing for the opposite sex rarely pose a problem. For literary characters, undetected disguise is part of the illusion of fiction. Moreover, in courtly romance, as I will argue, ideals of youth and beauty often transcend sex, ascribing the same physical attributes to young men and women. Even in historical cases, however, deception seems to have been made possible in most cases by the youth of the women. Since in the Middle Ages boys began their careers as apprentices, novices, servants, or squires at a relatively young age, a woman's beardlessness and slight build might have gone unnoticed, at least for a few years.

The popularity of the motif in religious and secular literature cannot be studied in isolation. Discrepancies between representation of disguise and social convention concerning transvestism soon become apparent. The passage from Deuteronomy quoted above in the epigraph clearly forbids all forms of cross dressing—a prohibition later repeated by the church in the canons of the Council of Gangra (ca. 341), the decrees of Burchard of Worms (†1025/26), and the influential *Decretum* of Gratian (twelfth century), to cite only a few sources.[33] In medieval and early-modern Europe, city ordinances about clothing sometimes mention male guise specifically, as in the *Kleiderordnungen* of Speyer (1356) and Strasbourg (1493) in which women are forbidden to wear men's clothing.[34] The evidence of official decrees against female cross dressing implies that women actually wore men's clothing or even attempted to pass as men with some frequency. That such behavior was condemned by medieval ecclesiastical and secular law is not surprising, since such conduct would have been considered a subversion of normal social order. The ambiguity arises when, from a historical perspective or in literary treatments, authors praise disguised women as exemplary characters. The reason for this apparent contradiction may lie not only in the perceived heroism of the women's extraordinary deeds but also, strangely enough, in the status accorded women by the medieval church and society. Women who aspired to be like men were distancing themselves from womankind. It could be argued, therefore, that by imitating men they were simply trying to improve themselves.

An ambivalence toward female cross dressing marks medieval literature in general. The stories of disguised women draw attention to the strict gender codes, yet the positive image of the transvestite presupposes a tolerant view of the transgression—at least from a distance. This humane tone was lost in the sixteenth and seventeenth centuries, when the struggle for the "pants" on the German stage became a forum for advocating repressive gender codes and the "Hic Mulier/Haec Vir" (1620) controversy raged in England.[35]

In general, historical and fictional depictions of women who cross dressed substantiate the conventional understanding of women's place in medieval society. Descriptions of the protagonists' situations before and after disguise depict a strict gender hierarchy in which women are governed by men. The illusion of maleness, however, often calls into question suppositions about gender differences. Whether historical or fictional, women in male dress are noteworthy precisely because they are unlike other women; their freedom to participate in a variety of activities contrasts with the constraints on the lives of ordinary women and offers a variety of models that challenge previous understandings of medieval definitions of gender.

Chapter Two

"FEMALE MEN OF GOD":
CROSS DRESSING IN
MEDIEVAL HAGIOGRAPHY

> Dâ diu sêle her nider sleht, dâ heizet si
> vrouwe; aber dâ man got in im selber
> bekennet und got dâ heime suochet, dâ ist si
> der man.
>
> [When the soul is downcast, then it is called
> woman; but when one recognizes God in
> oneself and seeks out God there, then it (the
> soul) is a man.]
> —Meister Eckhart[1]

O dd as it may appear initially, many female saints manifested
or attained their holiness through cross dressing. Dressed as
men, holy women lived as hermits or monks, undetected in most
cases until death. Although relatively neglected today, these saints
were so popular in the Middle Ages that it is almost impossible to
assemble all of the many versions of their lives. In these legends, the
church was not promulgating a doctrine of transvestism, human
sexuality, or, for that matter, women's rights. Cross dressing itself is
rarely an issue. Nonetheless, these unusual manifestations of
Christian culture reveal elements of the church's teaching on gender
roles and sexuality, as well as the remarkable influence of gender
imagery on Christian legend. With few exceptions, the transvestite
saint, by inverting signs of gender, illustrates problematic views on
the inferiority of women as well as anxiety about female sexuality.

As protagonists in over thirty legends, holy transvestites comprise
an unusual group in hagiographic literature.[2] Unlike other saints,
few of them suffered martyrdom and most are credited only with
posthumous miracles. In almost every case, recognition of holiness
is earned primarily through the denial of womanhood. It is as if, to

the authors of these lives, a woman's willingness to repress femininity bespeaks a lofty advocation, one which indicates sanctity.[3]

Legends of transvestite saints exist in numerous texts and variants. (Brief accounts of their lives appear in the *Hagiographic Appendix*.) Most of the early versions are set in the eastern Mediterranean, particularly in the cities of Alexandria, Constantinople, and Antioch. It appears that this hagiographic type flourished in Greek monastic communities from the fourth through the sixth century. Of the thirty-four disguised holy women I have found, twenty-four have probable Greek origins.[4] Several studies have tried to determine the archetype for the transvestite saint's legend. Following the view that early Christians adopted many pagan rites and metamorphosed deities into saints, Hermann Usener posits that Pelagia, a repentant courtesan, is the original transvestite saint and represents a relic of the hermaphroditic Aphrodite of Cyprus, a goddess whose worship entailed cross dressing.[5] Ludwig Radermacher disputes this thesis, arguing that an earlier text, the Thecla legend, harks back to literary themes of Hellenistic novels.[6] More recently, Evelyne Patlagean has anchored the transvestite motif in the Gnostic doctrine of salvation, which, she claims, offers evidence for viewing these female monks as androgynous ideals that represent the reconciliation of disparate forces (that is, male and female) necessary for salvation.[7] Subsequent studies have left the etiological question unresolved, as it must remain.[8]

Most of the Greek lives involving gender disguise were translated into Latin in the early Middle Ages and enjoyed wide circulation in calendars, legendaries, and collections of moral tales.[9] Several are included in the so-called *Vitae Patrum* (*Vitae maiores sanctorum virorum et mulierum*), a collection of twenty-eight Latin translations, most of which date from before 500.[10] Among the earliest western writers to mention transvestite saints are Bede (ca. 673-735), Hrabanus Maurus (ca. 780-856), Ado (†875), Notker Balbulus (†912), and Flodard (†966).[11] Even earlier, Aldhelm (ca. 640-709) had praised two transvestite saints, Eugenia and Thecla, in his *De laudibus virginitatis*.[12] Although no single medieval collection contains the lives of all the disguised saints, many occur in such popular works as Vincent de Beauvais's *Speculum historiale*, (1264), Jacobus de Voragine's *Legenda aurea* (1267), and Petrus de Natalibus's *Catalogus sanctorum* (ca. 1370-1400).[13]

Transvestite saints were also popular in vernacular hagiography. The first vernacular accounts of them are found in the *Old English Martyrology* (ninth century) and Aelfric's *Lives of the Saints* (ca. 1000).[14] In the thirteenth through fifteenth centuries, translations of legendaries containing accounts of disguised saints circulated throughout Europe. Stories of Euphrosyne, Marina, and Pelagia occur in French, German, Low German, and Italian versions, in both poetic and prose renditions.[15] The numerous translations and adaptations of Voragine's *Legenda aurea*, which includes the lives of Eugenia, Margareta, Marina, Natalia, Pelagia, Thecla, and Theodora of Alexandria, firmly established the disguised saint in western hagiography.[16]

Hagiography is not easily classified; most medieval readers perceived saints' lives as authentic "historical" sources, yet the literary tendencies and repetition of motifs and themes betray a certain amount of fictionalization, particularly in the earlier lives. The elements of flight, disguise, calumny, and dramatic anagnorisis give the lives of these saints a highly literary quality. They often read more like romantic novels than holy legends. Radermacher and, more recently, Zoja Pavlovskis have compared the stories of Thecla and Pelagia with Greek romances, finding parallel themes in the romances of Longus, Xenophon, Achilles Tatius, and Heliodorus.[17] In the Middle Ages, the literariness of the lives was recognized by Christine de Pizan (1364-1430) and Jacopo Filippo da Bergamo Foresti (1434-1520), who included several disguised saints in their tales of illustrious women.[18] Christine de Pizan stressed the constancy of Marina, Euphrosyne, and Natalia in order to support her contention that women not only are equal to men but even surpass them in virtuousness and strength of character.[19]

Medieval Europe had its own indigenous transvestite saints: a small group of historical women who, perhaps influenced by the lives of the female monks, concealed their sex and entered male communities. Hildegund von Schönau (†1188) lived most of her life as a man; she traveled abroad, served as a papal messenger, and even entered a monastery as a monk (see Chapter 3). Angela of Bohemia, the sister of Premysl Ottokar I (1198-1230) was said to have escaped from her bridal chamber by disguising herself as a man. She traveled in this guise until she arrived in Jerusalem where she became a nun. Other women, such as Christina of Markyate (ca. 1096-1160) and Juana de la Cruz (1481-1534), dressed as men in order to flee enforced marriages and later led holy lives as women. Agnes of Monçada was inspired by Vincent Ferrer (†1419) to dedicate herself to the contemplative life and did so by disguising herself as a man and living as a hermit. Even Catharine of Siena (1347-1380) considered following the path of the transvestite saints until, according to her own account, Christ informed her that a woman could praise God as well as a man.[20]

Catherine of Siena's affirmation of femaleness may reflect the more positive view of women in an era when Mary was venerated and women were developing their own relations with the mystical divine. But during the first several centuries of Christianity, masculine religious imagery predominated. Caroline Walker Bynum notes that cross dressing reveals men's concept of female spirituality and that "women's basic images of religious self were *not* inverted images, not male images."[21] Although formulated rather categorically (especially considering the important example of Perpetua, who writes that she dreamed that she was metamorphosed into a man, indicating that male imagery could affect women's perceptions of themselves as Christians),[22] Bynum's argument counters the tendency in some recent scholarship to perceive female monks as women who adopted, and adapted to, male ideals. Since, in the majority of cases of disguised saints, we are dealing with the creations of male writers, not the lives of actual women, any analysis of the women's motives and attitudes lacks grounding. It is precisely in their function as religious symbols, however, that disguised women in early Christian hagiographic literature deserve more attention. Anson considered the motives of the male monks, positing that the depiction of a female monk expresses the "secret longing for a woman in a monastery" and serves as a convenient scapegoat that embodies and, at the same time, purifies the sexual temptations of monks.[23] This psychoanalytical approach is speculative at best. As the personification of male perceptions of Christian heroism, however, the transvestite saints reveal much about gender definitions and cultural biases based on gender and also disclose, in some cases, male sympathies for women and the social restraints placed on them.

It is not an overstatement to assert that, for early believers, to be Christian was to be male or malelike. The *Gospel of Thomas* (ca. 140) quotes Christ as saying, "Every woman who makes herself male will enter the kingdom of heaven."[24] Later, Augustine (354-430) praises Perpetua's dream of sex inversion as a sign of her "manly spirit" and describes his mother as one who wore the clothes of a woman but had a "virile faith."[25] Ambrose (333-397) emphatically claims that the woman who serves Christ above all becomes like a man ("vir"):

Quae non credit mulier est et adhuc corporei sexus appellatione signatur; nam quae credit occurrit in virum perfectum.[26]

[She who does not believe is a woman and should be called by the name of her corporeal sex; but she who believes comes closer to the perfect male.]

Evidence for the identification of devout women with men can be found in the writings of numerous other early Christian writers.[27] Basil of Caesarea (†379) addresses his work on asceticism to women as well as men, because, he says, many women become equal to, or better than, men through religious zeal.[28] Using similar language, Palladius (†ca. 430), the author of the *Historia Lausiaca*, says he will celebrate women who are more like men than the name implies because of their devotion to Christ; elsewhere, he praises saintly women for their male strength as athletes and calls them "female men of God."[29] In the roughly contemporaneous *Apophthegmata Patrum*, a female hermit named Sarah is said to have claimed spiritual superiority in a double image of inversion when she told some brothers: "It is I who am a man, you who are women."[30] Use of male descriptors as the ultimate praise of women is not unique to the early Christians—Horace, for example, refers to "mascula Sappho,"[31] and the notion of women as defective males goes back to Hippocrates and Aristotle[32]—but the tendency becomes more pronounced among the church "fathers" than at any other period.

Evidence for the view that the consummate Christian is male can be found in metaphors for faith within the scriptures of Christianity. Ephesians 6:10-17 describes virtues in terms of battle gear: truth girds the loins of the true Christian; his breastplate is righteousness; his boots are the gospel of peace; his shield is his faith; and his helmet is salvation.[33] The newly confirmed Christian is frequently called a soldier of Christ, and the combat motif is prevalent in early writings on the Christian ideal. Martial imagery also pervades the *vitae* of many female saints who do not cross dress, as in the battle between St. Margaret and the dragon, and there are countless references to martyrdoms of women as athletic contests or battles.

The elevation of the male is not surprising, since, according to most medieval theologians, women were not created equal to men, the preferred version of human creation being Genesis 2:21-23, where Eve is made from Adam's rib. Because they were not made "in imagine Dei," women were usually considered inferior by nature, a point illustrated, it was said, by Eve's fatal mistake.[34] The defeminization of holy women is a natural consequence of the widely held view of woman as an afterthought of the creator and the cause of humankind's expulsion from paradise.

Even the simplest, one might say most primitive, narratives of disguised saints emphasize the "natural" inferiority of women. In nearly identical stories, Antonina and Theodora receive a sexual punishment for flouting cultural norms: both must become prostitutes in a brothel for their unwillingness to sacrifice to the gods. Their guards, Alexander and Didymus, take pity on their prisoners and allow them to escape by exchanging clothes.[35] In both legends, the deception is discovered and the characters suffer martyrdom. Symbolically, these women overcome their sexual vulnerability and, by extension, frailty only through male impersonation. The legend of Theodora and Didymus further emphasizes the sexual subordination of women. In what is supposed to be a humorous scene, a surprised customer supposes that Didymus is a metamorphosed Theodora. This, quite illogically but most tellingly, inspires a dreadful fear that he might be turned into a woman:

> ... quidam ingressus est ex istis, et invenit pro virgine virum; et stupefactus intrare, dixit, "Putas et virgines in viros demutat Jesus? [...] Audiebam quoniam demutavit aquam in vinum, et fabulam existimabam id quod facilius erat: nunc autem quod majus est video, quoniam in virum demutavit virginem, et timeo ne me demutet in mulierem.[36]

> [One of them entered from among the customers and he found a man in the place of the virgin. Stupefied, he said, "Do you think Jesus changes virgins into men? I have heard that he changed water into wine and I considered this, which is easier, a fable: now, however,

I see something greater, since he has changed a virgin into a man,
and I fear lest he should change me into a woman."]

From the earliest Christian writers to Meister Eckhart's statement
quoted at the beginning of this chapter, numerous sources could be
cited to support the contention that male metaphors and the concept
of the "animus virilis" (manly spirit) signified virtue and spiritual
development for both sexes.[37] While not stripped of gendered
meaning, maleness became a moral quality as well as a biological
fact. (This is obvious not only in the examples cited above but also
in the language itself, as in the related etymologies of "virtus,"
"virtuosus," and "vir" and the positive sense of "virilis" as an adjective
connoting strength.) This is not to say that early Christian authorities
encouraged cross dressing. On the contrary, Jerome (†419/20), who
specifically uses the word "vir" to describe the Christian ideal for
women in his commentary on Ephesians,[38] makes it clear that this is
meant only figuratively in his admonition elsewhere to Eustochium,
a young Christian girl, to avoid women who wear male clothes, cut
their hair, and reject nature.[39]

If disruptions of gender hierarchy were not encouraged, why then
do so many hagiographers write about women disguised as men?
The answer can be found in the gender imagery of authoritative
texts of Christianity. As actualizations of male metaphors for faith,
cross-dressed women symbolically depict the power of Christianity
to "transform" its adherents. Radical transformation—water to wine,
death to life, male to female—informs Christian doctrine on many
levels, as the brothel customer in the story of Theodora noted. The
female monks also provide a means of praising female spirituality in
a particularly androcentric context. And finally, the act of inverting
sex, which repudiates sexual relations, reflects the growing emphasis
in the early centuries of Christianity on celibacy and sexual
renunciation.[40] Ultimately symbolic figures perhaps, the disguised
saints are nonetheless presented as imaginative and adventurous
characters who reject prescribed gender roles yet retain, because of
the authors' notions of essential femaleness, stereotypical feminine
traits. A paradox, one of many in these lives, is that a doctrine of
male spiritual superiority produced so many sympathetic and popular
female saints.

Several incidents from the lives of transvestite saints substantiate
the view that male disguise symbolizes female attainment of superior

spirituality. When Eugenia presents herself as a man to the divinely informed abbot Helenus, he answers knowingly, "recte vir diceris, quia, cum sis femina, viriliter agis."[41] [You rightly are called a man, since, although you are a woman, you act manfully.] In the legend of Euphrosyne, the abbot prays to the recently departed saint to help her brother monks so that they might also "manfully" (*viriliter*) gain entrance to heaven.[42] The moral valence of maleness provides the premise for praising disguised women even when such praise incorporates condescension toward women, as in the prayer of astonished witnesses at the discovery of Pelagia's true sex: "Gloria tibi Domine Jesu Christe, qui multas divitias absconsas habes super terram, non solum viriles, sed etiam muliebres."[43] [Glory to you, Lord Jesus Christ, you have many hidden treasures on earth, not only male but even female treasures.]

The story of Thecla, as recorded in the apocryphal *Acts of Paul and Thecla*, perhaps best illustrates the extent to which male constructs for Christian belief inform legends of disguise.[44] Probably the earliest example of female cross dressing in Christian literature (second century), the account is fraught with symbolic implications. Thecla, a pagan maiden from Iconium, is so moved while hearing St. Paul preach on virginity that she will not leave her room or eat. Her strange behavior incurs the displeasure of her mother and fiancé. Finally, at her mother's request, the local authorities sentence Thecla to be burned to death. A miraculous rainstorm rescues her from this predicament and enables her to join Paul's entourage. During another near martyrdom, this time in the circus at Antioch, Thecla baptizes herself. Thereafter, she cuts her hair and dresses as a man. Although first wary of Thecla's disguise, Paul eventually accepts her as a true disciple of Christ and allows her to take up the apostolic mission.[45]

The assumption of male clothing after baptism is not unique to the story of Thecla. In the *Acts of Philip*, Charitine puts on male clothing after conversion and follows Philip.[46] No more is said of her, but such a connection between baptism and maleness is stressed frequently in early Christian writings. In Paul's letter to the Galatians 3:27, baptism is described as "putting on Christ." More significantly, in Colossians 3:10 he says that the Christian has "put off the old man with his deeds and has put on the new man, who is renewed in the image of him that created him." The putting on of Christ as a garment, a masculine vestment, was intended for both sexes. The Pauline metaphor appears to have been incorporated into the earliest baptismal ceremonies in the removal of clothing and, after immersion, the putting on of new white robes, apparently the same for men and women.[47] The initiate is described as transformed, reborn, and united with Christ.

Thecla's self-baptism in the amphitheater shows striking parallels to the early Christian baptismal ceremony. Her story reflects the stages of preparation prescribed in descriptions of early baptism: instruction, apostaxis (rejection of Satan), syntaxis (profession of faith), disrobing, immersion, anointing, and symbolic robing.[48] Others have linked Thecla's disguise with "putting on Christ;"[49] closer examination, however, reveals not only that her male disguise symbolizes acceptance in a male-dominated religious movement but also that her ordeal mirrors the formal baptismal ceremony.

Thecla follows Paul as a disciple, continuing the religious instruction first experienced from her window in Iconium. One could argue that she rejects paganism when she leaves her family and fiancé, but the apostaxis is more graphically illustrated when she physically attacks a pagan suitor in Antioch.[50] Later, she professes her faith before the Roman magistrate (syntaxis) and is led off to be stripped and thrown to the beasts in the circus. Unashamed of her nakedness—just as baptismal initiates are supposed to be—she awaits her fate.[51] In the midst of various tortures, Thecla jumps into a reservoir full of aquatic monsters, saying, "Now it is time to baptize myself."[52] Even this detail is significant. That baptismal waters should be represented by a pool of monsters is not incongruous with Christian thought. There is evidence that Christ was believed to have conquered demons of the waters by his baptism.[53] It was asserted that baptism aided the catechumen in overcoming similar terrors, especially those deleterious to salvation. When Thecla enters the water the monsters are struck dead. Immediately after her immersion, she is enveloped in a divine cloud that covers her nakedness and protects her from further persecution. This cloud might be perceived as akin to the anointing, which sometimes served as a confirmation of the efficacy of baptism, but more likely it signifies divine protection. The anointing is more graphically symbolized in the next event when the women in the audience throw down nard, cassia, and balsam to deaden the senses of the wild beasts surrounding her.

As a palpable sign of her spiritual salvation, Thecla is saved from physical death. Soon after the dramatic baptism, she cuts her hair and puts on male clothing, thus realizing the symbol of the baptismal robe as the sign of the new man in the male image of God. The correlation between Thecla's acts and the baptismal ceremony with its attendant symbolism leaves little doubt that the motif of male disguise could be used to objectify the masculine metaphors inherent in the Christian rite of baptism.

An equation between preaching and maleness is also evident in Thecla's apostolic mission to convert her homeland. Apparently still dressed in male clothing, perhaps to emulate the original twelve apostles, she converts Iconium.[54] Because she becomes spiritually equal to men through persecution and baptism, she earns the right to proselytize in the tradition of male missionaries. We find this pattern again in the *Acts of Philip*, in which Mariamne, Philip's sister, expresses concern for her brother, who has been assigned the task of converting the recalcitrant Greeks. Jesus tells her to put off her womanly attire and follow Philip as his assistant in proselytizing: "καὶ σὺ Μαριάμνη ἄλλαξόν σου τὴν ἰδέαν καὶ ὅλον τὸ εἶδος τὸ γυναικεῖον, καὶ βάδιζε ὁμοίως μετὰ Φιλίππου."[55] [And you, Mariamne, change your appearance, rid yourself of your feminine identity, and go along with Philip.] Later, Mariamne is crucified in a culmination of the masculinizing force of *imitatio Christi*.

In other *vitae* maleness is equated with sexual renunciation and virginity. One of the primary motives for disguise, as configured by the hagiographers, is escape from sociosexual entrapment. A number of women, the so-called *monachoparthenoi* (virgin monks), in particular, don male garb to evade an arranged marriage, an unsympathetic husband, or a persistent suitor. One of them, Hugolina, flees the threat of incest. Agnes of Monçada, Angela of Bohemia, Apollonaris, Euphrosyne, Eusebia, and Margareta wish to circumvent marriage. Anastasia, Callisthene, Glaphyra, and Susanna, unwittingly incite powerful rulers to lust. Disguised as men, they escape, but are often pursued from place to place. In all these cases, disguise is presented as the means of breaking away from a prescribed role as sexual object. Male disguise becomes a natural expression of the renunciation of sex because it effectively shields the female body from sexual union with men.

Most of the saints are described as beautiful young women wooed by male suitors. For the attractive woman who wishes to elude marriage, male disguise also functions, at least in part, as a means of disfiguring feminine beauty. An important example of masculinity as disfigurement is the bearded saint. This saint is known variously throughout Europe as Wilgefortis, Uncumber, Ohnkummer, Kümmernis, Barbata, Gehulff, Liberatrix, Librada, and even Veränderung.[56] The many versions of the legend share a basic plot. A noble and beautiful girl, having dedicated herself to Christ, vows to preserve her virginity. When she refuses to marry the man to whom she is betrothed, her father (or suitor) attempts to coerce her. After praying to God to render her unattractive to the bridegroom, she miraculously sprouts a long beard. In most cases, the marriage is merely called off, although in some versions the father becomes so angry that he crucifies his daughter.[57] The physical metamorphosis of the bearded saint distinguishes her from transvestite saints because she is not disguised as a man but merely "disfigured" by a beard. While the bearded saints were granted divine disfigurement, other holy women took matters into their own hands: Medana, an Irish saint, plucked out her eyes when a soldier told her they inspired his love; Oliva of Italy amputated her hands for a similar reason, and Euphemia and Rodena cut off their noses to repel bridegrooms.[58] The patristic emphasis on female virginity and opposition to sexual appeal, if not sexuality itself, underlies the mutilation, self-deprivation, self-inflicted torments, and, I would argue, male disguise of numerous female saints.

By cutting her hair, a decisive action of all the transvestite saints, she willingly deprives herself of a primary sign of female beauty. In most instances, the *monachoparthenoi* also practice strict asceticism to defeminize themselves. Of Hilaria, it is said that "her flesh had withered through mortification and the beauty of her body had altered."[59] Euphrosyne so disfigures herself through self-denial that her own father does not know her: "non enim cognovit eam, quia species vultus emarcuit prae nimia abstinentia, vigiliis, et lacrymis."[60] [He did not know her because the beauty of her face was marred by excessive fasting, late vigils, and crying.] After effacing her sex with male disguise, Apollonaris lives in a swamp until her body is emaciated, tanned, and pockmarked from mosquito bites.[61] In several lives, fellow monks find tight bands around the body of the dead monk, which, they discover, the woman used to diminish the size of her breasts. The threat of sexual intercourse and devotion to the ideal of virginity it endangers become the chief motives for male disguise. It protects female virginity by obscuring femaleness. Maleness, in turn, is perceived as a defacement of female beauty, which, when coupled with a disregard for the body that roughens, emaciates, and disfigures, indicates saintly concentration on things spiritual.

Within the narrative, male disguise also foils most attempts to reimpose traditional roles on women, since change of identity allows them to eradicate sociosexual strictures. In some of the lives, the saints consider entering a nunnery but fear their relatives or suitors will find them and force them to marry (Euphrosyne, Hilaria). Initially, these stories appear to be concerned largely with male sexual oppression of women. While that is to a limited extent true, there are also many indications in these legends that impute potential sinfulness entirely to femininity.

Narrative confusion and conflation of gender identities characterize these lives, which often reveal male perspectives on female sexuality beneath the veneer of disguise. Although male disguise seems to represent a desire for asexuality, the narrators tend to impose problems of sexuality on the disguised saints. Maleness alone does not always render them unattractive. When Euphrosyne enters the monastery, her fellow monks are so attracted to the new "eunuch" that the abbot, as a precaution, confines her to her cell: "Pulchra est facies tua, fili (i.e., Euphrosyne disguised as Smaragdus), timeo ne sit ruina infirmis fratribus; volo autem, ut sedeas solus in cella tua."[62] [Your appearance is beautiful, son. I am afraid lest it be the ruin of infirm brothers; therefore, I want you to remain alone in your cell.] Although Euphrosyne soon disfigures herself through harsh observances, other female monks remain objects of sexual attraction. While disguised as monks, Eugenia and Susanna inflame the love of women. When the saints reject all amorous advances, the spurned women take revenge, like Potiphar's wife, by falsely accusing them of rape or attempted seduction. Although both saints are described as paragons of monastic virtue, the false charges are quickly believed. Presumed guilty, the female monks are brought to trial and vindicated only when they reveal their true identity. Susanna, Eugenia, and other calumniated saints document a suspicion of sexual sinfulness in women, in a curious twist, even when they are thought to be men. The potential for scandal concerning the relationship of these women with men in the monastic communities is never developed in hagiographic writings, although it does appear in later satirical works.[63] Rather, these legends center on the sexual guilt inherent in femininity.

Perhaps in an effort to prove that femaleness and its attendant sinfulness cannot remain hidden, the authors consistently introduce sexuality into the lives of these female monks. The sexual vulnerability of the disguised woman is a recurrent theme in the lives, and it is of particular significance in the legends of the calumniated female monks. The examples are numerous. Eugenia allows herself to be alone with a sick woman whose lust she soon arouses. Susanna's contacts outside the monastery inspire a charge of rape from a spurned woman. Marina and Theodora, both of whom must spend the night abroad while on monastery business, are charged with seducing an innkeeper's daughter. In her role as the monk Pelagius, Margareta is placed, against her wishes, in charge of a nunnery; when a nun becomes pregnant, Pelagius is the obvious suspect. Apollonaris is ordered to exorcise the devil from her sister. Although she tries to avoid the compromising position of being alone with a woman, she cannot escape the situation, which later leads to trumped-up charges of rape. It is ironic and noteworthy that, although true sex invalidates charges of sexual transgression, this type of disguised woman is consistently viewed as being sexually suspicious. The transferral of feminine vulnerability in sexual encounters to the woman in her masculine role suggests that hagiographers were influenced in their portrayals by male notions of female frailty. The calumniation, which is obviously untrue, provides an excellent forum for displays of Christian virtue, but it also reflects a deep-seated view of women as the cause of sexual transgression.

Those who relinquish femininity, especially the penitents and *monachoparthenoi*, are depicted as being obsessed with self-abnegation. Despite the governing precept of male superiority, disguise emerges, paradoxically, as a sign of humility, since it reflects a voluntary disregard for the self in favor of serving God. In the cases of calumniated saints like Marina, Margareta, and Theodora of Alexandria—falsely accused female monks who bear sexual guilt in silence—willingness to suffer for the sins of others obviously evokes the figure of Christ. For some of these saints, however, the virtue is feminized in the type of responsibility they assume for the alleged sin. Even Marina, a woman whose father disguised her as a boy in order to enter a monastery with her, suffers in a distinctively feminine way for imputed sexual sins. Accused of fathering a child, Marina answers the charge enigmatically: "Peccavi pater, poenitentiam ago huic peccato, ora pro me."[64] [I have sinned, father, I do penance for this sin, pray for me.] The illegitimate child is then left with the alleged father, and Marina raises the child while retaining her male persona. The role she assumes, however, has more in common with that of the unwed mother. Cast out from the community, she begs for alms and nurtures the child of a sinful liaison. When readmitted to the monastery after a period of penance, she is still regarded as being tainted with sin. Moreover, she must perform the most menial tasks—all of which concern housekeeping—and continue to raise the child. Thus, when punished for the transgression of a man, she nonetheless conforms to the model of the female sinner. This inconsistency with the narrative setting, in favor of traditional gender biases, betrays ingrained notions of sexual inequality and, more important, illustrates a central aspect of disguise literature: the disguised woman, despite narrative claims of total integration among males, remains a woman in the narrator's (and reader's) mind.

Sexual sinfulness becomes the thematic focus in the legends of penitent transvestites. The sympathetic figure of the repentant prostitute, such as Thais, Mary of Egypt, Afra of Augsburg, and Mary Magdalene, enjoyed broad popularity in medieval legendaries. Among the transvestite saints, Pelagia of Antioch and Theodora of Alexandria reject not only their past lives of sin, but also their female nature. Male disguise functions as an antidote to their sins as women.

According to her legend, Pelagia was the most beautiful and seductive courtesan in Antioch.[65] She attracts the attention of a saintly bishop, variously called Nonnus or Veronus, who, surprisingly, uses her as a positive example to reprove other bishops. In a far-fetched analogy, he faults himself and other churchmen for not spending as much time on the salvation of their flocks as Pelagia does on her appearance. Eventually, he becomes the agent of Pelagia's salvation. The transformation from prostitute to penitent is developed in two stages. First, Pelagia repents, confesses, and receives baptism. But the penance Pelagia imposes on herself is stricter than what the bishop prescribes. Dressed in the hair shirt and cloak of the man who converted her, she secretly leaves Antioch to become a recluse in a cave on Mt. Olivet.

The appropriation of maleness seems to symbolize the denial of female sexuality, the cause of Pelagia's sinfulness. Yet, more than simple gender inversion, male disguise may represent an artifice for neutering. Pelagia and many other transvestite saints (Anastasia, Euphrosyne, Eugenia) are presumed to be eunuchs because they do not have beards. Such a perception of the incompleteness of gender reversal implies that male impersonation is symbolically equivalent to castration in these cases. Indeed, Freudian psychologists construe the cutting of a woman's hair—an important moment in the lives of all the transvestite saints—as a symbol of castration.[66] Jerome seems to make the same connection when he speaks of "aliae virili habitu, veste mutata, erubescunt esse feminae quod natae sunt, crinem amputant, et impudenter erigunt facies eunuchinas."[67] [Other women, having changed their clothes, in male attire, they blush to be women as they were born, they cut off (literally "amputate") their hair, and they impudently lift up (*erigo* can also mean "make erect" in a sexual sense) their eunuchlike faces.] Although Pelagia's identity as a holy man can be viewed as a simple antipode to her past as a sinful woman, disguise, in this case at least, indicates not merely an inversion of natural gender but rather an attempt to eradicate gender entirely. By confining herself in complete solitude, Pelagia effectively renders sex irrelevant; her goal, like that of the voluntary eunuch, is asexuality (she is called "monachus et eunuchus").

Before self-made eunuchs were anathematized at the Council of Nicea (325), castrated men were considered particularly pious and certainly above suspicion in sexual scandals. There is evidence that women who abjured sex were likened to self-made eunuchs. Methodius (third century), for example, dubbed virgins the female equivalent of God's eunuchs.[68] Although most disguised saints desire to elude male sexual entrapment, Pelagia's rejection of corporeal identity, like that of the holy eunuch, implies a suppression of her own sexuality and points to an epicene ideal.

Theodora of Alexandria also assumes a male identity after sexual transgression. Theodora, a married noblewoman, is persuaded to commit adultery when her seducer convinces her that God does not see sins that are committed in the dark. Overcome with remorse, she puts on men's clothing and leaves her husband. At a nearby monastery, she passes for a monk named Theodorus and achieves renown for her holiness. The devil, angered by her piety, contrives to have Theodora falsely accused of fathering a child. Accepting the blame, she is driven from the monastery and, like Marina, takes on the feminine role of nurturing the child. After her return from penitential exile, the abbot has a strange dream in which Theodora's sex and sanctity are revealed. He rushes to her cell, only to find her dead.

Theodora's male disguise allows her to escape from her husband when she feels unworthy of him, but it also represents a rejection of her female past. During her five years in exile, the devil comes to Theodora in the form of her husband, offering forgiveness and begging her to return to him. Believing him to be her husband, she says "Nunquam amplius tecum manebo, quia filius Johannis militis jacuit mecum et volo agere poenitentiam de eo, quod in te peccavi."[69] [I will not stay with you anymore because the son of John the soldier lay with me, and I wish to do penance for this because I sinned against you.] Despite her rejection of sexual identity, however, Theodora is obviously not considered a eunuch and she cannot achieve asexuality. An innkeeper's daughter tries to seduce "Theodorus" and later avenges the rebuke by accusing him of fathering her child. It is perhaps a sign of an author's contrivance that, although Theodora avoids any scandal over her own adulterous affair by changing identity, she must later bear the onus of another's sexual misconduct. Unlike the false accusations against Marina and other *monachoparthenoi*, the charge against Theodora is consequential; because of the nature of her sin, she continues to be haunted by sins related to sexuality.

While many of the transvestite saints leave their homes and families with no further thought of their worldly past, others, such as Athanasia, Eugenia, Euphrosyne, and Hilaria, use disguise to redefine familial relationships. These women earn recognition and praise from their male family members only after effacing gender. Once again, the authors of these lives present the disguised figure within the confines of female experience. In this case, familial obligations as daughters and wives, although skewed by perception, are met by the women in male disguise.

In the legend of Athanasia and Andronikos, disguise redefines the intimate relationship of husband and wife. According to the legend, the couple joined separate religious communities after the deaths of their children. As fate would have it, the nun, Athanasia, and the monk, Andronikos, both decide to make pilgrimages at the same time. Athanasia recognizes her husband when they meet, but Andronikos is misled by her pilgrim's clothes and tanned skin. Although her original motive for male disguise was travel, Athanasia keeps her identity concealed since her husband's monastic vows otherwise would be jeopardized. Andronikos develops such great affection for his traveling companion that he begs "him" to enter the same monastery. They live as brother monks and best friends in the same cell for decades until the truth is revealed at Athanasia's death. According to the narrative, disguise successfully eliminates the sexual aspects of their relation so that Athanasia and Andronikos can fulfill their religious vocations without sacrificing natural affinities.

In a similar story, gender undermines a relationship between father and daughter. Unable to reason with a father determined to betroth her against her wishes, Euphrosyne flees her home and, disguised as a monk, enters a monastery. Later, as the monk Smaragdus, she is able to explain her vocation in several conversations with her unwitting but sympathetic father. For more than thirty years she consoles him, assuring him that his daughter has found peace and promising that he will be reunited with her before he dies. When she reveals her identity on her deathbed, he laments his ignorance. One detects some underlying criticism of paternal authority in matters concerning a daughter's sexuality, particularly in the depiction of Euphrosyne as a wise and intelligent counselor who helps her father understand his daughter's choice of lifestyle—a role she can play only from behind a male façade. In the legends of both Euphrosyne and Athanasia, the female role of fostering domestic harmony is maintained, yet the women consciously enjoy the nearness of their loved ones, whereas the men, unfettered by preconceptions of gender roles, are consoled by what they perceive to be new friendships. This configuration reveals a certain amount of respect on the part of the authors for female companionship as well as a sympathetic response to the adverse effects of the tension of sexuality on women in their relationships with men.

The woman's femaleness, then, remains her most important feature. The somatic focus and the emphasis on "female" qualities reveal the authors' inability to divorce the woman from her "innate" femaleness in these narratives that praise the "manly spirit" of extraordinary women. The climax always occurs at the scene of recognition, which, more often than not, exposes the female body. Eugenia bares her breasts to disprove false charges, whereas many saints patiently keep their secret until death, causing an equally dramatic spectacle of anagnorisis when the monks prepare her body for burial. In the end, it is femaleness that is at the center of these hagiographies.

The motif of male disguise unifies the legends, but the range of possible interpretations of the motif complicates any consideration of the group as a uniform literary or sociological phenomenon. According to the authors of the *vitae*, disguise is motivated most often by a woman's unwillingness to conform to her sexual role in society, which, they admit, is often oppressive. Despite their disregard for women's prescribed roles in society, the disguised saints are presented as positive models. This incongruity can be explained by looking at the meanings of disguise in a Christian context and at the portrayal of the disguised women. The transvestite saints embody restraint, self-denial, and humility. They rarely infringe upon male dominion; more often, they retain stereotypical feminine characteristics, including sexual vulnerability and sinfulness, maternal instincts, and concerns for family.

The ambiguity of inversion that results, in part, from an incongruity between narrative assurances that the women were considered men and gendered identifications in the portrayal of the women had the unintended consequence that the transvestite saints have been interpreted as strong and independent models of female heroism by later generations from the Middle Ages to the twentieth century. Far from being examples of early feminism, however, the disguised saints are manifestations of male dominance in the structure, philosophy, and language of the church.

As Mary became a more dominant force in Christian worship, she offered a female model for saintly women, but Mary's life includes little of the heroism associated with the early saints and martyrs. It is interesting to note, however, that Marian lore includes at least one episode involving disguise. In the thirteenth-century legend

"Du chevalier qui ooit la messe et Notre Dame estoit pour lui au tournoiement," Mary disguises herself as a knight and fights in her supplicant's stead.[70] This story is a late addition to Marian legend with no basis in biblical or early religious writings, but it further illustrates the positive forms of transvestism in portraits of female heroism.

In addition to the emergence of the maternal model of Mary as a feminine image of holiness, the mystical movement of the High Middle Ages also provided alternatives for expressing female spirituality. Mysticism redefined the relation of the soul to God to allow for individual religious experiences. Many of the female mystics feminized the relation, using erotic imagery for the union of the soul with the divine.[71] This new avenue of religious experience obviated the need for male metaphors and legitimated woman's relationship to God.

The general issues raised in the lives of the transvestite saints provide a basis for the rest of this study. As the discussion broadens to historical and secular literature, paradoxes inherent in disguise literature will recur as the inability of authors to suspend knowledge of true sex results in fascinating, if sometimes contradictory, portrayals of women. The motives, if not the meanings, of disguise serve similar functions in the life of Hildegund, the legend of the female pope, and secular literature. Influences from these saints' lives on later disguise literature also can be found in such literary figures as the female pope and the fabliau character Frère Denis, both of whom dressed as monks, albeit for less than holy reasons. Furthermore, the enormous popularity of disguised roles in Renaissance and baroque drama might ultimately stem from the model of the transvestite saint. This field of inquiry has not been explored, but a recently discovered fifteenth-century French play about Euphrosyne, as well as the later dramatization of the legend by Calderón de la Barca, *El Josef de las mujeres*, first printed in 1660, suggests the possibility of such an origin.[72]

Chapter Three

THE LIVES AND DEATH OF
HILDEGUND VON SCHÖNAU (†1188)

> Femina fuit hic homo; nemo cognovit,
> quamquam hoc infirmitas crebra clamaverit.
>
> [This man was a woman; no one knew it,
> although infirmity proclaimed it repeatedly.]
> —Engelhard von Langheim[1]

Five accounts from the late twelfth and early thirteenth centuries record the life of Hildegund, a woman who enjoys the remarkable reputation of being the most celebrated monk of the Cistercian abbey of Schönau. Disguised as a man, she joined the monastery in 1187 under the alias Joseph. While still in her first year as a novice, she fell ill and died, although not before giving a fascinating account of travel and adventure throughout the Middle East and Europe. More surprising than these peregrinations, however, was the discovery, made by monks preparing her for burial, that the novice was a woman.

Hildegund's deathbed account and the shocking postmortem disclosure of her sex were recorded almost immediately. According to the earliest account, the monastery publicly announced the discovery and initiated investigations to determine the woman's identity. Within a few years, five *vitae* had appeared.[2] Her biography has been included in chronicles and hagiologies from the thirteenth through twentieth century, attesting to the general acknowledgment of Hildegund's authenticity and saintliness.[3] The story became a notable event in Schönau's history, and it quickly attracted attention throughout Germany.

Holding a tenuous position between history and hagiography— as many saints' lives do—the five contemporaneous *vitae* present special problems for literary and historical analysis. Hildegund's historical existence seems probable, although the facts of her life may have been exaggerated, both in her own account and in the work of her biographers. Influenced by such factors as the traditions of the transvestite saints and their loyalty to the Cistercian order, Hildegund's biographers nevertheless do not obscure their subject behind a veil of absolute sanctity. Blending the mundane with the miraculous, the biographers not only record Hildegund's account of divine encounters but also claim to incorporate eyewitness reports of her conduct in the monastery. Far from unambiguous panegyric, the accounts offer some critical perspectives that are difficult to assess. The hints in the account of psychological duress resulting from renunciation of gender are either authentic accounts of Hildegund's problems or interpretations imposed by cultural uneasiness about women on the part of the authors.

The portrait of this woman bears little resemblance to the saints with whom she is obviously intended to be grouped. Although the *vitae* record her successful performance as a man in secular and religious settings and even attribute divine sanction to her disguise, an underlying criticism of female cross dressing pervades the accounts. The possibility of cultural maleness, while depicted, is undermined by interpretations that consistently purport to confirm that biological sex determines behavior. Portrayed as a woman caught between the antinomies of her sinful female "nature" and the divinely mandated male persona she has been all her life, the historical Hildegund fades into a cipher for expressing the cultural dilemma of assessing the cross-dressing woman.

The earliest account was written only a few months after her death on 20 April 1188. Even before her given name had been discovered, Engelhard of Langheim (†ca. 1210) included her story as the final chapter in, of all places, an example book for nuns.[4] Praising her as a saint, Engelhard stops short of advocating such a course to sainthood for his female audience.[5] He claims to have his information from a witness to the recent events at Schönau. Although other unknown sources cannot be ruled out, Engelhard's version probably inspired a poetic account of Hildegund's life written in dactylic hexameter.[6] This "Vita Hildegundis metrica" (153 lines) is extant in two manuscripts, and its inclusion in Hugo von Trimberg's list of essential reading for students, the *Registrum multorum auctorum* (1280), suggests that it enjoyed at least some circulation for several generations.[7] Like Engelhard, the poet, an unnamed Cistercian monk from Windberg, does not know Hildegund's name. It may have been composed, therefore, soon after 1188. It certainly was written no later than 1191, since the author addresses Abbot Gebehard of Windberg, who died in that year.[8] The third version of Hildegund's life survives in a fourteenth-century legendary, now in the collection of the Royal Library of Brussels; the original, however, probably dates from around 1200.[9] This assumption has been supported recently by the discovery of an earlier exemplar of this text in a late twelfth-century manuscript in Heidelberg.[10] The account appears to draw on both earlier lives, in particular the "Vita Hildegundis metrica," from which it borrows entire lines in hexameter.[11] Within a framework that includes narrative commentary, these three accounts introduce character and setting before quoting Hildegund's first-person deathbed account of her life. Since the information comes from Hildegund in her role as Brother Joseph, no mention is made of her disguise or the reason for it. But the nature of the adventures she relates and the consistent use of male pronouns make it clear that everything she describes was experienced in the guise of a male.

The remaining two accounts dispense with direct quotation of Hildegund's own testimony, incorporating it instead into a third-person narrative, with frequent passages of dialogue. Of all the versions, the best known is found in Caesarius of Heisterbach's *Dialogus miraculorum*.[12] Writing some thirty years after her death, Caesarius says he relied on Brother Hermann, one of Hildegund's fellow novices, as his source for certain facts about her life in the cloister. The anecdotal style and more detailed depiction of her conduct among the monks, however, may indicate that local legends about Hildegund had arisen since the earliest accounts were written. It seems likely that Caesarius used a version similar to the one in the Brussels/Heidelberg manuscripts for the details of Hildegund's last words,[13] although he also includes information not found in other accounts. Similarly, the fifth version is full of unique anecdotes concerning her life among the monks, as well as new, and sometimes conflicting, details about her adventures before entering the monastery.[14] It is difficult to date this independent version. The author, who claims to have been Hildegund's tutor, is obviously writing several years after her death because he refers to events that

occurred at least as late as 1191.[15] Although this account by
Hildegund's colleague should be the most reliable, the author's
tendency to digress, his literary inclinations, and his insistence on
Hildegund's sanctity detract from its worth as biography.
Nonetheless, it is this account, the only one to claim direct experience
of the affair, that makes the clearest connection between biological
sex and gender identity and that ascribes a psychological burden of
gender disguise.

Common to all accounts is a description of Hildegund's
experiences from childhood until her arrival at Schönau. Without
revealing her sex, Hildegund told her life's story to her confessor
before she died.[16] All accounts agree that she was born near Cologne
and that her mother died when Hildegund was still young. Her
father decided to take her with him on a pilgrimage to Jerusalem.
One version, that of her fellow novice, explains that her father dressed
her as a boy in order to facilitate travel.[17] On the return trip, the
father fell ill and, after commending his child to a servant, died at
Tyre.[18] The servant betrayed his charge, however, and, absconding
with all her belongings, deserted her in a strange land. Although
reduced to begging, Hildegund may have acquired some education
in the East, for she says, "Mendicabam et scholas frequentabam."[19]
[I begged and attended the schools.] Hildegund eventually found
refuge with a German pilgrim, who, thinking her a young man,
invited her to join his entourage and eventually brought her back
to Germany. According to her fellow novice, however, Hildegund
first went to Jerusalem and joined the Knights Templar for a year
before returning with an old acquaintance of her father.[20]

Deemed by all to be an intelligent young man, Hildegund was
soon entrusted to carry a secret letter from the archbishop of Cologne
to the pope in Verona.[21] During the journey, in some woods outside
Augsburg, she fell in with a thief who tricked her into holding some
stolen goods while he escaped his pursuers. When those following
him found their property in the hands of the innocent courier, they
beat her and dragged her before a magistrate. Since guilt seemed
overwhelmingly clear, she was condemned to hang. The priest who
came to hear her final confession, however, believed the courier was
innocent and instigated a search for the real culprit. When the
apprehended thief denied all charges, the priest suggested a trial by
ordeal. Hildegund and the thief carried burning iron, but only the

thief was burned. He was hanged and the messenger was freed. But, as she resumed her journey, angry relatives of the thief captured the youth and hanged her in revenge.

Hildegund claimed she was not strangled because an angel supported her for three days (two days in Caesarius). During this time, the angel comforted her with a heavenly scent. While in the presence of the angel, Hildegund heard a beautiful melody sung by sweet voices. The angel explained that Hildegund's sister Agnes had just died and was being taken up into heaven. He promised her that three years from that day (two years in some accounts) she too would ascend to heaven amid such music. As he was speaking, some shepherds came and decided to bury the poor young man. When they cut the rope, however, the body did not fall heavily because the angel slowly lowered Hildegund to the ground. Terrified at this sight, the shepherds fled.[22] The angel then pointed to a city not far away, telling her it was Verona. Thus, Hildegund claimed she was miraculously transported from Augsburg to Verona, a distance that normally required a journey of seven days. After successfully completing her mission, she returned to Germany and soon entered the monastery of Schönau as an act of thanksgiving.

Explaining that the appointed time for her death was near, she revealed these things and added that a miracle would come to light after her death. According to all accounts, she died, as she predicted, on Easter Wednesday. The wonder she had foretold, her true sex, shocked her fellow monks, who had never suspected their colleague. The results of the abbot's investigation to determine the identity of the disguised monk are found in the Brussels/Heidelberg version, Caesarius's *Dialogus miraculorum*, and the account of the fellow novice. It was learned that she was Hildegund, daughter of a man from Neuss, a village outside of Cologne.[23] In addition, evidence was adduced to substantiate the story of her father's pilgrimage to Jerusalem.

Little has been written about Hildegund. The scanty scholarship that exists is limited almost exclusively to editorial comments and perfunctory retellings of the story.[24] When one looks beyond the story itself—however fascinating it may be—to the way the story is presented, one finds that the mixture of hagiography, fictionalization or even sensationalism, and biography in these accounts presents problems for interpretation. Possible auctorial motives, including

institutional allegiances, gender biases, and the conflicting concerns
for historical accuracy and literary appeal, are revealed in the limited
narrative commentaries. Most telling is the authors' apparent
difficulty in presenting Hildegund's life: on the one hand, they try
to place her within the tradition of the female monks, and on the
other hand, they wish to depict and, more important, interpret her
reactions to concealment of gender.

Given Hildegund's basic story, complete with self-proclaimed
miracles, it is not surprising that she was venerated as a saint.
Nonetheless, according to most accounts, only the discovery of her
sex inspired the monks of her order to set down her life in writing.
After introducing a young man named Joseph who not long ago
entered the monastery of Schönau, Engelhard von Langheim
dramatically reveals the reason for his interest in this figure: "Femina
fuit hic homo; nemo cognovit."[25] [This man was a woman; no one
knew it.] Hildegund also emphasizes her disguise, rather than her
wondrous experiences, when she hints at the great miracle that will
become apparent after her death: "Cum defunctus fuero, apparebit
in me unde stupeatis, et divinae virtuti gratias merito referatis."[26]
[When I am dead, there will appear in me something that astounds
you, and may you give thanks, as you should, to God.]

The view of Hildegund's disguise is similar in all five versions.
The authors admire Hildegund and praise God for hiding such a
saintly woman among them. The positive reception accords with
the tradition of transvestite saints. Historical pretensions in the
accounts of Hildegund do not rule out hagiographic influence, since
each author styles her a saint, and hagiography, as a highly imitative
form of medieval literature, tends to express saintly characteristics
in conventional terms. A woman who disguised herself as a man
and entered a monastery could not avoid comparison with other
female monks. Engelhard hints at the phenomenon, and Caesarius
of Heisterbach actually refers to earlier female monks by name. Given
the wide circulation of legends of disguised saints, however, there is
little doubt that Hildegund's biographers—and perhaps Hildegund
herself—knew of their existence.

The chief similarity between the descriptions of Hildegund and
the transvestite saints is the positive portrayal of disguise. As in the
legends of the transvestite saints, the woman's ability to suppress
her femaleness in order to live undetected among men remains a

principal reason for veneration. The importance of the hagiographic tradition of female monks for the acceptance of Hildegund's holiness should not be underestimated; such prototypes for sainthood would have outweighed any doubts about her worthiness and justified sanctification. Some aspects of Hildegund's life find parallels in the legends of other transvestite saints. Like Marina, she is disguised by her father and raised as a boy. Later, she is accepted into a community of men as an equal. The primary reason for disguise, as in the cases of Athanasia, Eusebia, Glaphyra, and others, is travel, in particular a pilgrimage to the Holy Land. The adventures of Hildegund as a papal courier differ from the monastic existences of the earlier female monks. Nonetheless, some details suggest the legends of calumniated female monks, as in the episode with the thief when Hildegund is charged with wrongdoing on the basis of circumstantial evidence. Finally, for Hildegund and most of the transvestite saints, the moment of anagnorisis comes when the monks prepare to wash the corpse for burial.

Added to these narrative similarities is the tendency of the authors to use masculine metaphors to describe the woman's spiritual state. Influenced by the male imagery of Christian semiosis, Hildegund's biographers consider male disguise a sign of spiritual strength. Using the language of battle, Engelhard says that for love of Christ the fragile girl forgot her sex, and, entering the battle, she triumphed over evil.[27] The author of the "Vita Hildegundis metrica" credits her with taking up arms against her gender: "arma resumens / Pugnat, et in fragili vicit patientia sexu."[28] [Taking up arms, she fights, and patience prevailed in the fragile sex.] The Brussels/Heidelberg manuscripts ascribe a divine gift of a "manly spirit" to Hildegund: "Deus [...] ei in fragili femineo sexu tam virilem tamque fortissimum donavit animum."[29] [In her frail feminine sex, God gave her a manly and very strong spirit.] Caesarius is less direct in equating male disguise with superior spiritual fortitude, but he praises Hildegund's "fortitudo mentis," which, he says, is found in few women.[30] Finally, her confrere claims that she actually surpassed men in virtue.[31] Thus, as was the case with earlier transvestite saints, approbation of a woman requires male metaphors and comparisons. This contrastive approach to creating a positive image of women is not limited to cases of gender inversion, but it consistently informs descriptions of women in disguise.

The authors are careful to mention Hildegund's virtuousness to reinforce this positive image. Engelhard cites the universal respect of the monks at Schönau.[32] The poet celebrates Hildegund as "clara Dei"[33] [the light of God], whereas the author of the Brussels/Heidelberg version goes so far as to call the case of Hildegund the greatest miracle since Mary gave birth to Christ.[34] Her fellow novice, who seems most concerned with establishing her sanctity, even credits Hildegund with a posthumous miracle.[35] Such effusive laudation is a common feature of hagiography; through the spectacle of miracles and praise of abstract virtues, the figure is made to conform to the ideal of sainthood.

As evidenced by the efforts of no fewer than five monastic biographers, the case of Brother Joseph redounded to the credit of Schönau. Local veneration of Hildegund, particularly among lay women, is noted by Caesarius, who observed that Schönau's renown increased on account of the disguised monk.[36] That the monks at Schönau viewed Hildegund's presence as cause for celebration is stated most directly in the account of the fellow novice. He repeatedly interprets Hildegund's presence as the fulfillment of divine will and credits Gottfried, the abbot of Schönau, as the first to express this view. Moments after the discovery, Gottfried tells his monks to thank God for such a miracle:

> Videtis, inquit, Fratres, corpus, quod coram vobis positum est? Non est hoc, ut putavimus, viri corpus, sed feminae. Deus omnipotens apud nos hominem habere voluit, qui nobis usque ad hanc horam omnino incognitus fuit: cuius animam Angeli sancti susceperunt, et ad gaudia vitae perennis in hac hora sine dubio perduxerunt. Agamus ergo gratias ei, qui nobis hunc thesaurum tam desiderabilem dereliquit; et in coelo talem Patronam habere voluit.[37]

> [Do you see, brothers, the body placed before you? It is not, as we thought, the body of a man, but of a woman. Omnipotent God wished to have a person among us who was completely unknown to all of us until this very hour; whose spirit the holy angels received and led, without doubt, into the joy of eternal life in this hour. Let us give thanks to him, therefore, who left behind such a welcome treasure for us and wanted us to have such a patroness in heaven.]

Despite universal praise of Hildegund, a careful reading of the lives finds that panegyric falters in the narrations and assessments of her deeds. Although the narrators' tone and presentation of the material remain positive in every case, their choice of anecdotes and the implications of many of their comments qualify the stated goal of praising a saintly woman. With the exception of the prediction of her own death date (a common topos in the documentation of saints), Hildegund exhibits few saintly characteristics. She performs no miracles while in the monastery, nor any acts of charity or mercy. According to almost all accounts, her demeanor ranged from withdrawn to downright recalcitrant. Her testimony of miracles and the discovery of her true sex ensured veneration, but the reported anecdotes fail to aggrandize her novitiate. If we are to believe the descriptions of her failing health, agitated mental state, and unruly conduct while a novice, the remarks about Hildegund's fortitude and saintliness seem mere platitudes at odds with her performance in the monastery.

It is possible that the monks insisted upon Hildegund's saintliness to exculpate the Cistercian order from any charges of sexual impropriety.[38] Perhaps the Cistercian authors feared the reputation of their order would suffer as a result of the woman's presence in the monastery. That such a situation could engender antifraternal satire is evident from Rutebeuf's ribald treatment of a similar situation in Frère Denise (mid-thirteenth century).[39] In the tale, a lecherous Franciscan brother advises the innocent Denise to put on men's clothing and enter his order if she wants to gain sainthood. (It is indicative of the popularity of the transvestite saints' lives that disguising oneself as a monk could be presented as a path to sainthood.) The Franciscan's goal, however, is to seduce Denise so she will become his secret concubine within the walls of the monastery.[40] Much later, Heinrich Cornelius Agrippa von Nettesheim (1486-1535) criticized monasteries for keeping prostitutes in the cloister under the guise of monks.[41]

The monks' ignorance not only exonerated the community but also illustrated their obedience to an important tenet of the Cistercian rule. In a work outlining the paths to good and evil, Bernard of Clairvaux (1090-1153) singled out *curiositas* as a primary cause of sin: "Iure igitur in gradibus superbiae primum curiositas vindicat sibi, quae etiam inventa est initium omnis esse peccati."[42] [Thus, curiosity justly claims first place in the gradations of pride, since it is also found to be the beginning of all sin.] Bernard specifically warned monks not to meddle in the affairs of their fellow brothers.[43]

Accordingly, injunctions against sinful *curiositas* are prevalent in twelfth-century Cistercian writings.[44] To the medieval reader, the apologetic tone in the accounts was not necessarily a defense of the monks at Schönau but rather a commendation of their piety, since it would have been sinful to have suspected Brother Joseph. Engelhard even suggests that adherence to the Bernardine rule made it impossible for the monks to suspect Hildegund. Her fear of discovery, he claims, was unfounded, since "si cui hoc suggereret vel suus cogitatus vel angelus malus, ad radicem mox ubi oriretur aresceret; numquam ad signum, numquam ad nutum pro multa domus disciplina procederet."[45] [If anyone's own thoughts or some evil angel suggested this to him, the idea would have soon withered at the root where it arose; it never would have extended to a sign or nod because of the great discipline of the monastery.]

In all accounts, Hildegund's femininity is viewed as the cause of her strangeness. The narrators are obsessed with her femaleness, and they also portray her as one consumed by thoughts about her own gender. Engelhard first speculates that lack of privacy in a monastic environment unsettled her to the point of making her ill: "Hinc tamen frater Joseph securus esse non potuit, suspectum se suspicans et fluctuans jugiter nec habens solatium preter Deum et priorem solum."[46] [Brother Joseph could not feel secure, thinking herself suspected and always vacillating in her resolve, she had no solace except God and the prior alone.] Hildegund's femaleness, so obvious yet unperceived, permeates every account. The emphasis on misunderstood indications prefigures revelation of Brother Joseph's true sex and, more important, suggests a residual resistance to accepting the woman. Although they invoke common male metaphors used for saints of both genders, such as "soldier of God," "conqueror of Satan," and "God's athlete," the authors are unwilling to defeminize Hildegund; instead, they expose her femaleness openly in their anecdotes, insisting all the while that God blinded the monks to the truth. The majority of incidents reported portends revelation of biological sex. Double entendre, not uncommon in disguise literature, occurs throughout the accounts, especially in the fellow novice's version. He says that Joseph once interrupted their lessons to ask what would happen if a woman were discovered in the clothes of a man among the monks. She wanted to know if the monks would simply expel her or if they might provide for her well-being by placing her in a convent. We are led to believe that, with this rash statement, Hildegund was trying to determine whether she might safely give up her disguise. She was discouraged by his indignant answer: "Quae mulier tam petulans, tam lasciva, tam insana, quae hoc auderet praesumere?"[47] [What woman so impudent, so wanton, so insane, would dare to undertake such a thing?] (A clear indication of the double standard of Christian transvestism: a dead female monk was considered a saint, but a woman discovered in monk's clothes would be wanton and insane.) Another time, Joseph spoke disapprovingly of the practice of washing corpses before burial and requested that his own body not be disrobed or washed after death.[48] Before administering the last rites, the prior asked Brother Joseph if he had ever had any relations with women. The novice replied, "Neque feminam, neque virum cognovi unquam."[49] [Neither woman nor man have I ever known.] Caesarius also includes this remark and a similar episode when the abbot observed that Brother Joseph's voice had not yet broken; the disguised novice honestly answered that it never would.[50]

Hildegund not only tended to speak enigmatically but also behaved so strangely that her observance of monastic discipline is questioned in several anecdotes. Caesarius's source, Brother Hermann, claims that Joseph once induced him to break the vow of silence in order to discuss which of them was more handsome. Hermann remarked, "Videtur mihi mentum tuum dispositum sicut mentum mulieris."[51] [It seems to me that your chin is like a woman's.] Indignant at this insult, Joseph ran away. Later, both were beaten for disobedience. Hildegund's less than humble nature also exhibits itself in a description of an escape attempt that was foiled by an old monk's vision. The monk told the author, Joseph's tutor, that Brother Joseph's resolve was wavering. Her friend and teacher ran to her cell and told her what he had heard. Although she grew pale at first, when she determined that her sex had not been revealed she smiled and commented disdainfully, "'Eia', inquit, 'Propheta vester non habet oculos ad videndum quod adhuc latet; meum non est ei datum videre secretum.'"[52] ["Ah," she said, "your prophet does not have eyes for seeing that which is hidden; it was not granted to him to see my secret."] Her physical weakness, regarded as a sign of her sex, is also mentioned by several authors. Engelhard admits that Hildegund tried to overcome her natural infirmities but failed to withstand the rigors of Cistercian life, which not only required a good knowledge of Latin (hence the assignment of the tutor, who would later become her biographer) but also entailed physical labor (the "ora et labora" mandate). He claims that Hildegund was conspicuously weak, "maxime apud nos, ubi cuncta sunt fortia."[53] [Especially among us, where all are strong.] As quoted in the epigraph, he also notes that her infirmity frequently "proclaimed her sex."

Seeking additional causes for her strange conduct, several authors make vague references to Hildegund's struggles with the devil. Only Caesarius of Heisterbach says he knows nothing of Hildegund's temptations. But even he claims that Joseph was a source of sexual temptation for other brothers. Equating women with the devil and sexuality, and transferring the sin of male lust to the woman, he quotes one of the monks at Schönau as saying, "Homo iste vel femina est vel diabolus, quia nunquam illum aspicere potui sine tentatione."[54] [This man is either a woman or the devil, for I could never look at him without being tempted.] Engelhard von Langheim lauds her victorious efforts against the devil, implying, thereby, that she suffered from demonic temptation, and the Brussels/Heidelberg version says she engaged in a difficult struggle with the devil.[55] Her fellow novice and biographer is more specific, claiming that the devil envied her progress and began to torment her with some success: "ille damnatus [...] poterat [...] venenoque pestifero tam castum pectus inficere."[56] [The damned one was able to infect her chaste breast with pestiferous venom.]

For the most part, the lives are characterized by the crossed purposes of establishing Hildegund as a saint and demonstrating the inferior nature of women, which, according to most of these narrators, can never be successfully concealed and can only remain hidden from others if God wills it. Based on her conduct, at least as represented by her contemporaries, it seems that she was torn between the cultural contradictions of giving up her disguise and continuing to live as a man. According to her fellow novice, she contemplated entering a nunnery when she returned to Cologne, but, perhaps because she had lived as a male for so long, she decided to retreat to a private house of prayer while attending a nearby school.[57] It is hinted that the owner of this house, a respected holy woman, knew the secret.[58] Thus, it is suggested that Hildegund found a refuge in which she could reveal her female nature but retain her outward male identity. This solution, however, was short-lived, for she was soon persuaded to join the community at Schönau. There, fear of discovery and the conflict between nature and environment, according to the narrator, led to erratic behavior and, finally, desperate escape attempts.

The fellow novice's description of Hildegund's final attempt to flee implies a connection not only with temptation and fear of detection but also with her gender. His account of the abortive attempt is worth quoting in full:

> Tandem, non valens sustinere daemonum conflictus, de claustro exivit, ad portam venit, habitum ibi deponere voluit: ubi virtus divina potenter eam revocavit flagello quodam: nam sanguinis fluxum tam vehementer pati coepit, quod eam redire necesse fuit. Et hoc usque ter factum est. Quod cum fieret tertia vice, tam vehementer est afflicta dolore ventris, quod in infirmitorium est delata, et infirmario commendata.[59]

> [Thus, not strong enough to withstand the afflictions of demons, she left her cell. She went to the gate and wished to take off the habit there. But (when she got there) a more powerful divine force (*virtus*) recalled her as if with a whip. For she began to suffer such a terrible flow of blood, that it was necessary for her to return. And this happened again three times. When it happened for the third time, she was so sorely afflicted with pain of the abdomen/womb that she was taken to the infirmary and entrusted to a doctor.]

No other account describes the nature of Hildegund's last illness. Although the taboos surrounding menstruation obfuscate closer inquiry, it appears that amenorrhea, or the cessation of the natural menstrual cycle that can result from ascetic practices, was not uncommon among medieval religious women.[60] Of the transvestite saints, it is specifically said of Hilaria that she did not menstruate.[61] Another holy woman in male dress, Jeanne d'Arc, was reportedly amenorrheic. Obviously, the lack of this monthly sign of femininity indicates successful renunciation of sex. Whether or not Hildegund was amenorrheic, this report of her final ailment implies a reversion to femaleness. Like the public childbirth that unmasked and destroyed the legendary female pope, a condition indicative of female sexuality undoes Hildegund and results in death and disclosure of sex.

It is possible that the author simply reported the historical fact, albeit with claim of supernatural cause, that Hildegund died from uterine hemorrhaging. Based on the general agreement in the accounts that Brother Joseph's short stay in the monastery was marked by an increasingly debilitating physical weakness, it is perhaps plausible to accept loss of blood as the cause of death. Or she may have suffered secretly with this condition until it reached such an extreme state that she determined to flee rather than risk medical examination and certain discovery. Equally likely, however, would be the view that it is the author's embellishment that, in one more way, emphasizes femaleness.

On several occasions, the authors of the *vitae* claim it was God's will that Hildegund remain disguised in the monastery until death. It is ironic, therefore, that just as Hildegund is about to defy God's will by reclaiming her womanhood, she is struck down by a palpable sign of her sex. Although all the accounts attribute essential inferiority to women, her tutor consistently depicts Hildegund's monastic life as a struggle between divine destiny to rise above her sex and the desire, instilled by the devil, to return to her own womanly (i.e., sinful) nature. Not surprisingly, this dramatic menarche or resumption of menstruation—the clearest manifestation of femaleness—is expressly connected with sin. The transgression is not Hildegund's deceptive presence in a male enclave but rather that she allows herself to be persuaded by Satan to reject the spiritual superiority of her adopted maleness. When she knowingly disobeys the will of God by leaving the monastery, God punishes her, like Eve, with female fecundity.

The inconsistencies of Christian ideology with its focus on gender and gender attributes as moral qualities and its view of women as objects of sex (both procreative and erotic) create a tension in hagiographic portrayals of women in male disguise. According to the symbolism of Christianity, the disguised woman who renounces gender and strives to be like men achieves a greatness impossible for other women. Yet an uneasiness with the female presence among men vowed to celibacy informs the recurring association of women and sexuality.

In Hildegund's case, femininity, representing as it does an imperfect state of being, comes to be viewed as demonic temptation: the desire to be a woman is sinful, and womanhood itself, it seems, is the cause of death. The problem of interpretation confounds the authors of her life because of their insistence that Hildegund's presence in the monastery fulfilled God's plan on the one hand and their perception of biological sex as a determining factor in physical, mental, and spiritual development on the other hand. In the end, they are unable to draw a convincing portrait of Hildegund as a woman with the "manly spirit" required for saintliness. Although their interpretations may reflect, in part, a psychological trauma arising from disavowal of gender, the condescending and contrived view of Hildegund's performance, whether in labor, Latin, or spiritual fortitude, undermines, at every turn, the goal of sanctifying her.

Consistently misunderstood, Hildegund's words, actions, and appearance, as reported, betray only an idea of femininity. The authors stress that male disguise became a heavy burden for Hildegund. And yet, at least to their minds, it symbolized her spiritual salvation. Is it a mark of authenticity that Hildegund does not accept disguise unequivocally? In many ways, Hildegund's internal conflict contrasts sharply with the portrayal of other women disguised as men in medieval literature. In general, disguised figures are in control of the situation, having donned their guise to achieve some personal advantage. Hildegund's ambivalence and lack of confidence are unique.

As interpreted by her contemporaries, the dilemma of disguise for Hildegund lay in lack of identity, denial of physical nature, and fear of discovery. The portrait that emerges from descriptions and analyses of her behavior depicts a young woman singled out by God for distinction yet plagued by doubt, fear, and regret. This uneven characterization, a result of the clash between biography and hagiography, between genuine admiration and androcentric outlook, makes Hildegund von Schönau one of the most complex of the transvestite saints. The depiction of her personal struggle with maleness renders her more human than the earlier disguised monks, yet it also confuses the purpose of her hagiographers, who, it seems, also suffer from the dilemma of disguise.

Chapter Four

TRANSVESTISM ON TRIAL:
THE CASE OF JEANNE D'ARC

> Le ciel pour la former, fit un rare melange
> Des vertue d'une Fille, et d'un Homme et d'un Ange.
>
> [To create her, heaven made a rare mixture
> of the virtues of a girl, a man, and an angel.]
> —Jean Chapelain[1]
>
> This witch or manly woman (called the maid of
> God) [...] was not inspired by the holy ghoste nor
> sent from God (as the Frenchemen beleve) but an
> enchanteresse, an organe of the devill, sent from
> Sathan to blind the people and bryng theim in
> unbelife.
> —Edward Hall[2]

Jeanne d'Arc (ca. 1412-1431), perhaps the most thoroughly documented medieval transvestite, illustrates the ambivalent attitudes toward cross dressing in the Middle Ages. She was controversial in so many ways—not the least of which was her preference for male dress—that numerous authorities and writers, both opponents and partisans of Charles VII (1403-1461), analyzed her case. Much of the documentation of her life results from the protracted trial at Rouen that led to her condemnation and execution. In a strictly legal sense, the Burgundians and English did not execute her at Rouen for political or military reasons; she was convicted of heresy in an ecclesiastical court and turned over to civic authorities for execution after it was claimed she had relapsed into heresy. Not countenancing the obvious political questions, the ecclesiastical court adjudicated two matters: the veracity (or source) of her supernatural auditions and the legality of her cross dressing.[3] The court at Rouen, however, was not the only institution that passed judgment on her transvestism. Charles VII, a committee in Poitiers, the theologian Jean Gerson (1363-1429), the poet Martin le Franc (1395-1460), and most of the witnesses at her posthumous trial for rehabilitation discussed the meaning and legality of her dress. As a source for her notoriety, cross dressing was only second in importance to her resounding military victories.

In 1429, a young woman calling herself Jeanne la Pucelle, having discarded a plain red dress, put on men's clothing and set out from Vaucouleurs for Chinon with a remarkable message for Charles VII of France. She claimed to have been sent from God to save France and to lead Charles to Rheims for his official coronation. Although her patriotic sentiments were in accord with the hopes of the Armagnac party in its struggle against the English and Burgundians, Jeanne was viewed with suspicion at the outset of her public life. Wary of her strangeness, Robert de Baudricourt, the governor of Vaucouleurs, brought along a priest to exorcise her when he finally agreed to a meeting.[4] He twice refused to grant her escort—after all, she was merely a country girl from Domremy—and finally sent her to Chinon with the ambivalent words, "Vade, et quod poterit venire, veniat."[5] [Go, and come what may.] At Chinon, she met with more suspicion, not only because of her claim to have a divine mission but also because of the male clothing she had worn since leaving Vaucouleurs. After some delay, Jeanne was able to speak with Charles and, in no time at all, seems to have convinced him of her power. Nonetheless, Charles sought the advice of his counsel before accepting the aid of a visionary girl wearing men's clothing.

Even before attempting to determine the legitimacy of her claim to divine inspiration, Charles reacted to Jeanne's transvestism, asking some women of the court to examine her body. According to testimony from the rehabilitation hearings (1450-56), he wanted to know "si esset vir vel mulier, et an esset corrupta vel virga"[6] [if she was a man or woman, and whether she was corrupted or a virgin]. The results, like those of a similar examination conducted later by women of the Burgundian side, confirmed Jeanne's femininity and virginity. In both cases, this test represented more than simple verification of sex and sexual status; it contributed to the general validation of her claim of divine inspiration. The suspicion of masculinity, however, persisted to her death, when her executioners showed the crowds her body before it was completely burned.

No observers report that Jeanne had a masculine or even androgynous appearance. Quite the contrary, several contemporaries mention her feminine attributes, in particular her beautiful breasts.[7] The only contemporary likeness of Jeanne, a sketch in the margin of an account of the siege of Orléans dated May 1429, shows an obviously female figure in profile with breasts and a small waist.[8] The male clothing set her apart from other women, whereas her transparent femininity distinguished her from the men with whom she fought. By distancing her from her sex without concealing it, cross dressing became Jeanne's trademark, so to speak; it was the outward sign of transcendence and uniqueness.

For ecclesiastical investigation, Jeanne was taken in the spring of 1429 to the University of Poitiers, where theologians questioned her not only about her faith and mission but also about her masculine attire. While the proceedings of these interrogations have not survived, the conclusions are recorded in several contemporary documents. Either because she impressed them or because they understood what Charles wanted, the Poitiers investigators advised Charles to test her claims by sending her to Orléans as she requested.[9] In June 1429, Perceval de Boulainvilliers, a nobleman loyal to Charles, recorded their findings as to the orthodoxy of her faith: "Et in his omnibus, reperta est fidelis catholica, bene sentiens in fide, sacramentis et institutis Ecclesiae."[10] [In all these things, she was found to be a faithful Catholic, well observant in the faith and in the institutional sacraments of the church.]

According to Jeanne's testimony at Rouen, she was questioned about her male dress at Poitiers:

> Interrogata an recordetur quod magistri qui examinaverunt eam [...] interrogaveruntne ipsam in mutatione sui habitus: respondit: "Ego non recordor; tamen ipsi me interrogaverunt ubi ego ceperam istum habitum virilem; et ego dixi eis quod ego ceperam apud oppidum Valliscoloris."[11]

> [Asked whether she remembered that the experts who examined her had asked her about the change of her dress. She answered, "I do not remember. However, they did ask me when I began to wear men's clothes, and I told them I began in the village of Vaucouleurs."]

She also implied that a written account of the trial existed when she told her hostile judges to send for the book at Poitiers to learn what she had answered about her transvestism. Judging from all accounts of that inquisition, however, its favorable opinion would not have been welcome evidence in Rouen.[12] The Poitiers investigation is enacted in the *Mystère du siège d'Orléans*, a play performed in Jeanne's honor by the people of Orléans as early as 1435. In the drama, Jeanne explains her transvestism straightforwardly:

> Puis que c'est le voloir de Dieu
> Et qu'i m'est permis en l'office,
> Me fault gouvener en ce lieu
> Pour luy acomplir son service
> Et l'estat qui est plus propice
> Pour guerroyer et batailler,
> En abit d'omme est plus notice
> Que de femme pour travailler.[13]

> [Because it is the will of God and it is permitted for me in this office, it is right for me to act in this place (i.e., a man's place) to accomplish His service. And the state is more propitious for waging war and fighting battles, since male dress is better suited than that of women for the work.]

At about the same time, Enea Sylvio Piccolomini (soon to be Pope Pius II), who was not present at any of the proceedings, seems to quote from official notes when he comments on her defense of cross dressing at Poitiers:

> Rogata cur vestes viriles mulieri prohibitas induisset, virginem sese ait; virgini utrumque habitum convenire; sibi a Deo mandatum esse vestibus ut virilibus uteretur, cui et arma tractanda essent virilia.[14]

> [Asked why she had put on men's clothes, which are forbidden for women, she said she was a maiden and it was fitting for a maiden to have both styles of dress; that it was mandated by God that she wear masculine clothing, for whom manly arms would also have to be used.]

In an early literary account of Jeanne's life, the *Chronique de la Pucelle* (ca. 1467), the author also claims to quote Jeanne's answer to questions about her clothing at Poitiers. To the defense that it was necessary for warfare, Jeanne adds that male clothing protects her from sexual advances or abuse:

> Je croy bien qu'il vous semble estrange, et non sans cause; mais il fault, pour ce que je me doibs armer et servir le gentil daulphin en armes, que je prenne les habillemens procipes et nécessaires à ce; et aussi quand je serois entre les hommes, estant en habit d'homme, ils

n'auront pas concupiscence charnelle de moi; et me semble qu'en cest estat je conserveray mieulx ma virginité de pensée et de faict.[15]

[I believe this seems strange to you, and not without cause; but since I must arm myself and serve the gentle Dauphin in war, it is necessary for me to wear these clothes, and also when I am among men in the habit of men, they have no carnal desire for me; and it seems to me that thus I can better preserve my purity in thought and deed.]

This additional defense, if Jeanne actually used it, would have exonerated her from any charges of wrongdoing, since protection of virginity, as even one of her enemies admitted, legitimated transvestism in the eyes of the church:

> De quinta propositione, quod ex mandato Dei assumpsit habitum viri, etc., hoc non est verisimile, sed magis scandalosum, indecens et inhonestum, maxime mulieri et puellae, quam se esse dicit, nisi hoc faceret ad praeservationem violentiae inferendae, propter virginitatem servandam.[16]

> [Concerning the fifth article, that she assumed male clothing at God's order, etc. This is not believable but rather scandalous, indecent, and dishonest, especially for the woman and girl that she says she is, unless this were done to preserve her from coming into violence, especially for protecting virginity.]

The protective power of transvestism takes on almost magical properties in the accounts of her fellow soliders at the rehabilitation trial. They all swear that they were never moved by lust or desire for her, although they lived in close quarters and even slept near her. [17]

Although the Poitiers proceedings, which may have contained evidence for ecclesiastical approval of transvestism, are lost, several testimonies of theologians survive from the first months of Jeanne's career. All of them address the matter of male disguise.

A treatise long attributed to Heinrich van Gorkum (ca. 1386-1431) considers the authenticity of Jeanne's mission and the appropriateness of her male dress.[18] *De quadam puella* was probably written in the late spring of 1429 soon after Jeanne proclaimed her purpose in Chinon and before the battle of Orléans in May of that year. Although the general tenor of the introduction implies approbation of the unnamed girl—she is referred to merely as "puella"—the work adduces arguments for and against her. This cautious approach may have seemed warranted since, after all, Jeanne was an unknown and unproven ally. The ambivalent attitude, however, prefigures the polarity in subsequent interpretations of her appearance and mission.

Drawing together material from the Bible and patristic authorities, the author presents six arguments that support and six that refute her worthiness. On the positive side, he cites biblical precedents that sanction her dress as well as her role as a politically active woman. Salvation, he says, often comes "per fragilem sexum et innocentem aetatem"[19] [through the fragile sex and innocent youth]. As examples, he mentions the Virgin Mary, as well as such women as Deborah, Esther, and Judith, who delivered their people from military threats. Furthermore, there is nothing wrong, according to the implications of some biblical stories, with putting on different clothing:

> Nec mirum si in statu equestri sit alterius luminis quam in solito statu mulierbri: quia etiam David, volens Dominum consulere induebat ephod et sumpsit psalterium; et Moises, dum virgam gestabat mirabilia faciebat, quia, sicut dicit Gregorius: "Spiritus Sanctus frequenter se interius conformat exterioribus concurrentibus."[20]

> [Nor is it surprising if in the habit of a knight she should be of a different glory than in the ordinary habit of a woman, because indeed David, wishing to consult the Lord, put on the ephod (priestly dress) and took up the psaltery; and Moses when he waved the rod performed miracles, since, just as Gregory says, "the Holy Spirit within frequently conforms itself to the exterior appearances it comes upon."]

Thus, it can be deduced that male clothing gave her special power: "vestibus et armis virilibus induta, ascendit equum; quae dum in equo est, ferens vexillum statim mirabili viget industria quasi peritus dux exercitus ad artificiosam exercitus institutionem. Tunc quoque sui efficiuntur animosi."[21] [Dressed in male clothes and arms, she mounts her horse; when she is on the horse and carrying the banner, immediately she becomes invigorated with miraculous industry, like an experienced leader of an army well versed in the skillful arrangement of an army; and then the men are also inspired with courage.] Elsewhere, however, the author claims that as soon as she dismounts, she resumes her womanly attire and reverts to the status of an innocent girl.[22] No evidence corroborates this point. Uneasy perhaps with male dress, the author of De quadam puella wants Jeanne to appear to accept her modest position as a woman. While he believes that cross dressing can manifest divine empowerment, he explicitly limits it to extraordinary circumstances.

The six counter-arguments cite biblical laws that forbid male impersonation, arguing that the girl has broken the law of Deuteronomy (22:5) against transvestism as well as Paul's injunction against women cutting their hair (1 Cor. 11:6). In direct opposition to the favorable comparisons to biblical heroines, here it is claimed that Esther and Judith actually adorned their femininity to conquer their foes, whereas this girl defeminizes ("effeminare") herself and immodestly "transforms herself into a worldly man of arms."[23] Despite numerous exceptions to these laws, including Paul's own disciple Thecla, the charge of breaching biblical law finds no contradiction in the propositions for endorsement.

Another apologetic work from 1429, *De mirabilia victoria cujusdam puellae*, puts forth a stronger case for Jeanne's transvestism. The treatise, which is generally attributed to Jean Gerson, has enjoyed broad circulation, and was read at Jeanne's rehabilitation trial.[24] In many ways similar to *De quadam puella*, this tract is less structured but contains a more detailed defense of Jeanne's male dress. It may have been prepared at the request of the Poitiers investigators, many of whom were former colleagues of Gerson at the University of Paris and had remained loyal to him after his exile.[25] Gerson refutes the argument that transvestism violates biblical law on several grounds, claiming that: 1) the law of Deuteronomy proceeds from a legal code that has been superseded by the new law; 2) the law against transvestism is a moral law directed only against indecent clothing; and 3) the law does not forbid masculine clothing in extraordinary cases. To these proofs Gerson adds examples of such martial heroines as Camilla (the warrior-heroine of the *Aeneid*) and the Amazons.

Although ancient female warriors may be apt parallels to Jeanne, they offered little support against charges of transgressing canon law. This problem was addressed, however, in the contemporaneous *Sibylla Francica* (1429), the work of an unnamed German cleric.[26] The author, who explains the prophecies that purportedly foretold Jeanne's appearance, endorses her male dress on the authority of Thomas Aquinas. In the *Summa theologiae*, Aquinas had determined that women may put on men's clothing without sin if necessity dictates:

Et ideo de se vitiosum est quod mulier utatur veste virili, aut e
converso; et praecipue quia hoc potest esse causa lasciviae. Et
specialiter prohibetur in Lege (Deut. 22:5), quia gentiles tali mutatione
habitus utebantur ad idololatriae superstitionem. Potest tamen
quandoque hoc fieri sine peccato propter aliquam necessitatem, vel
causa se occultandi ab hostibus, vel propter defectum alterius
vestimenti, vel propter aliquid aliud hujusmodi.[27]

[And thus, of itself it is sinful for a woman to wear male clothing, or
vice versa, especially since this can be a cause of lasciviousness. And
it is particularly prohibited in the law (Deuteronomy 22:5) because
the gentiles used to make use of such changes of attire for the
superstition of idolatry. Nonetheless, this can be done without sin at
any time because of some necessity, or to hide from enemies, or
because of lack of other clothing, or for some such thing of this
nature.]

To this strong endorsement, the cleric adds the Christian example
of the transvestite saints, in particular St. Marina. The comparison
is obviously meant to link Jeanne to a type of cross dressing that
was acceptable to the church: "Et si Deo placuit Marina virgo
militans in habitu spirituali virili, [...] quanto magis ista virgo sibylla
in armis bellicis non offendit; sed ad defendendum et praecavendum
pro republica et communi bono poterit militare?"[28] [And if the brave
virgin Marina pleased God in the habit of a spiritual man, how
much less does this prophetic virgin in warlike arms offend; rather,
she will be able to fight to defend and protect the state and the
common good.]

The arguments and examples of Gerson and the *Sibylla Francica*
were taken up again during the rehabilitation hearings. Writing briefs
in support of the rehabilitation trial, such experts in canon law as
Thomas Basin, Martin Berruyer, Jean Bochard, Guillaum Bouillé,
and Jean Bréhal, cited the passage from Thomas Aquinas quoted
above as a crowning argument in favor of Jeanne's transvestism.[29]
They also expanded the list of models of Christian cross dressing to
include Pelagia, Natalia, Theodora, Euphrosyne, Eugenia, and
even Thecla in their defense of Jeanne's male dress.

In another early tract dated May 1429, Jacques Gelu (ca. 1370-
1432), archbishop of Embrun, reinforced the theological excuses for
transvestism with the practical argument that male clothing is more
appropriate for waging war: "Decentius enim est ut ista in habitu
virili committantur, propter conversationem cum viris, quam alias."[30]

[For it is more decent that these things (military activities) be done in male attire than otherwise because of the contact with men.] This mundane defense, which Jeanne herself is said to have used, is also echoed in the fifteenth-century poem *Champion des dames* by Martin le Franc. Martin's champion answers his adversary's disdain for Jeanne's transvestism rather prosaically, observing that the traditional long dress worn by women is impractical: "La longue cote (tu n'as doubtes), / Es fais de guerre n'est pas boine."[31] [The long robe (you cannot doubt it) is not suitable for acts of war.]

Whether excused for its practicality or defended as a sign of divine aid, those loyal to the Armagnac cause were disposed to approve of Jeanne's male dress. It was also claimed that she fulfilled certain prophecies about a virgin who would save France, and the French felt that they were in need of a miracle. The first poet to celebrate Jeanne's success, Christine de Pizan, alludes to these prophecies—attributing them to Merlin and Bede—in her *Ditié de Jehanne d'Arc* (July 1429).[32] Yet, although Christine praises women in male dress elsewhere in her writings,[33] she does not dwell on Jeanne's transvestism. A long-time champion of women, Christine prefers to present Jeanne as proof of female superiority and a source of honor for the feminine sex. As recorded by both French and English sources, however, the prophecy of Merlin indicated that a female savior would come to France in masculine dress: "Virgo puellares artus induta virili / Veste, Dei monitu, properat relevare jacentem / Liliferum regemque."[34] [Having dressed girlish limbs with male clothing, a virgin hastens, at God's admonishment, to raise up the fallen, the lily-bearing king.]

Not surprisingly, the Burgundians and English viewed Jeanne in a different light. They equated her male clothing with her success at the battles of Orléans, Jargeau, and Patay, where she wrought destruction on the opposing forces. What the Armagnacs viewed as divine aid, the English forces considered demonic magic. Her transvestism particularly rankled the English, whose polemics against Jeanne almost always include references to male dress as a sign of wantonness or evil. As early as August 1429, the guardian of Henry VI, John of Lancaster, the duke of Bedford, chastened Charles for relying on "that disorderly and deformed travesty of a woman who dresses like a man!"[35] In a letter to the king of England written about the same time, he pronounced her "a disciple and lyme of the Feende,

called the Pucelle, that used fals enchauntements and sorcerie."³⁶ At
Rouen, Jeanne's captors emphasized the scandalous implications of
her male dress, in which she allegedly consorted with men, shed
blood, and received the sacraments at the instigation of the devil.³⁷
In an official letter to the pope, emperor, and cardinals, the faculty
of the University of Paris went so far as to compare Jeanne to the
false Christ of the Apocalypse.³⁸ The demonic is also alluded to in
the so-called *Journal de Bourgeois de Paris* (1414-49), where
transvestism not only blurs gender distinctions but also renders
Jeanne's humanity suspect. In an oft-quoted statement, the author
hints that Jeanne may be a monster: "une créature qui estoit en
forme de femme [...], que on nommoit la Pucelle. Que c'estoit,
Dieu le scet."³⁹ [A creature that, in form, was a woman, whom they
called la Pucelle. What it was, God knows.] Although it did not
become a primary charge at Jeanne's trial, she was also accused of
being a witch during the Rouen proceedings: "Ipsa foemina est
mendosa ac divinatrix."⁴⁰ [This woman is evil and a witch.] English
fear of her power induced them to delay the siege of Louviers until
after her execution because they believed they could not succeed
while she lived.⁴¹ That the English perpetrated the notion of Jeanne
as sorceress is evident from Shakespeare's later portrayal of her as an
evil woman whose success came from spells, incantations, and
Faustian pacts with the devil.⁴²

Ultimately, Jeanne's luck failed and she was captured by
Burgundian forces at Compiègne on 23 May 1430. Ransomed to
the English for a prince's price, she was handed over to church
officials for prosecution on charges of heresy.

In the introduction to the trial against her, Pierre Cauchon
(†1442), the chief prosecutor, excoriated Jeanne for her male dress:

> Fama vero jam multis in locis percrebuerat mulierem ipsam illius
> honestatis que muliebrem sexum decet, prorsus immemorem,
> abruptis verecundiae frenis, totius foeminei pudoris oblitam, deformes
> habitus virili sexui congruos, mira et monstruosa deformitate gerere.⁴³

> [Indeed, already in many places, the report has been spread about
> that this woman, completely forgetful of the honesty that beseems
> the female sex, having broken the bonds of shame, oblivious to all
> feminine modesty, with astonishing and monstrous brazenness, wears
> immodest garments belonging to the male sex.]

Throughout the trial, Jeanne's male dress is the subject of countless interrogations. As a matter of contention, it is second only to questions about her voices. Almost every description of the defendant criticizes her "scandalous" appearance. The judges questioned her about the origin and reason for her male dress, repeatedly asking if she considered transvestism a crime. Early in the trial, it was decided that she would not be permitted to hear mass unless she renounced her male dress. In the preliminary lists of accusations and admonishments, the charge of transvestism occurs almost thirty times, and two of the final twelve charges against Jeanne concern male dress. Above all, article five condemns her transvestism as blasphemy:

> Item, dixisti quod, de praecepto Dei et ejus bene placito, tu portasti et continue portas habitum virilem; et quia habebas praeceptum Dei de portando hunc habitum, cepisti brevem tunicam, gipponem, caligas ligatas cum multis aguilletis; portas etiam capillos tonsos in rotundum supra summitatem aurium, non dimittendo aliquid super te, quod sexum foemineum approbet aut demonstret, excepto eo quod tibi natura contulit; et saepe recepisti in hoc habitu sacramentum eucharistiae; et, quanquam pluries admonita fueris de dimittendo, nihilominus noluisti facere, dicens quod malles mori quam dimittere hunc habitum, ad minus nisi hoc esset de praecepto Dei; et quod, si tu esses adhuc in isto habitu, cum aliis de parte tua, esset unum de magnis bonis Franciae. Dicis etiam quod, pro nulla re, faceres juramentum de non portando hunc habitum et arma; et in omnibus his, dicis te bene fecisse et de mandato Dei.
>
> Quantum ad istud punctum, clerici dicunt quod tu blasphemas Deum et contemnis ipsum in sacramentis suis; transgrederis legem divinam, sacram Scripturam et canonicas sanctiones; male sentis et erras in fide; te jactas inaniter et es suspecta de idolatria et exsecratione tui ipsius ac tuarum vestium, ritum gentilium imitando.[44]

[Likewise, you have said that you wore and still wear men's clothing at God's command and at his good pleasure, and because you had orders from God to wear this habit, you have put on a short tunic, doublet, and boots tied up with many pointed laces. You even wear you hair cut round above the ears, not displaying anything about you that confirms or demonstrates sex, except what nature has given you. And often you have received the sacrament of the eucharist in this apparel. And although you have many times been admonished to put it off, nonetheless you did not want to do it, saying that you would rather die than relinquish this dress, unless this were at God's command; and that if you were still in this dress with those of your own side, it would be for the great good of France. You also say that for no reason would you take an oath not to wear this dress and carry these arms; and in all these things you say you have done well and at God's command.

As far as this point is concerned, the clergy declare that you blaspheme God and disdain him in his sacraments, that you transgress divine law, holy scripture, and canonical sanctions, that you think wrongly and err from the faith, that you utter inanities, and you are suspected of idolatry and blasphemy of yourself and your clothing, according to the customs of the heathens.]

The Rouen judges continually voiced their disapproval of Jeanne's appearance, demanding that she put off the male clothing. They never forced her to do so, however, as they easily might have done. Her insistence on maintaining this visible sign of lawlessness actually advanced their case against her. To dress as a man, they argued, violated nature and biblical mandates, as well as secular and canon law. Although the veracity of Jeanne's visions might be debated, the reality of her appearance offered incontrovertible proof of transgression.

Jeanne was no less concerned about retaining male dress, since, for her, male clothing signified obedience to a higher authority. Although her answers varied, she consistently returned to the opinion that her transvestism represented God's will.[45] When asked who advised her to wear men's clothing, she said, "Non cepit ipsam vestem, neque aliquid fecit, nisi per Dei praeceptum et angelorum."[46] [She did not put on this dress nor did she do anything, except at the command of God and the angels.] In response to the repeated accusation that transvestism is blasphemy, she replied, "Ille habitus non onerabat animam suam, et quod ipsum portare non erat contra Ecclesiam."[47] [This attire did not burden her soul, and that to wear it was not against the church.] At one point, however, she agreed to put on women's clothing in order to receive communion,[48] but the judges conveniently overcame this threat to their case by requiring her to give up male dress permanently. Later, she returned to her defiant posture, claiming that God had the power to let her hear mass in men's clothing without them.[49] She even taunted her judges by agreeing to resume feminine dress if permitted to leave. Yet she also assured them that she would revert to male clothing as soon as possible in order to attack the English again.[50]

Tired, perhaps, of incessant interrogations about her clothing, Jeanne once retorted that the dress was "a little thing, indeed the least."[51] Given her categorical refusal to put on women's clothing, however, one must assume that this was said out of exasperation with the question or to put cross dressing into proper perspective vis-à-vis the goal of saving France. If anything, Jeanne's dress became more important in the course of the trial than it had been before her capture. The refusal to abandon male dress arose not only from the personal conviction that God required it; her insistence on its religious validity also implied an unwillingness to accept the authority of the court. This implication did not escape the notice of her prosecutors, who charged her with insubordination. Jeanne was not politically naive; she clearly understood that the Burgundian clerics were carrying out the will of the English, who wanted her destroyed. She denied the rightful jurisdiction of the Burgundian church officials and shrewdly demanded, on several occasions, that the pope adjudicate her case.[52] Contrary to ecclesiastical legal code, however, she was denied this appeal on the untenable grounds that the distance between Rouen and Rome was too great.

The church was hopelessly divided in its opinion of cross dressing in general and in Jeanne's case specifically. Both her clerical supporters and detractors could base their partisan views on a variety of acceptable sources. Ecclesiastical authorities often contradicted one another, with opinions ranging from positive assessments of transvestite saints, to punishment of cross dressing as a venial sin, to the contention that it was heretical. The important concordance to canon law, the *Decretum* of Gratian (twelfth century), drew upon the decrees of the Council of Granga to anathematize female gender inversion: "Si qua mulier suo proposito utile judicans, ut virili veste utatur, propter hoc virilem habitum imitetur, anathema sit."[53] [If a woman, judging it useful according to her own decision, put on male clothing, she is anathematized because this is imitating male dress.] Despite Gratian's view that it deserved excommunication, medieval penitentials often recommended more lenient punishments. The penitentials of St. Hubert (ca. 850) and Robert of Flamborough (†ca. 1224) prescribe a three-year penance for transvestism.[54] Furthermore, the judges and the theologians from the University of Paris undoubtedly knew of Aquinas's moderate stance on cross dressing as well as the tales of exemplary transvestite saints. Just as the clerics

at Poitiers overlooked negative opinions of cross dressing to approve
Jeanne's mission, so the court at Rouen ignored any positive examples
because they did not suit their political aims. Interestingly, however,
they neglected to cite the most damning example of female
transvestism, the female pope, since to do so would have discredited
the church. To rid themselves of an enemy, they were content to
disregard ecclesiastical practice, the tradition of hagiography, and
even the authority of Aquinas in favor of the letter of the law, which
condemned female transvestism as blasphemy.

Although Jeanne's transvestism alone might have served as cause
enough for condemnation, it also led to the additional charge of
disobedience to the temporal church. She rejected the
admonishments of the clergy to resume feminine attire on the
grounds that she wore male clothing at God's behest. Thus, she
distinguished between the church on earth (Ecclesia Militans) and
the divine order (Ecclesia Triumphans), rather than accepting the
concept of a unified church in which the Church Militant acts as
the intermediary to the Church Triumphant. The last article of the
condemnatory charges against Jeanne specifically brands her a
schismatic apostate for her refusal to submit her deeds to the Church
Militant:

> Nec de istis vis te referre judicio Ecclesiae quae est in terris, nec
> alicujus hominis viventis, nisi soli Deo. [...] Quantum ad istud, clerici
> dicunt quod es schismatica, male sentiens de unitate et auctoritate
> Ecclesiae, apostata et hucusque pertinaciter errans in fide.[55]

> [Nor do you wish to submit yourself in these matters to the judgment
> of the church that is on earth, nor of any living man, but only to
> God alone. [...] Because of this, the clerics say that you are schismatic,
> thinking wrongly about the unity and authority of the church, and
> apostate for thus far persistently erring in faith.]

As was the case with so many of the mystics toward whom the church
maintained an apprehensive and sometimes hostile posture, claims
for personal contact with the divine were met with opposition since
they diminished the role of ecclesiastical officials. In Jeanne's case,
political forces inspired such charges, but her insistence on the
superiority of her voices allowed the clerics at Rouen to base their
case on theological doctrine.

Jeanne's unswerving contention that she spoke with God's
messengers irked her prosecutors not only because it challenged

their authority but also because it implied that God was on the side
of the Armagnac party. When asked why one of her voices, St.
Margaret, spoke French instead of English (St. Margaret was a
popular English saint), she said, "Why should she speak English
when she is not on the side of the English?"[56] On several occasions,
she proclaimed that it was God's will for the French to drive out the
English from their land. Her claim of divine inspiration implied
that God wanted to provide the Armagnac party with a champion
who might conquer the English. The idea of a partisan God might
be rejected pragmatically by theologians, but the Rouen churchmen
failed to conceal their political leanings in their assessment of Jeanne's
visions. They dismissed the possibility of heavenly visitors who aided
France's campaign against the English, concluding instead that
Jeanne had been misled by demonic phantoms in the guise of angels.
With such an interpretation, they discredited the Armagnac side
without denying the supernatural contacts attributed to her.[57]

On 24 May 1431, Jeanne d'Arc allegedly signed a letter of
abjuration that denied her voices and admitted that she had
blasphemed God and transgressed divine and canon law by wearing
male clothing and cutting her hair short:

> je confesse que j'ay très griefment péchié, en faignant men-
> çongeusement avoir eu révélacions et apparicions de par Dieu, par
> les anges et saincte Katherine et saincte Marguerite, en séduisant les
> autres, en créant folement et légièrement, en faisant supersticieuses
> divinacions, en blaphemant Dieu, ses Sains et ses Sainctes; en
> trespassant la loy divine, la saincte Escripture, les droiz canons; en
> portant habit dissolu, difforme et deshonneste contre la décence de
> nature, et cheveux rongnez en ront en guise de homme, contre toute
> honnesteté du sexe de femme.[58]

> [I confess that I have sinned grievously in falsely pretending to have
> had revelations and apparitions from God, from his angels, and from
> St. Catherine and St. Marguerite; in seducing others; in believing
> madly and easily; in making superstitious divinations; in blaspheming
> God, his angels and his saints; in trespassing divine law, holy scripture,
> and canon law; in wearing a dissolute habit, misshapen and dishonest,
> against the decency of nature, and hair cut round in the style of a
> man, against all honesty of the feminine sex.]

Condemned to life imprisonment, she was led back to the English
military prison and outfitted with a woman's dress. Four days later,
her accusers were summoned to her cell by the report that she had

put on men's clothes again. The clothing dramatically signified Jeanne's "relapse," and, indeed, her apparel was the chief topic of the short interrogation that preceded her condemnation as a relapsed heretic: "Interroguée pourquoy elle l'avoit prins, et qui luy avoit fait prandre: respond qu'elle l'a prins de sa voulenté, sans nulle contraincte, et qu'elle ayme mieulx l'abit d'omme que de femme."[59] [Asked why she had put it on, and who had made her put it on, she responded that she put it on of her own will, under no compulsion, and that she liked male attire better than female.] According to her, she had never meant to forswear it or anything else.

When pressed about the clothing, she answered enigmatically "pour ce qu'il luy estoit plus licite de le reprendre et avoir habit d'omme, estant entre les hommes, que de avoir habit de femme."[60] [That it was more lawful and fitting to have male clothing while she was among men than to have women's clothing.] This excuse has led some historians to suppose that Jeanne was sexually molested and perhaps even raped after her abjuration.[61] The contention is supported by several Rouen witnesses for her rehabilitation who testified from 1450 to 1456 before yet another ecclesiastical court. During the inquiries that eventually reversed the church's judgment of 1431, Guillaume Manchon (†1456), the official court reporter at the original trial, proved a valuable source of information. He testified that Jeanne excused her return to male clothing saying that she would not have done so if she had been taken to an ecclesiastical prison with female guards, as had been promised at the abjuration.[62] Manchon and several others admitted that Jeanne complained of sexual harassment from her English guards.[63] One witness, Martin Ladvenu, said that Jeanne herself told him of this and also of an attempted rape by an English lord: "Quidam magnus dominus Anglicus introivit carcerem dictae Johannae, et tentavit eam vi opprimere; et haec erat causa, ut asserebat, quare resumpserat habitum virilem."[64] [A certain great English lord entered her cell, according to Jeanne, and attempted to rape her; and it was on account of this, she maintained, that she had resumed male dress.] As we have seen in the cases of the female monks and the bearded saints, masculinization is often equated with deformity and serves as a protection for feminine virginity. Yet Jeanne's male clothing would not have protected her from rape. Witnesses for her rehabilitation stress this insupportable claim, however, overlooking the fact that she was shackled and could have done nothing to defend herself.[65]

Modern scholars, most notably Marina Warner and Anne Llewellyn Barstow, have posited that her guards felt free to attack her only after she had denied her authority and resumed her female dress.[66] This argument—which attributes prodigious powers to transvestism—is based on the notion that the English were extremely superstitious and feared contact with a witch. There is, however, also evidence that her enemies mocked her authority and threatened her with sexual violence before her abjuration. Jeanne's comrade, the Duke of Alençon, reports that her insistence on the title "la Pucelle" actually incited a Burgundian sympathizer to threaten her with rape: "quidam homo...dixit ista verba: 'Esse pas là la Pucelle?' negando Deum quod si haberet eam nocte, quod ipsam non redderet puellam!"[67] [A certain man said these words, "Is this not the virgin maid?" Swearing by God, he said that if he could have her for a night, she would not remain a maid.] In an apparent play on "la Pucelle," the English commander Glasdale called Jeanne "la Putain" (the whore).[68] Unless she was protected by an official order, as some claimed,[69] it seems unlikely that her enemies would not have attempted to rape her, since her virginity was viewed as the source of her strength and success against the English.

Whether or not Jeanne was sexually abused in prison, her reversion to masculine clothing has more significance than mere physical protection. It symbolized her denial of the entire statement of abjuration. According to her, she had not understood the statement she had signed, and, if she agreed to anything contrary to all that she had maintained during the trial, she claimed she had done so for fear of fire.[70] Yet after reaffirming her belief in her voices (in an answer glossed with the comment "responsio mortifera" [a fatal response]), she made a remarkable statement: "Si les juges veullent, elle reprandra habit de femme; du résidu elle n'en fera autre chose."[71] [If the judges wished, she would put on women's clothing again; as for the rest, she would not do otherwise (i.e., she would not deny).] This willingness to abandon the outward sign of her struggle against the judges' authority seems strange unless one understands that Jeanne realized, like the author of the marginal note quoted above, that she would soon be executed. Indeed, earlier in the trial she had asked that, in the event of her condemnation, she might be given "une chemise de femme, et un queuvrechief en sa teste."[72] [A woman's dress and a hood for her head.] When asked why she wanted to die in women's clothes when she rejected them so adamantly in life, she simply said of the requested dress: "il luy suffist qu'elle soit longue."[73] [It would suffice if it were long.] Despite her ambivalence toward male dress in her final hours, Jeanne's return to transvestism after the abjuration gave the judges the visible proof they needed to declare her a relapsed heretic.

Some witnesses maintained that Jeanne was tricked into resuming male clothing. Jean Massieu reports that soon after she had put on a woman's dress as ordered after her abjuration, her guards stripped her of it and threw into her cell a sack containing her male attire.[74] She protested that such apparel was forbidden her, but, in the end, she was forced to put on the clothes in order to leave her cell to relieve herself. Thus, the judges fulfilled the promise purportedly made by a cleric to the Earl of Warwick after Jeanne's escape from death through abjuration, "Domine, non curetis; bene rehabebimus eam."[75] [Don't worry, lord, we will get her again successfully.]

Regardless of the cause of the return to male dress, transvestism remains a primary reason for condemnation. During the rehabilitation hearings, witnesses to the event in Rouen were asked why she was charged with being a relapsed heretic after she had clearly stated her willingness to submit herself to the pope. Everyone of them cited the reversion to male dress as the reason.[76] Pierre Cusquel stated this succinctly: "Populus dicebat quod nulla erat alia causa condemnationis suae, nisi resumptio habitus virilis."[77] [The people said there was no other cause for her condemnation, except the resumption of masculine clothing.]

Even among the supporters of Jeanne's rehabilitation one senses an uneasiness toward her cross dressing. For the most part, they overlooked her own explanation for transvestism when they defended it as a protective device or blamed her enemies for forcing her to put on men's clothes after the abjuration. They shied away from extolling her transvestism but offered various excuses to legitimate it within the Christian tradition. For example, the rehabilitation proceedings include a defense for receiving the sacraments in male dress grounded in hagiographic precedence:

> non debet haereticum judicari si in eo habitu sacramenta sumpsit,
> quoniam necessitate officii et ministerii suscepit, et bona de causa

induebatur. Sicut nec beatae Marinae quis imputabit ad culpam, si in monasterio monachorum, perpetuo in virili habitu, incognita vixit, cum monachis communicans in sacramentis [...]. Simile de beata Eugenia, quae in virili habitu diutissime et castissime vixit.[78]

[It ought not to be judged heretical if she received the sacrament in this habit (male dress), since it had been taken up out of necessity for her duty and office, and it was worn for a good cause. Just as no one will fault blessed Marina, who was accused of a crime, if, continually in men's clothes, she dwelt incognito in the monastery of monks, communicating in the sacraments with the monks. Similarly, concerning blessed Eugenia, who lived for a very long time and very chastely in men's clothes.]

Jeanne apparently never made such excuses during her trial, although they were attributed to her by later authors. In fact, she failed to use any of her supporters' defenses for transvestism at her trial. She neglected to cite examples of biblical heroines and transvestite saints, although it is likely that she had heard of such precedents either from French encomiasts in their tributes to her or from her own religious upbringing. Instead, she persisted in the unprovable claim that God was the source of her transvestism. Perhaps she ignored biblical and hagiographic precedents because they were not her models. Unlike Jeanne, Judith and Esther used womanly charms to succeed, and although she also has been compared with female monks, her goal was not the imitation of meek men.[79] The transvestite saints' lives of self-effacement in the cloister had little in common with Jeanne's military career. Even Camilla, Penthesilea, and Semiramis, the classical female warriors, whom Jeanne, with her limited education, may not even have known, offered no analogy to her divinely ordained transvestism. Jeanne was obviously not concerned with precedents; she emphasized the importance of her male dress without apology because it distinguished her, served as a source of strength, and, she maintained, represented God's will.

Although the outward appearance of the dominant sex gave her the trappings of authority, Jeanne had no desire to masculinize herself. On one occasion, she refused to say if she wished she were a man.[80] Her name, "la Pucelle," and her concern for publicly declaring her femininity attest to her identification with the female sex, yet her innocent posture and virginity align her more closely with the sexless state of childhood. Some have argued that she achieved an androgynous ideal.[81] While it is true that Jeanne's own emphasis on female traits and her insistence on male dress set her apart from either sex, her goal was neither androgyny nor any type of sexual transcendence. Rather, her male dress became a sign of the authority she claimed from her mystical auditions.

As attested by figures as diverse as the female monks, the infamous female pope, and the heroines of secular literature to be discussed in the next chapters, medieval sources express widely divergent opinions about female cross dressing. Jeanne d'Arc's case is unusual not only because transvestism became a focal point for contemporaries who assessed her extraordinary accomplishments but also because it demonstrates the basic inconsistencies in attitudes toward cultural gender in the Middle Ages. In the act of debating Jeanne's male dress, her supporters and opponents also established their positions on gender roles and the effect of sex on behavior. Jeanne defied stereotypical gender models to a certain extent, but in the inversion of roles she conformed to the sexual hierarchy by adopting male dress and androcentric symbols of heroism and strength. In her insistence on transvestism as divinely mandated, she reaffirmed the notion of maleness as a moral quality indicative of spiritual advancement. The masculine paradigm for heroism, however, was incomplete because of Jeanne's clear presentation of herself in female terms as a virgin and innocent vessel for a divine plan. From these incongruent elements emerged a hero clearly defined by her female sex yet unconfined by gender constructs for women. The case of Jeanne d'Arc, in every forum in which it was argued, illustrates both the oppressiveness of gender ideology in the Middle Ages and the willingness, in cultural, theological, and legal discourse, to overrule the gender code, at least to a degree. Her paradoxical status, like the dichotomous views on her cross dressing from equally legitimate historical and canonical sources used to defend or impugn her, reveals the fundamental contradictions in medieval cultural and biological views of gender.

Chapter Five

THE FEMALE POPE AND
THE SIN OF MALE DISGUISE

> O Deus inclite, quid non audent mulieres?
> [Great God, what will women not dare?]
> —Giovanni Boccaccio,
> on the female pope[1]

The legend of the female pope presents the curious ecclesiastical fiction that a woman, disguised as a man, wielded absolute authority over the male-dominated church. Medieval authors were fascinated with this woman, as evidenced by the numerous accounts in chronicles, biographical literature, short didactic or polemical works, travel guides, and drama. According to most accounts, she was a young woman of English or German descent (variously named Johanna, Agnes, Glancia, Gilberta, or Jutta), who assumed male identity in order to attend a university with her lover. Her scholarly diligence led to rapid advancement through the clerical ranks until she reached the pinnacle of the ecclesiastical hierarchy by being unanimously elected pope. After a two-and-a-half-year reign under the name Johannes, the pope's true nature was made manifest when, during a ceremonial procession, she fell to the ground and gave birth to a child. The outcome of this revelation varies in the numerous accounts. Some say an angry mob killed the impostor, others that she was imprisoned or simply deposed and exiled; the majority, however, claim she died in childbirth. Although the legend was conclusively debunked in the seventeenth century by David Blondel, the authenticity of the papess remained largely undisputed throughout the Middle Ages and Renaissance.[2]

The female pope is generally said to have lived in the mid-ninth century but is attested in no documents dating from before the thirteenth. Defenders of the historicity of the account, such as the sixteenth-century Protestant historian Johannes Wolf (1537-1600), who compiled a bibliography of literature on the papess, frequently claimed earlier sources.[3] Indeed, accounts of the papess do appear in manuscripts of earlier texts, including the important ninth-century *Liber Pontificalis* attributed to Anastasius Bibliothecarus, but this and other such references to the female pope all have been proven to be later insertions.[4]

While historians have explored the possible origins of the myth, they have seldom considered the multifarious interpretations of this fictional breach of male dominance in the church.[5] Most accounts fall under the rubrics of curiosity literature, historical reporting, moral didacticism, or anti-Catholic polemic, though some versions, especially the dramatic interpretation of Dietrich Schernberg, are too complex to be so neatly classified. The antifemale basis of the myth is always present but emphasized to greater or lesser extent depending on the author's purpose.

The *Chronicon universalis Mettensis* (ca. 1250), usually attributed to Jean de Mailly,[6] is the earliest extant recording of the legend. However, it can also be found in roughly contemporaneous works, such as the *Erfurt Chronicle* (ca. 1250) and Stephen de Bourbon's *De septem donis Spiritus Sancti* (ca. 1260).[7] Perhaps the most influential source for propagating the myth was the *Chronicon Pontificum et Imperatorum* of Martin Polonus (†1278), also known as Martin of Troppau.[8] Scores of manuscripts of Polonus's chronicle exist, and echoes from it are found in works by many medieval historians. Because Polonus had served as the papal confessor under Clement IV (†1268) and had access to the records of the curia, his history of the papacy was regarded as an official document. The entry for the female pope, however, does not appear in early manuscripts but seems to have been added to a later redaction, probably produced after Polonus's death in the last quarter of the thirteenth century.[9] Nonetheless, the interpolation served as a model for many later chroniclers and remained the most authoritative evidence throughout the Middle Ages and Renaissance. Inserted after the entry for Leo IV (847-855), the account established the reign of the papess in the mid-ninth century:

> Post hunc Leonem Iohannes Anglicus nacione Maguntinus sedit annis 2, mensibus 7, diebus 4, et mortuus est Rome, et cessavit papatus mense 1. Hic, ut asseritur, femina fuit, et in puellari etate Athenis ducta a quodam amasio suo in habitu virili, sic in diversis scienciis

profecit, ut nullus sibi par inveniretur, adeo ut post Rome trivium legens magnos magistros discipulos et auditores haberet. Et cum in Urbe vita et sciencia magne opinionis esset, in papam concorditer eligitur. Sed in papatu per suum familiarem impregnatur. Verum tempus partus ignorans, cum de Sancto Petro in Lateranum tenderet, angustiata inter Coliseum et sancti Clementis ecclesiam peperit, et post mortua ibidem, ut dicitur, sepulta fuit. Et quia dominus papa eandem viam semper obliquat, creditur a plerisque, quod propter detestationem facti hoc faciat. Nec ponitur in cathalogo sanctorum pontificum propter mulieris sexus quantum ad hoc deformitatem.[10]

[After Leo, Johannes Anglicus, a native of Mainz, held the throne for two years, seven months, and four days, and died in Rome; the papacy was then inoperative for one month. This pope, it is asserted, was a woman, and in her girlhood she went with her lover to Athens in the guise of a man. Thus, she became proficient in diverse sciences and no one could be found equal to her, so that afterward, teaching the trivium at Rome, she had great masters as students and auditors. And because her life and learning were highly respected in the city, she was unanimously elected pope. But while pope, she became pregnant by her friend. Indeed, ignorant of the time of delivery, she gave birth in an alley between the Coliseum and the church of St. Clement when she was going from St. Peter's to the Lateran. After she died, they say, she was buried there. And since the lord pope always avoids this same street, it is believed by many that he does so because of the curse of the event. Nor is she placed in the catalog of holy pontiffs because the sex of the woman is so great a disgrace.]

In the chronicles of the thirteenth and fourteenth centuries, the account of the female pope is often entered into the papal lists in much the same form as it appears in Martin Polonus's chronicle, usually without comment in keeping with the lapidarian style of such works. In some cases, however, the growing fascination with the story is evident in its embellishments. For instance, in the *Erfurt Chronicle* the devil plays a major role:

Fuit et alius pseudopapa, cuius nomen et anni ignorantur. Nam mulier erat, ut fatentur Romani, et elegantis forme, magne sciencie et in ypocrisi magne vite. Hec sub virili habitu latuit, quousque in papam eligitur. Et hec in papatu concepit, et cum esset gravida, demon in consistorio publice coram omnibus prodidit factum, clamans ad papam hunc versum: "Papa, pater patrum, papisse pandito partum."[11]

[There was another pseudo-pope, whose name and dates are unknown. For it was a woman, as the Romans admit; she was a woman of beautiful appearance, great learning, and her life was great in deception. Hidden in men's clothing, she was elected pope. During her reign, she conceived, and when she was pregnant, a demon made the fact clear to everyone in front of a public assembly, crying out at the pope this verse: "O pope, father of fathers, make known the childbirth of the papess!"]

The devil's alliterative jingle is found, with some variation, in numerous accounts; sometimes spoken by a demon as above but more often cited as the inscription on the tombstone of the papess, as in the *Chronicon universalis Mettensis*, Stephen de Bourbon's account, and the popular *Flores temporum* (1320).[12] The female pontiff's collusion with the devil was not an uncommon element of the story. Although the accounts do not include a pact with the devil, it is taken for granted that demonic forces assisted in her rise to power.

The legend soon began to appear in etiological explanations as well. Beginning as early as Polonus, the story of the female pope was used to explain why papal processions avoided a certain street in Rome (called the "via papissae" or "vicus papissae"). Robert d'Uzès (†1296) embellished the story in his *Liber trium virorum et trium spiritualium virginum*, where he cites the scandal of the female pope as the reason for the commode-shaped throne (the so-called "porphyra") used at papal investitures. The actual origins of this ceremonial seat have been adequately explained,[13] but according to Robert the pope had to sit on this odd throne, "ubi dicitur probari papa, an sit homo"[14] [where it is said the pope is tested (to see) whether he is a man]. Later accounts were so bold as to claim that two witnesses announced the results of their investigation, crying out to the crowd, "testiculos habet," to which the assembly replied, "Deo gratias!"[15]

Moving beyond the curious and anecdotal, some writers recognized the critical force of the legend and used it as a topical but powerful argument in polemics against ecclesiastical irregularities. William of Ockham (†ca. 1349) deduced from the legend that the church was not infallible.[16] Similarly, Jean Gerson cited the affair as evidence of ecclesiastical error in the past and urged the divided church to put aside questions of right or wrong and strive for reconciliation: "Sed etiam in talibus Ecclesia fallere dicitur et falli, sicut dum multo tempore feminam pro papa coluit."[17]

[But, indeed, in great matters the church has erred and has been deceived: as when, in that turbulent time, it chose a woman as pope.]

Although no one believed she reigned with divine approval, for the reformers of the fifteenth and sixteenth centuries the female pope was indeed a godsend. She offered an authentic case of irregularity and immorality in the papacy that even church authorities did not dispute. Reformers decried the hypocrisy of the papacy on the basis of several bad popes, but the incontrovertible fact that a woman had been pope was consistently used to undermine papal authority. In addition to citing the papess in theological disputes concerning ecclesiastical hierarchy, numerous reformers also transferred her femaleness and its attendant characteristics to male popes in order to denigrate them.

Perhaps the most celebrated criticism of the papacy based on the legend was that of Jan Hus (1369-1415). He frequently cited the example of the papess to refute claims of apostolic succession and to prove that the papacy was not a *sine qua non* for the existence of the church. He challenged church authorities to decree that the female pope, whom he called Agnes, had indeed been head of the church for over two years or to admit that the church had existed as an acephalous institution at that time. If the former were true, then it was impossible to know if God's choice always occupied the throne of St. Peter, since electoral cardinals, so it seemed, had erred. On the other hand, if, as Hus believed, the church had operated without a divinely ordained head under Agnes and numerous other bad popes, it became clear that salvation in no way depended on belief in the supremacy of the pope, since, as he argued: "tunc nullus potuisset salvari, quamvis non tunc fuit papa."[18] [No one could have been saved at that time since there was no pope then.] Hus referred to the papess almost a dozen times in his writings, invoking her in arguments against papal authority and apostolic succession.[19]

As the reform movement became more widespread, antipapal polemic grew virulent and the issue of the papess was often used to lambaste the church.[20] During his trip to Rome in 1510, Martin Luther (1483-1546) was surprised to see a stone monument purportedly of the female pontiff with her child. He ridiculed the church for countenancing this dark moment of its history: "Es nimmt mich Wunder, daß die Päpste solch Bilde leiden können; aber Gott

blendet sie, daß man sehe was Papstthum sei: eitel Betrug und
Teufelswerk!"[21] [I am amazed that the popes can suffer such images;
but God blinds them so that one sees what the papacy is: vain deceit
and devil's work!] Like most people, Luther accepted the authenticity
of the papess; to him, it was just one more example of misguided
and evil church hierarchy.

In his *Vera christianae pacificationis et ecclesiae reformandae ratio*,
John Calvin (1509-1564) questioned the sacrament of priesthood
and the idea of perpetual succession from the apostles on the basis
of several heretical priests and bishops, before crowning his argument
with the sarcastic assertion: "Verum his omissis, Ioannam papissam
transsiliant oportet, si continuare suam ab apostolis seriem volent."[22]
[Even omitting these, it will be necessary to leap over Papess Johanna,
if they would continue their series from the Apostles!] Similarly, the
English reformer and author of the *Book of Martyrs*, John Foxe (1516/
17-1587) nagged the church with the memory of the female pope in
a polemical treatise entitled *Papa Confutatus*, reproaching the popes
with "Ioanna [...] cuius nunc successores se fateantur necessario
oportet." [Joan, whose successors they must needs confess themselves
to be even yet.][23] The female pope offered dramatic evidence for
interruption in the male line from St. Peter, thereby supporting the
view of several reform theologies that rejected the notion of apostolic
succession in favor of a heritage of apostolic tradition. Similar attacks
were made by several reformers, including Heinrich Cornelius
Agrippa von Nettesheim (1486-1535), Philipp Melanchthon (1497-
1560), John Bale (1495-1563), Paul Vergerio (1497-1564), and Matthias
Illyricus Flacius (1520-1575).[24]

Defenses of the papacy took on several forms in the fifteenth
and sixteenth centuries, but the most common was to deny the
very existence of the female pope. Johannes Aventinus (1477-1534)
argued that the story had evolved as a satire of John IX, who,
according to Aventinus, was dominated by his mistress, Theodora.[25]
This view of the myth was later taken up by others, although not all
agree on which pope was the object of the satire. Onofrio Panvinio
(1520-1568), the learned and prolific librarian of the Vatican, appears
to have been the first to look critically at the manuscript transmission
of the legend.[26] In his lengthy annotation to Platina's *Historia de
vitis pontificum romanorum* (in which Platina himself voiced some
doubts about the authenticity of the account), Panvinio noted that

the entries about the female pope in the *Liber Pontificalis* (ca. 860)
and Otto von Freising's chronicle (ca. 1147/56) were later insertions.
He also pointed to inconsistencies in the story, and questioned the
woman's ability to conceal gender so completely, especially when
pregnant.[27] Using Panvinio as a point of departure, Florimond de
Raemond (1540-1601) exposed the myth of the female pope in his
Erreur populaire de la Papesse Jane (1587).[28] Nonetheless, popular belief
in legends dies hard. Although Raemond had offered ample evidence
of manuscript tampering and incongruities in the basic facts, it was
not until the seventeenth century, through the work of the Protestant
historian David Blondel (1591-1655),[29] that the myth was recognized
as such, at least among the educated public.[30]

No one, Catholic or Protestant, questioned that a woman was
not a worthy successor to St. Peter. It is a reflection of the deep-
seated belief in female inferiority and the view that female ministry
was contrary to the law of the New Testament (a view not upheld
by early Christian practice) that the reign of the papess was universally
considered an abomination. Though disapproving of her male
disguise, most accounts also criticize the church for having allowed
the scandal to occur. The woman herself is usually presented as
learned and accomplished, if perhaps a bit misguided. Cultural
trappings of male gender are acknowledged to be transferable, but
her female "nature," according to the premise of this story of a
pregnant pope, cannot be entirely suppressed. Misogynist
undercurrents rise to the surface in several accounts, especially in
literary versions that enlarge upon the chronicle entries.

In *De mulieribus claris*, Boccaccio praises the female pope for her
erudition but criticizes her presumption.[31] He explains that a woman
named Gilberta dressed as a man to study with her lover in England.
After his death, however, she continued in male disguise and
renounced her femaleness because "se cognosceret ingenio valere et
dulcedine traheretur scientie."[32] [She recognized that her intellect
was strong and she was drawn by the sweetness of learning.] The
moral sense of gender encoded in language and androcentric imagery
informs Boccaccio's contrastive description of Gilberta's successful
disguise: "Et cum, preter scientiam, singulari honestate ac sanctitate
polleret, homo ab omnibus creditus."[33] [And since, in addition to
learning, she was esteemed for her great honesty and saintliness, she
was believed by all to be a man.] Despite such ingrained biases,

Boccaccio's assessment of Gilberta remains positive until she becomes pope. In Boccaccio's configuration, her femaleness placed no impediments on her intellect or character. But once she accepted the papacy, he says, God could not suffer such audacity. He abandoned the woman, and she fell prey to Satan and sexual desire. The connection between femininity and sexual sin becomes the dominant theme. As in the legends of the calumniated female saints, male disguise fails to defeminize or eliminate the element of sexual suspicion ascribed to female characters who cross dress. Although Boccaccio can praise the virtuousness and learning of a disguised woman, her ascension to the papal throne constitutes a grave sin because "nulli mulierum a christiana religione concessum."[34] [This is permitted to no woman in the Christian faith.] He explains her rapid moral descent as the result of loss of favor with God. The implication, however, is that God condones male disguise for education but not if it is used to assume positions of power within male institutions.

In his poem "Der Babst mit dem Kind," the German dramatist and *Meistersinger* Hans Sachs (1494-1576) uses the legend as an example of female deceitfulness.[35] As in every other account, the woman's prodigious knowledge is the cause of her elevation to the papal seat. Echoing Luther, Sachs claims that the cardinals and prelates were blind to the truth. He directs the thrust of his polemic against the papacy, but he also blames the female pope, observing that the church fell victim to "weiplich list" [womanly deceit], an attribute apparently common to all women in Sachs's view.[36] The parallel to the fall of man is made clear: like Adam, the church was deceived by a clever woman under the influence of Satan. Unsympathetic to the church's error, Sachs implies that curial mismanagement and corruption ensured the success of the woman's deceit.

Despite the antipapal and misogynist force the legend had gained even by the fifteenth century, one writer chose to ignore the ecclesiological ramifications of admitting a female pope. On the eve of the Reformation, Dietrich Schernberg, a clerk in the chancellery at Mühlhausen and later vicar of nearby St. John the Baptist, wrote a play illustrating the moral lessons of the legend.[37] Schernberg's *Ein schön Spiel von Frau Jutten* (ca. 1480) interprets the story as an unusual example of sin, retribution, and salvation. The play survives only in a sixteenth-century edition by Hieronymus Tilesius, a radical reformer from Mühlhausen, who published the work with the expressed purpose of discrediting the papacy. According to Tilesius's introduction, Schernberg's choice of material was damning enough in itself because it unmasked the hypocrisy of the papacy. He also railed against the emphasis on the intercession of Mary as belittling Christ's role as savior. In the *Nachwort* to the edition, Christian Irenäus follows Sachs's interpretation of the incident as an example of the essential sinfulness of women, claiming: "Weiberlist / sagt man / übertrifft alle list / des wir in dieser Historia ein mercklich Exempel haben."[38] [Female deceitfulness surpasses every other deceit; of this we have a clear example in this history.] Nonetheless, Tilesius appears to have left Schernberg's text largely unaltered, except for some orthographic updating.

The play has received little attention from Germanists because it is generally considered an inferior literary work. Richard Haage, whose dissertation on *Frau Jutta* offers the most complete discussion of the play, summed up the general critical opinion in his wistful comment: "Was hätte ein wirklicher Dichter aus dieser Gestalt machen können?"[39] More recently, Manfred Lemmer, who has produced an edition of the 1565 printing, recognizes Schernberg's contribution to the development of the legend but laments that Schernberg's play, like many medieval dramas, is wooden and highly imitative.[40]

Although most scholars who have studied the legend of the female pope have failed to mention his play, Schernberg must be credited as the first to dramatize the life of the papess and the first to depict her afterlife.[41] Other additions or changes include scenes in heaven and hell, transferral of the university from Athens to Paris, a scene depicting the cardinals' reaction to the revelation, and, above all, the introduction of Mary as a motivating force in salvation. His description of Jutta in hell and heaven is original, and, although his direct source for the earthly life of the papess cannot be ascertained, it appears to be based on annalistic rather than literary accounts.[42]

In the play, Jutta decides to leave her home in England dressed as a man in order to study in Paris. Her decision is apparently independent of outside influences; unlike the chronicle accounts where the woman assumes a male guise to follow her lover, Schernberg's Jutta urges her lover, Clericus, to join her in her pursuit of knowledge. Learning of Jutta's plan, the devil Luciper sends his minions Spiegelglantz and Sathanas to encourage her scheme. No pact with the devil is made, however, and Jutta does not renounce Christianity. In keeping with other versions of the story, her rise to power is meteoric. Although she is not portrayed as a bad pope, her gender illegitimates her reign and enrages Christ. When he prepares to send Death to kill the sinner, however, Mary pleads for compassion and obtains the concession that Jutta will be offered a choice either to suffer earthly humiliation and death or to earn eternal damnation after death. In a parody of the annunciation, the angel Gabriel delivers the ultimatum and announces Jutta's pregnancy. Jutta chooses humiliation, and, in return, receives hope for salvation. Nonetheless, her soul is carried off by devils at her death. She endures numerous tortures but does not lose hope. Unceasingly, she calls on the intercession of Mary, never doubting that she will be saved. Finally, after Mary pleads with Christ a second time, Jutta's soul is brought to heaven by the archangel Michael.[43]

Schernberg depicts Jutta as a character unwilling to accept the societal constraints placed on women. Although she does not seek the office of pope, but rather is drafted by her peers because of high regard for her scholarship and character, she nonetheless expresses her ambition and her desire for honor (*ehre*) on numerous occasions. In her opening speech, she cautiously considers disguise, if it can bring her honor:

> Das wolt ich gern vollenden /
> Wenn es würde kriegen ein gut ende /
> Das ich mit ehren müge bestahn /
> Und nicht schande darvon möchte han.[44]

[I would gladly bring this about, if it might come to a good end so that I might gain honor from it and not scandal.]

This concern for *ehre* appears in all her earthly actions until her final acceptance of humiliation and death. That the lure of worldly honor could lead characters astray from the pursuit of moral honor frequently appears as a problem in medieval literature. Schernberg, however, uses the theological view of pride as the primary and most tempting sin to offer what the legend did not previously have—a motive for the actions of the female pope.

Despite Tilesius's contention that Schernberg's material exposed the corruption of the church, the plot centers on the individual as sinner and on pride and the desire for wordly honor as a mortal sin. For Christian moralists, it was not uncommon to introduce bad members of the ecclesiastical institution as exempla, particularly as examples of the sin of *superbia*. Jutta belongs to a long line of fallen clerics, including such figures as the ambitious bishop Theophilus, whose story serves as a basis for Schernberg's *Jutta*, and Pope Sylvester, who, like Theophilus, was said to have made a pact with the devil. Such characters are not presented for the purpose of criticizing the church but rather to symbolize the fall and salvation of all human beings.

Schernberg's Jutta is a sympathetic heroine whose ambition, though sinful, makes her a strong and in many ways positive female character. In this, he followed other versions of the legend, which claim that this woman's sex in no way determined her capacity for secular or religious success. Schernberg also retained the posture of most chronicle accounts in viewing Jutta's sex as a sin, regardless of her intellectual talents and her capable reign as pope. The view of male disguise as sin was not uncommon in medieval society: penitentials, canon law, and popular cases, like that of Schernberg's near contemporary Jeanne d'Arc, criticized cross dressing, but positive portrayals of women in male dress, particularly in literature and hagiography, are far more frequent. Given the background of tolerance and even approbation of women who disguised themselves as men to perform courageous acts or to serve God, the play (and, for that matter, the legend), with its emphasis on disguise as sin, must be reconsidered. There is a clear pattern in medieval assessments of female transvestism: the closer the connection between the cross-dressed character and reality, the less positive the appraisal. The sin of the papess was not primarily that she posed as a man but that she dared to seize power over men. Disguise was merely her means of overturning the traditional order. The popular female monks were more palatable because they lived quietly in monasteries, usually undetected until after their deaths. Women as monks or even clerics presented little threat to the male-dominated church as long as they kept their identities concealed. It was her presumption to rule over men in the highest office in the church that male authors found outrageous.

Interestingly enough, it is not at all clear in Schernberg's interpretation that Jutta sinned knowingly. Several of her statements indicate that Jutta never felt she had transgressed until Gabriel confronts her.[45] When Gabriel informs her of God's displeasure, Jutta expresses immediate remorse: "Darumb rewet mich von hertzen sehre/ [/] Das ich erzürnet habe Gott den Herren."[46] [I am truly sorry that I have angered God, the Lord.] Her relationship with Clericus obviously transgressed societal rules as well as the celibacy vows of priesthood (a point Tilesius stressed in his preface), but this relationship is not developed nor explicitly criticized in the play. Indeed, it is mentioned only in a stage direction.[47] In the context of the play, Jutta's pregnancy is primarily a manifestation of her true nature and only secondarily the fruit of an illicit love affair.

While Jutta is not a bad character *per se*, the realm of evil is portrayed extensively, sometimes even flamboyantly. Although the devil was often introduced in earlier accounts as a taunting figure at the childbirth, Schernberg emphasized the connection with evil by including several scenes depicting demonic forces.[48] In the opening act, Luciper's grandmother and dancing devils parody the heavenly world of Christ, Mary, and the angels. Inverting the role of Mary as *mediatrix*, it is Lillis (i.e., Lilith) who asks her son to lead Jutta into sin. Later, two devils play a decisive role in Jutta's downfall by encouraging her resolve to dress as a man. Despite the ubiquity of evil, however, Schernberg indicates that Jutta is responsible for her actions because the desire to sin originated in her mind. The demonic does not compel her, though its pronounced presence in the drama makes the road to salvation seem perilous.

That her sin lay primarily in her sex is stated explicitly several times in the play. Christ first describes it when he explains the reason for his displeasure:

> Sindt sie sich hat vermessen /
> Vnd ihres Frewlichen wesens vergessen /
> Vnd hat in Mannes weise gegangen /
> Vnd also das Bapstumb empfangen.[49]

[Because she has acted audaciously and forgotten her feminine nature and went about in men's clothing and thus received the papacy.]

Gabriel also designates her disguise as her sin: "Wenn du hast gar sehr wider jhn (i.e., Gott) gethan / [/] Das du dich hast vergleichet einem Mann."[50] [Because you have sinned against him (God) in

that you have acted like a man.] Likewise, Death justifies his murder
of Jutta on the grounds that women ought not to impersonate men.[51]

Schernberg draws a clear connection between sin and femaleness,
however, in a specific analogy between Jutta and Eve. Jutta desires
knowledge and honor, but realizes that she has to become what she
is not, in her case male, in order to achieve this. Although she had
already considered a plan for disguising as a man, Sathanas convinces
her with a promise that evokes the serpent's words to Eve: "Ihr sollet
werden klug und weise. Auch sage ich euch mehre / Ihr sollet komen
zu grossen ehren" (lines 155-58). [You will become shrewd and wise.
I'll tell you even more—you shall experience great honor.] Thus,
like Eve, Jutta's aspiration for knowledge and honor leads her into
sin. Unlike Eve, Jutta is not promised that she will be like a god,
but, in the end, her ascension to the papal throne distinguishes her
as the absolute authority over Christians on earth. Jutta's sin of pride
mirrors Eve's first sin, which, it was said, was a transgression of God's
power and therefore a sin of pride. In the Middle Ages, pride was
acknowledged as a sin to which women were particularly prone.
Furthermore, when punishment comes to Jutta it is identical to
Eve's: she must endure a painful childbirth, which also substantiates
her womanhood. Finally, Eve, who was often singled out in medieval
accounts of the harrowing of hell because of her role in humankind's
downfall, was also pardoned after a period of penance and released
from hell.[52]

That Eve would offer a convenient model for another female
sinner is not surprising, of course, but Schernberg's unique
presentation of Mary as the critical force in Jutta's salvation introduces
a more complex view of the role of women in the story of salvation.
A common typological argument was that Mary, in giving birth to
Christ, regained for humankind what Eve had forfeited through
sin. Womankind, therefore, was vindicated by Mary's existence. By
casting the mother of Luciper as a force behind Jutta's downfall, by
equating Jutta with Eve, and by portraying Mary as the agent of
salvation, Schernberg feminized the *Heilsgeschichte* in this play about
Christian redemption.

Schernberg not only introduced numerous innovations to the
legend but also managed to make a blasphemous legend palatable
to the church. He amplified the story of the female pope as recorded
by medieval chroniclers to create what was perhaps the most didactic

version of the legend yet remained uncritical of the church and even faithfully upheld its doctrines by illustrating the gravity of the sin of pride, the legitimacy of male dominance, the necessity of prayer and repentance, and the efficacy of heavenly mediation for salvation.

The evolution of the myth from historical curiosity to the bane of Catholicism is nowhere as clear as in the crossed purposes of Schernberg and Tilesius. Within one generation after the play's composition, and certainly by the time Tilesius printed *Frau Jutta*, the mere mention of the female pope constituted an attack on the church. Schernberg's approach offered a new and more universal interpretation, but the literary potential of the legend as anything more than antipapal polemic was lost when the church adopted a defensive attitude in the wake of the Reformation.

Chapter Six

THE DISGUISED WIFE:
GENDER INVERSION AND
GENDER CONFORMITY

> We'll have a swashing and a martial outside
> As many other mannish cowards have
> That do outface it with their semblances.
> —Rosalind in *As You Like It*, I, iii

In secular literature, women often put on male clothing to circumvent impediments to social prestige or personal fulfillment. Yet, unlike the transvestite monks and the female pope, most of these characters do not attempt to achieve male sociopolitical status. Instead, they use the authority and privilege of maleness to reclaim female roles. The medieval wife who finds herself without a husband because of his absence or outright abandonment, loses her sexual and social identity. Medieval literature includes stories of many abandoned women who respond to this loss of status by adopting another personality and gender.

The removal of the woman from the domestic sphere and the consequent melding of male and female roles in the figure of the disguised wife create unusual fictional representations of partial androgyny. Rejecting female passivity, the deserted wife chooses a more active—and hence more traditionally male—response to loss of status. This "masculine" reaction is realized in her appropriation of the literary functions of a male character, such as the rescuer, minstrel, clever servant, trickster, or even her own husband, to achieve her goal. In the end, however, her extraordinary accomplishments are credited to her female persona as loyal wife. Thus, the disguised wife offers a model for heroism that appropriates the androcentric model of the hero and challenges, in fictional discourse, notions of biological determinism, indicating that medieval understandings of gender are not consistently deterministic.

Women who rescue their husbands through heroic acts are not uncommon in fiction and history. According to Livy, the Sabine women saved both their husbands and fathers through intervention on the battlefield. Medieval examples can also be found, as in the twelfth-century account of the women of Weinsberg, who, when ordered to leave their conquered city with whatever dear possessions they could carry, boldly walked out of town with their husbands on their backs.[1] In literature and history, women marshal troops, negotiate ransoms, and place themselves in mortal jeopardy to protect or rescue husbands.[2] Not surprisingly, heroines of disguise literature actually assume male identities when they appropriate male functions of protection and defense. Posing as men, they free their husbands through a combination of subterfuge and heroism. From a practical standpoint, their maleness is essential for success, whereas metaphorically the inversion signifies a reversal in both the nature of the task and the qualities of mind and body deemed necessary to perform it. The inverted plots provide a context for evaluation and analysis of cultural inscriptions of gender.

Rescue from imprisonment is often accomplished through disguise or, more precisely, through the exchange of clothes. This motive conveys an idea of transvestment as a source of social salvation. Such a ruse, it will be recalled, appears in the stories of the saints Antonina and Theodora. In a popular medieval tale of Greek origin, the Minyan women save their husbands from execution by exchanging clothing during a prison visit.[3] Similar tales abound in folklore and historical record.[4] Transvestment as salvation informs some uncomplicated stories, such as *Ritter Alexander* (1490) and *Der Ritter auß Steyermarck* (1507),[5] two German tales in which wives free imprisoned husbands. In these cases, a husband faces execution for having committed adultery with the one woman deemed to be more beautiful than his wife. His magnanimous wife saves him by switching clothes during a prison visit, allowing him to escape. Later, when brought to court, the woman vindicates her husband—albeit duplicitously—by baring her breasts to reveal her sex. Thus, the exposure of the body as female, despite cultural maleness, reestablishes social harmony. These examples illustrate a peculiar type of disguise literature in which the woman takes her husband's place, as it were, by remaining behind with his captors. The couples reverse genders superficially, but the woman's body remains a sign of her status as loyal wife. Whereas men in medieval literature rarely exhibit conciliatory attitudes toward their partner's adultery, the women in *Ritter Alexander* and *Der Ritter auß Steyermarck* not only overlook the husband's infidelity but also conspire to conceal it. Cultural gender transgression becomes an antidote to sexual transgression. Although this role reversal indicates the wifely virtues of subservience and self-denial, male disguise also augments, to a certain extent, the wife's stature. She alone can forgive her husband, but, thanks to disguise, she also has the power to deflect public recognition of the scandal. The woman becomes a hero in her own right, admired by the cuckolded husband and the court for her alleged desire to seek out the other woman in order to compare their beauty and for the daring disguise used to approach the woman. In *Der Ritter auß Steyermarck*, the unmasked wife boldly admits, in male terms, that she came in search of adventure: "umb Abenthewr so kam ich her."[6] That the woman's heroism arises from her dual identities becomes clear in *Ritter Alexander* when the husband of the other woman praises the disguised woman's purported deed, addressing her as "herr und frau":

> [er] sagt: "genad mir, herr und frau,
> eins von natur, das ander sunst
> nach der gebert, gestalt und kunst,
> wie sich geschicket hant die beid,
> das weib und man in einem kleid
> geschetzt sollen werden alhie."[7]

[He said, "forgive me, man and woman, one in nature, which otherwise come from birth, form, and artifice. How well both the woman and the man fit in one garment ought to be admired always."]

In both cases, gender inversion inspires renewed vows of loyalty from the husband. Curiously, both works end with admonishments not to unfaithful husbands but to women who should see a model in the story. Although gender transgression itself is not recommended, wives are enjoined to support their husbands when confronted with marital infidelities, as in the closing lines of *Ritter Alexander*: "Hiebei, ir weiber, nemet ler / und seit nit so heftig und schwer."[8] [You wives, learn from this example; don't be too strict or difficult.] Despite the regressive moral, in the context of the tales, gender inscription and the sexual code are, most emphatically, not absolute values.

Another popular figure is the woman disguised as a traveling musician. The least complicated example of this type occurs in the thirteenth-century French romance *Aucassin et Nicolette*.[9] After a short separation, Nicolette returns to Aucassin's land disguised as a minstrel and sings a song about their love before greeting Aucassin in her true form. Similarly, in *Ysaÿe le Triste* (fourteenth century), Marthe, a furtive writer of chansons, disguises herself as a minstrel to follow Ysaÿe, the son of Tristan and Yseult and the father of her own child.[10] Because both works combine prose and poetry—not an uncommon form in French romances—the introduction of a musician figure eases the integration of songs into the narrative.

The abandoned wife as rescuer also appears in the guise of a traveling musician. In fact, the theme of the faithful wife who, in the trappings of a mendicant musician, rescues her husband from imprisonment is widespread in the folklore of Germany and the Netherlands, with numerous retellings and adaptations from the fifteenth to the eighteenth century.[11] The earliest extant version is *Graf Alexander von Mainz* (first printed 1493).[12] In this tale, the disguised wife frees Alexander from enslavement in a foreign land by playing the harp so well that the pagan captor grants her request for his release. Without revealing her identity, she takes leave of Alexander just outside of Mainz, asking as a reward only a piece of his miraculous shirt, which has long remained white as a sign of his wife's continued fidelity. When Alexander arrives home, he joyfully greets his loyal wife, but during a celebration feast his mother undermines his faith by complaining of the daughter-in-law's long absence, implying that she has not been faithful since she did not meet her obligation to remain at home in chastity. The wife vindicates herself by appearing in the garb of Alexander's rescuer and producing letters concerning the rescue as well as the patch of white shirt to remind him of its continued spotlessness. In a dramatic scene of revelation, she exposes her body, which becomes a mark of her distinctive androgynous heroism (and purity) as well as a challenge to the gender inscription imposed by the unwitting mother-in-law and husband. The "image" of the pure female body supports this idea of cultural androgyny:

> "Alexander, du hast ein bider weib,"
> Ir kutten ließ sy vallen.

"Nun schawet alle meinen leib!
Ich hoff, ich sey bey meinen eren bliben."
Die frau sprach: "Alexander, mein fyl lieber herre,
Das ist das stück des hembdes dein,
Das setz ich wider in dein geren.
Lug, ob das der brieff müg sein,
den du mit deinen henden hast geschriben!
So ist das deß künigs brif,
Den uns der ritter bey dem pflug hat geben,
Do ich in grossen nöten liff,
Biß ich dir hab gefrist dein edels leben,
Dy solt du lesen hie gar offenbare!
So hören sy, wa ich bin gewesen
Dy zwen monat und das gantze iare."[13]

["Alexander you have an honest wife." She let her monk's habit fall.
"Now, everyone, look at my body! I hope I have retained my honor."
The woman spoke: "Alexander, my dear husband, this is a piece of
your shirt; I return it to you. Look, if this might be the letter which
you wrote with your own hand! And this is the king's letter that the
knight by the plow gave us when I faced great risk until I had
ransomed your noble life. These you should read here in public! Then
they will hear where I've been this past year and two months."]

Her transgression of the gender code, as charged by the mother-
in-law, is proven to be true, but the goal of restoring domestic order
legitimates it. Inspection of her body, moreover, restores her wifely
status. Although society's suspicions and the husband's doubts betray
an uneasiness with female activity outside the domestic sphere, the
resumption of disguise not only clears the wife of any charges of
disloyalty but also affords her the opportunity to reveal heroism.
The truth elevates her from her subordinate position as wife and
requires Alexander to express his indebtedness: "Ich wil dir
underdenig sein; / Dyweill ich leb, so wil ich dichs ergetzen."[14] [I'll
be your servant as long as I live; thus shall I repay you for it.]
Alexander's reaction to the epiphany represents a conscious
formulation of gender inversion (using the language of submission),
while indicating his reacceptance of her as wife. The conclusion
accommodates the complexity of her status.

An important variation on this story is *Der Graf von Rom*, a song
that enjoyed numerous reprintings from 1510 through the
seventeenth century and served as the model for many later
reworkings of the theme.[15] It differs from *Graf Alexander von Mainz*

in the omission of miraculous elements. Furthermore, the tension is heightened between husband and wife because the woman publicly refuses an opportunity to travel to the East to free her husband. Fearing a trick from the captor that might compromise her honor, she instead rescues her husband in the guise of a minstrel. Upon his return, however, the husband complains of her unwillingness to meet with his captors. He has also heard reports of her protracted absence, which, to his mind, indicate sexual misconduct. For the wife, the risk of sexual transgression is immense, since, once calumniated, she only barely eludes her husband's murderous wrath by reverting to her male persona. As soon as her husband acknowledges the minstrel as his rescuer, she reveals her identity, thereby reclaiming her status as honest wife and eliciting the admiration of the community for her heroic action.

The disguised woman as rescuer also occurs in local German legends about historical women. Anna Eltz, the wife of Philip Hausten of Ulm, and the anonymous wife of Konrad von Tannenberg were credited with similar escapades in male disguise.[16] Whether these women actually rescued their husbands or merely served as convenient figures around which to build imitative legends, they and several other literary examples attest to the appeal of this kind of heroism, which tests the boundaries between male and female cultural identities.

Although distinguished by gender inversion, these women consistently conform to a literary paradigm for male heroism: the tradition of minstrel disguise as subterfuge for wooing and rescue.[17] The best-known hero as minstrel is Tristan, but men also use minstrel disguise in courting and rescue expeditions in Wace's *Brut*, Gerbert de Montreuil's *Roman de la Violette*, *King Horn*, and *L'Estoire de Merlin*, to name only a few examples. Further, the female minstrels have much in common with the heroes of German *Spielmannsepik* who travel to the East, attempt daring rescue missions, and usually win (or win back) their mates through disguise.[18] In *König Rother* (1150-60), Rother poses as a *Spielmann* at the pagan court where his men are imprisoned; he later returns in disguise to rescue his wife, who, fittingly enough, has been abducted by another cunning minstrel.[19] Likewise, in *Salman und Morolf* (mid-twelfth century), Morolf, who is a minstrel, uses disguise to recapture his brother's wife from a foreign kingdom.[20]

For the female minstrel-rescuers, disguise temporarily inverts the highly gender-conscious Bridal Quest. The feminization of the motif would seem to undermine the husband's status, but several devices mitigate the reversal's impact. First of all, the transgressive woman is always exceedingly modest, and, furthermore, she speedily returns to her role as obedient wife. In fact, she admits her "male" exploits and heroic androgyny only to blunt further threats to her wifely status.

False accusations, like those encountered by the female minstrels, become the focal point of stories of women rejected by their husbands. In these tales, the woman's status as wife is threatened not by the husband's absence but by unfounded charges of sexual misconduct. These abandoned women dress as male servants and, through the empowerment of cross dressing, manage to regain their husbands' favor. By assuming the male identity of a servant, however, the woman demonstrates her worthiness without a radical abrogation of male power. During the period when she has lost her status as wife, the woman resembles the heroes in stories of such displaced nobles as Rennewart, Florence of Rome, and Kudrun, who are forced to play the role of servants for a time. For the disguised wives, servitude does not entirely efface identity and status because their innate nobility and female identity remain important aspects of their characterization. And in the end, such characters, despite their male heroism, return to their female status.

Perhaps the best-known example of the calumniated wife in disguise is Imogen in Shakespeare's *Cymbeline*, but the story has numerous medieval antecedents. The theme occurs in Christine de Pizan's *Livre de cité des dames* (1405),[21] the anonymous German *Ein liepliche histori und warheit von vir Kaufmendern* (1489),[22] and *Fraw Genura*, a play by Hans Sachs (1548).[23] All these versions are based on the tale of Zinevra in Boccaccio's *Decameron* (II, 9).[24]

Boccaccio's story uses fictional disguise to question gender inscription of women, but the challenge to cultural gender is, in the end, only fragmentary. Every detail, it seems, speaks to the issue of the female body and cultural gender differentiation. Unlike Sachs and Shakespeare, who introduce male disguise at the point of crisis, Boccaccio questions male-female polarity in the opening scene. Zinevra's husband, Bernabó, foolishly enters into a bet with his fellow merchant Ambrogiuolo, wagering that his wife cannot be seduced.

Bernabó praises her as the paragon of womanhood, using masculine imagery, however, for his hyperbolic commendation. His male metaphors are drawn not from Christian ideology, as was the case with the transvestite saints, but from courtly romance. He insists that his wife exhibits the noble qualities of knights:

> [...] affermando sé di spezial grazia da Dio avere una donna per moglie la più compiuta di tutte quelle virtù che donna o ancora cavaliere in gran parte o donzello dee avere.[25]

> [Declaring that as a special grace from God he possessed a lady for his wife who was more richly endowed than any other woman in all of Italy with all those virtues that a lady should possess, and even, to a great extent, those virtues that a knight or a squire should possess.]

Continuing in this vein, he boasts that Zinevra's manners outshine those of pages and merchants:

> Oltre a questo, niuno scudiere, o famigliare che dir vogliamo, diceva trovarsi il quale meglio né più accortamente servisse a una tavola d'un signore, che serviva ella, sí come colei che era costumatissima, savia e discreta molto. Appresso questo la commendò meglio saper cavalcare un cavallo, tenere uno uccello, leggere e scrivere e fare una ragione, che se un mercatante fosse.[26]

> [Besides this, he asserted that it was impossible to find any servant or page who could better or more skillfully serve at a gentleman's table than she could, since she was most well-mannered, educated, and most discreet. Moreover, he praised her for her ability to ride a horse, handle a falcon, read and write, and keep accounts better than any merchant.]

The villain Ambrogiuolo counters with the pronouncement that men are the noblest of God's creatures, more perfect and constant than women. But, he asks, since men cannot remain steadfast when propositioned by women, how can the lesser sex be expected to resist temptation? Bernabó's reply again compares women with men:

> Ma quelle che savie sono hanno tanta sollecitudine dello onor loro, che elle diventan forti più che gli uomini, che di ciò non si curano, a guardarlo; e di queste così fatte è la mia.[27]

> [But those women who are wise have so much concern for their honor that they become even stronger than men, who care very little for their own, in defending it; and my wife is one such woman.]

The female body has ambivalent meaning in the story. Unable to seduce the faithful Zinevra, Ambrogiuolo steals some of her belongings and hides in her bedroom, where he observes a mole on her breast as she sleeps. Bernabó, who believes such knowledge could come only from an adulterous affair, declares himself bested and orders Zinevra killed.[28] The wifely body, once exposed as sinful can no longer exist. Fleeing the country under a male identity as Sicurano, Zinevra finds a position in the court of a sultan and soon puts her masculine potential to actual use. In fact, almost every attribute of Bernabó's prefatory comparative description is reflected in Zinevra's conduct as a man: on two occasions, Sicurano is praised for his impeccable serving skills; he handles falcons for the sultan; and, consistent with Bernabó's assessment of Zinevra's mercantile talent, Sicurano becomes the overseer of trade at the sultan's port. Above all, he advances his career through loyalty to his lord—the very trait that earned Zinevra her spotless reputation as Bernabó's wife.

Masculinized even before she puts on male disguise, Zinevra does not undergo a harsh transformation from female to male persona. Instead of creating a dual personality—a common trait of disguised figures—Boccaccio conflates male and female attributes to create a character that challenges gender difference. The signifiers of heroism remain masculine, but Boccaccio transfers them to his female protagonist, thereby reconfiguring the woman's cultural identity; by imputing masculine traits to her, he undermines the idea of biologically determined gender status. Male disguise gives Zinevra's "natural" talents a more congruous identity within Boccaccio's moral hierarchy of gender, although initially her body appears problematic. In the end, however, she affixes male heroism to her female body in the expected scene of anagnorisis, tearing open her shirt to reveal her breasts and thus vindicating the female body (and restoring wifely status with this exposure), while claiming moral heroism of the male.

A more daring, although lesser-known, example of the calumniated wife as servant comes from the thirteenth-century Franco-Flemish *Conte du Roi Flore et de la belle Jehane*.[29] In this romance, male disguise enables Jehane not only to regain her honor but also to redefine the nature of wifely loyalty. Unrecognized in male attire, the calumniated Jehane lives for seven years with her husband, Robiert, as his squire, Jehan. Her concealment of identity is unusual, since she becomes, in effect, a sexless wife who serves her husband with selfless love and loyalty.

Superficially, the story is similar to Zinevra's. In both cases, the crisis arises from a husband's foolish wager.[30] Likewise, the claims of the calumniators are based on knowledge of distinguishing marks on the female body (in the sexually charged areas of the breast and lower body). But the plots diverge in the circumstances surrounding the intrigue of the villain, Raoul, and the reaction of the husband, Robiert. Boccaccio's Ambrogiuolo dares only to gaze upon Zinevra's naked body while she is sleeping. Raoul, on the other hand, bursts into Jehane's rooms while she is bathing in an attempt to rape her and thereby win his bet. Both Zinevra and Jehane overcome the antagonist's advances, but Jehane physically defends herself as well by hitting her attacker on the head with a board. Verbal defenses after calumny, however, are of no use, despite the impeccable reputations of the women. Neither Bernabó nor Robiert confronts his wife with the accusation, since, as we are told repeatedly in such tales, the testimony of a man quickly erodes a husband's earlier convictions about his wife's loyalty. Indeed, only male disguise gives the maligned enough status to make countercharges against their accusers.

Unable to defend herself against false charges of sexual misconduct, Jehane drops out of society by changing her identity. The narrator addresses the gender prejudices that cause Jehane's abandonment and loss of identity. Regardless of her spotless reputation and the questionable character of the man who charged her, the narrator observes, the woman is presumed guilty. The disregard for Jehane's probity, according to the narrator, reflects a general social injustice against all women: "Car on set bien ke renoumée est si enviers toutes femmes ke se une fame s'ardoit toute, ne seroit elle mie creue d'un tel mesfait cant on li a mis sus."[31] [For it is well known that all womankind has a reputation such that no matter what she might say or do, she would not be believed once such an evil deed had been attributed to her.]

Because Jehane serves Robiert as her lord, one might argue that her transformation from wife to obedient servant strips male disguise of its empowering function. To be sure, comparisons of the marital relationship with that of the master/servant abound in medieval literature and theology.[32] In Jehane's case, however, the analogy of the wife to the servant would be overly simplistic. Although she functions in the subordinate roles of daughter, wife, and servant, the poet emphasizes Jehane's innate superiority throughout the romance. Robiert and Jehane are not equals in social rank; Jehane is the daughter of a knight, whereas Robiert is introduced as a squire of lesser nobility. As a reward for loyal service, Jehane's father favors Robiert with the hand of his daughter, knighting him before the marriage takes place. Nonetheless, the disparity of their social backgrounds is a matter of concern in the first part of the romance. Jehane's mother vows that the marriage shall not take place. She calls her relatives together to oppose it, but, in the end, they accede to the lord's wishes. Later, a servant, who is aiding Raoul in his attempt to seduce Jehane, advises her to accept the love of a valiant knight over that of her cowardly and unworthy husband.[33]

Societal hierarchy overlays sexual hierarchy: although a woman, Jehane is, also by birth, nobler than the man Robiert. Gender inversion is, to a certain extent, a reaction to the incongruity of their social standings. Robiert's inferiority and ineffectiveness manifests itself in his actions after the charge of adultery; he takes no action against Raoul or Jehane, preferring to leave the scene. Perhaps we are to think he holds himself partially to blame since he entered into the wager with Raoul, but this is not stated explicitly. Jehane, as his social and moral superior, takes on the cultural markings of this position when she pursues Robiert in male disguise. Without his lands and reputation, Robiert wanders about helplessly. Jehane, on the other hand, makes the best of her plight. Having joined Robiert in her guise as the squire Jehan, she decides that they will settle in Marseilles. Through her energies and entrepreneurial talents, she also takes on the responsibility for earning a livelihood for both of them. This relationship bears little resemblance to the typical relationship of master and servant or, for that matter, the stereotypical situation of husband and wife. In fact, Jehane's disguise has the effect of inverting traditional responsibilities. Jehan/Jehane prospers as a baker and innkeeper, quickly becoming a well-respected member of the city.[34] She earns the money and, it seems, makes all important decisions. Finally, when she learns that Raoul repents his crime, she announces that they are selling the business and returning to Robiert's country. Robiert remains a weakly defined character throughout the work. He apparently enjoys a life of leisure with fellow knights, leaving the matter of earning a living to Jehan. No mention is made of knightly activities like tourneying or seeking adventure in this part of the tale. Rather, he leads an indolent life of entertaining and amusing himself. The role reversal is not complete, since Robiert's rank and Jehan's apparent servility project the semblance of a traditional master/servant relationship. Nonetheless, Robiert himself recognizes his squire's worth when he says, "Je ne vous tieng mie à siergant, mès à compagnon et à ami."[35] [I do not consider you a servant but rather my companion and friend.] Robiert later expresses his dependence on Jehan in a vow that sounds like that of a loyal and subservient wife or servant: "Je ferai çou k'il vous plaira, et irai là ù vous vosrés."[36] [I will do as you please, and I will go where you wish.]

Jehane's cheerful acceptance of subordination modifies the figure of the displaced noble somewhat, since she never displays an inborn pride or arrogance like the subjugated noble in other works. Rennewart betrays his nobility and prodigious strength when he reacts with violent indignation to taunts from other servants.[37] Kudrun throws her master's clothes, which she has been washing for several years, into the river when reminded of her former nobility.[38] As in the case of the displaced nobles, Jehane's superior talents attract attention even in her lowly position as servant. Unlike other noble figures forced to play the role of servants, however, Jehane's change to a male persona enhances her influence. Free from the confining biases of sex, she proves her loyalty to Robiert in ways more tangible than a wife's claim of sexual fidelity. Biological sex has less effect on personality, talent, or accomplishments in the context of this work than hereditary social rank. When gender markers are obscured, "inborn" social status—the real focus of this work—replaces sex as the defining element of character.

The scene of recognition and the subsequent reversion to a traditional relationship curtail Jehane's power and influence. She becomes a silent figure, appreciated by Robiert for her service and loyalty but otherwise inactive. Their life together is described from the husband's view: we are told that Robiert participated in many tournaments, increased his wealth, and had no children by his wife.[39] In fact, Jehane is not even referred to by name in this brief part of the story. This sharp reversal of roles is jarring. It not only seems to mar the characterization of Jehane as an independent heroine but also clearly reverts to a social system that devalues females to such an extent that a woman of higher rank within the social hierarchy is nonetheless the inferior of any man in actual social situations.

A diminution of importance normally attends the resolution of tales of abandoned wives, but in the case of *Flore et Jehane* a coda reaffirms the heroine's uniqueness. After the death of Robiert, Jehane is elevated to a position of importance once again when King Florus of Ausay (hence the title of the romance) courts her expressly because he is impressed with reports of her previous exploits in male disguise. He sends an emissary to inform Jehane of his desire to marry her. But Jehane, now a self-sufficient widow, advocates cultural gender roles in this relationship, requiring him to do his own wooing if he would wed her: "mais dites à vostre roi, s'il li plaist, k'il viegne à moi [...] car li segnor doivent rekesre les dames, ne mie les dames les segnours."[40] [But tell your king, if he pleases, to come to me [...] for lords must court ladies, not ladies lords.] Florus agrees to her terms, impressed by his counselor's opinion that she is both wise and brave ("elle est et sages et vallans").[41] Qualities not usually attributed to women, therefore, continue to inspire his admiration. Further, although both Florus and Jehane were unable to have children with their earlier mates, together they quickly produce a daughter and son. In King Florus, it is implied, Jehane finds her equal. Unlike Robiert, Florus can appreciate her culturally "male" qualities without the screen of disguise. Although the closure of the tale suggests a traditional marriage, it remains an unusual attempt to overcome, in fiction, a gender hierarchy in conflict with social understandings of self-worth.

In two further cases of deserted wives, the cause of abandonment does not stem from charges of adultery but from the husband's dissatisfaction, either because his wife has failed to produce an heir or because he considers her his social inferior. In response, the wife assumes the role of the trickster to regain her husband. In the fifteenth-century French *Roman du Comte d'Artois*, a count leaves his wife, vowing never to return unless she conceives a son by him and obtains his ring and horse.[42] These tasks are intentionally designed to be unachievable, since the husband abjures further contact with his wife. Nonetheless, she follows him in male disguise and wins his confidence and friendship. Later, in a variation on the motif of the "substitute bride," the disguised woman arranges a tryst between her husband and his new love, but, disguised again, she takes the place of the mistress in bed. When certain of her pregnancy, she bids farewell to her husband, who unwittingly rewards his male confidant with a gift of his ring and horse. Thus, she fulfills the three tasks and is happily reunited with her husband.

A similar tale is told at the beginning of the fourteenth-century Icelandic *Magus saga jarls* (ca. 1300),[43] although here the disguised woman wins the required items from her husband in a game of *tafl* (similar to backgammon). The last condition, to become pregnant by her husband, is met when the husband goes to the victor's tent at night to avenge himself by seducing the man's wife. The woman is his own wife, unrecognized in the darkness of the tent.

In these stories of women as male heroes, we find once again that the narrators emphasize their femaleness at least as much as their heroism. Heterosexual intercourse is the goal of the heroine: she must have sex with her husband to achieve her ends. The tales lack a critical perspective on the wife's incognito intercession in the husband's planned adultery, ignoring the dishonesty of this sexual subterfuge perpetrated against the male. Instead, the husband expresses admiration for his wife's actions since they result in the conception of a son. The husband's rejection of the wife, although legitimated by society, disrupts social order. The wife's transvestism and deliberate subterfuge, on the other hand, are both clearly outside societal norms, yet they are acceptable because they restore marriage.

The woman's overriding concern for her status as wife and her ultimate gender conformity legitimate such inverted plots, but even these devices fail to diminish the perception of the woman as a powerful and untraditional heroine. The wife alternates between male and female roles in the course of the action: she plays the deserted wife, male servant or competitor, female lover, sexual conquest, and forgiving spouse; a range of characters, all of whom are focused on the restoration of her original social gender status. This strong determination, which disregards gender and societal constraints, is an important factor in the characterization of the abandoned wife as a hero.

A husband's enforced or voluntary absence serves as the impetus for disguise in all these stories of women's adventures outside the domestic sphere. Without a husband, the woman is no longer a wife; as the male disguise signifies, the absence of the husband literally results in a loss of sexual identity. In disguise, the women breach male hegemony but also conform to male ideals of heroism. Is the male ideal so dominant that it is the only fictionally interesting paradigm for the female heroine? The figure of the wife as a man fits into the general setting of the "verkehrte Welt," or world-turned-upside-down, but the restorative endings of these tales, like the typical endings of other inversion themes, often reveal a conformity to convention. Although a few works, most notably *Flore et Jehane* and Boccaccio's tale of Zinevra, articulate uncertainty about (perhaps even criticism of) gender inequity, for the most part the societal constraints that necessitate the use of male disguise are viewed as part of a natural order. In their use of temporary disguise, the women do not actually overstep culturally defined gender boundaries, despite their "manly" characteristics and heroic deeds. The restorative endings that impose a conventionality on these figures is qualified, however, by the admission that some extraordinary women (with innate "masculine" qualities), if unrecognized as such, are capable of succeeding in the male world. Nonetheless, they are praiseworthy because disguise results in their eventual return to the lower status of women.

A different type of disguised wife represents a source of disorder; she uses male disguise to dominate men in parodies of social structure. Contrary to the positive figures of other disguise literature, these characters conform to images of shrewd, unfaithful, and domineering women common in late-medieval fabliaux and carnival plays.[44] Cross dressing becomes a sign of the desire for dominance as a wife (an "unnatural" state), and, furthermore, it aids these women in schemes to outwit their husbands. Indignation at the idea of female authority sets the tone for much of the invective against Jeanne d'Arc and the supposed papess, but in fictional matters of less consequence than military dominance or papal authority, the empowerment of women could be used to comic effect. If presented with the proper tone, contravention of taboos becomes humorous. Instead of returning to positions as subservient wives, these women use disguise to gain the upper hand in the contentious struggle of the sexes for power within relationships.

Berangier au lonc cul, a fourteenth-century French tale, depicts a wife who uses male disguise to humiliate (and, thereby, dominate) a craven husband. There are two roughly contemporaneous versions of the story: an anonymous fabliau and a poem by Guerin.[45] In Guerin's social satire, the wife's superiority is emphasized from the outset; she comes from the knightly class, whereas her husband is the son of a usurer. As in *Flore et Jehane*, reversed gender hierarchy parallels actual social standing. Belittling his wife's noble birth, the newly made "chevalier" rides off to find knightly adventure. In both versions, he returns to boast of his prowess, claiming to have routed several knights and killed a few others. His wife's surprise soon gives way to suspicion when she notices that, although his sword and shield are badly damaged, his hauberk remains in perfect condition; furthermore, he has never gotten a scratch, much less a wound. One day she dresses as a knight to follow her husband into the woods, where she observes him as he hangs his shield on a tree and thrashes it with his sword. Decrying this affront to knighthood, she makes to attack him. When he begs for mercy, she gives him a choice:

> Comment que vos jostez à moi,
> ....
> Ou ge descendrai jus à pié,
> Si me prenrai à abaissier;
> Vos me venroiz el cul baisier,
> Trés el milieu se vos volez.[46]

[Either you joust with me or I'll dismount here and bend over thus; you come and kiss my ass, right in the middle, if you please.]

The cowardly husband chooses humiliation over knightly combat. Adding to the obscene humor, the disguised knight alludes to his/ her true sex, proclaiming his name to be Berangier "au lonc cul." Later, when the husband arrives home (already boasting again in the anonymous version), he finds his wife *flagrante delicto* with her knightly lover. His indignant objection gives way to shame when the wife threatens him with her new protector, Berangier. Thereafter, she can do as she pleases.

The misogyny that is rampant in fabliaux expresses itself in the crude punishment imposed by the wife and in her subsequent boldness in flaunting her sexual unruliness.[47] Moreover, although the boastful lies and foolish behavior of the pseudo-knight warrant comeuppance, the wife's subsequent abuse of authority shows her to be equally in need of reform. Despite its originality in the characterization of the "self-made" knight and the female defender of true chivalry, the plot ultimately devolves into clichés. Shamed and vanquished on the battlefield and in the bedroom, the man appears pitiful at the end. He is the cuckold to his wife's role as domineering adulteress; both have become stock characters in the troupe of fabliaux players.

Ritter Beringer, a fifteenth-century German adaptation of the bawdy fabliau, exhibits marked differences from both French versions.[48] In the same manner, the disguised wife punishes her husband, whose name is Beringer in this rendition, but a didactic ending replaces the cruel conclusion of the French versions. Furthermore, the couple seems to be of the same class and basically well disposed toward one another. The humiliation scene, during which the wife can scarcely keep from laughing ("ir ward zu lachen also not"), ends with her stern warning for him to improve his behavior. She does not, however, add insult to injury by engaging in extramarital affairs. Beringer returns from his encounter a changed man. He admits defeat and forswears "beyde stechen und turnieren" [both fighting and jousting].[49] Initially pleased with his reform, the wife later finds she must threaten him from time to time with the specter of her male persona, Ritter Wienant von Boszland "mit der langen ars krynnen." She retains superiority but does not abuse her power:

> sy [...] bot ims wol, die wyl er lebt.
> uß irem willen er nit me strebt.
> Er ward ir undertenig gar,
>
> ....
> ir truw die was stet.[50]

[She treated him well all his life. He never again strayed from her will, he was completely obedient, she was faithful to him.]

As Stiefel noted in his discussion of the sources for *Ritter Beringer*, "Der dichter [hat] die demütigung zu einer moralischen cur ausgenutzt."[51] This "moral remedy," administered by a wise and prudent wife to rehabilitate an offending member of society and strengthen marriage, articulates little misogynist sentiment, nor does it require an overly harsh condemnation of the husband. As in *Berangier au lonc cul*, the humor arises from the fact that a woman bests a man and a wife gains authority over her husband. But the wife's restraint in *Ritter Beringer* transforms the debilitating ending of the French fabliaux into the harmonious conclusion: "Sy lebten furbaß tugentlich."[52] [They lived virtuously ever after.]

Whereas the calumniated woman must resort to male disguise to defend her own honor, the woman in the Berangier stories takes the initiative, using disguise to dominate her husband. Nonetheless, as the crude appellations "au lonc cul" and "mit der langen ars krynnen" indicate, disguise is not complete in the Berangier stories. Indeed, female genitals provide the distinguishing characteristic of the wife's male persona. Unlike the transvestite saints, who fear exposure and for whom uncovering of the body often serves as the decisive act in the moment of a recognition, the wife in the Berangier stories combines male disguise and disclosure of the body. Female sex remains evident, although the sign of gender is misunderstood by the weak husband.

Hans Folz (1435/40-1513), the prolific German satirist, emphasizes female genitalia in *Der arme Bäcker*—his version of the bawdy humiliation scene of *Berangier au lonc cul*—but he also uses the material to reenshrine traditional sexual hierarchy.[53] Although incomplete, it is clear that Folz radically revised the theme to redeem the humiliated man and punish the presumptuous woman. Female gender inversion becomes a temporary anomaly punished and corrected by male authority. In his version, a woman dresses up like her husband and confronts a poor baker collecting firewood on her property. While performing the debasing act of kissing his lord's posterior, the baker realizes that he is dealing with a woman. To avenge himself, he disguises himself as a fool and visits the woman while her husband is away. Typical of women in misogynist literature, the wife's sexual appetite knows no bounds and she attempts to seduce the fool. However, as the poem breaks off, the baker wreaks revenge for his previous humiliation by sodomizing the woman.

The rough portrait of a greedy, immoral woman who bullies her social inferiors conforms to Folz's depictions of women in other works.[54] The strident misogyny and violent ending are new, and, moreover, Folz introduces the problem of the failure of disguise to the Berangier material. The baker does not seek revenge for his humiliation *per se* but rather for the attempt by a woman to dominate him sexually and socially. In spite of her higher social rank, the woman's sex implies, according to Folz, a moral inferiority that justifies the baker's retribution and necessitates the restoration of the sexual hierarchy. With unusual crudity, Folz's version vitiates the unruly woman who seizes power by means of male disguise.

In Dietrich von der Glezze's *Der Gürtel* (ca. 1270-90), the disguised woman combines characteristics of the devoted partner who follows her husband to foreign lands, the calumniated wife, and the unfaithful schemer.[55] Probably based on the mythological story of Procris and Cephalus,[56] this odd tale of disguise is fraught with contradictions. The author writes in the language and style of courtly romance but inverts traditional themes and motifs from romance literature to criticize the decay of chivalric virtues. Dietrich von der Glezze depicts a complex degeneration of courtly love that includes adultery, transvestism, homosexuality, and prostitution. Inversion occurs not only in transgressive sexual acts that degrade the ideal of *minne*, but also in the presentation of a woman as the questing figure. Contravening moral codes, gender roles, and literary tradition, the hero is an adulterous woman who cross dresses as a knight and ultimately stands as arbiter of virtue in the resolution and moralistic epilogue.

Equivocal presentation sets description, characterization, and plot development at odds with one another. The *maere*, which is addressed to a courtly audience,[57] praises such traditional chivalric values as *tugend* [virtue], *triuwe* [fidelity], and *êre* [honor], yet depicts a nobility willing to compromise virtue for material gain. From the start, the honor of the characters is emphasized. Konrad von Schwaben is described as an honorable knight and his wife's virtue, fidelity, and chastity are mentioned six times in the introductory description. Later, however, the wife commits adultery in return for four magic gifts: a falcon and hunting dogs from which no quarry can escape and a horse and belt that render their owner invincible. Initially indignant at a visiting knight's suggestion that she trade sexual favors for material goods, she rebukes him in absolute terms. Her staunch refusals ring with finality, but the persistent knight finally overcomes her defenses with the offer of the magic belt in addition to all the animals.[58] The implication that every virtue has its price scarcely conforms to the characterization of the woman at the beginning of the poem, yet the narrator's presentation remains positive.

The honorable Konrad, who retreats to a foreign court when he learns of his wife's infidelity, also contravenes his own ethical standards. Following Konrad in men's clothing and making use of the magic gifts, the unnamed wife, now called Heinrich von Schwaben, quickly gains renown for her hunting and jousting skills.[59] Konrad soon tries to induce Heinrich to sell him the falcon and dogs, but Heinrich refuses all offers of money. Finally, he agrees to part with the animals if Konrad will be his lover. When Konrad immediately agrees to the homosexual encounter, his wife reveals her identity, scolding him for his easy virtue. She maintains that homosexual love is more dishonorable than her own affair with the knight. More important, she criticizes Konrad's willingness to barter his honor for the least of the four gifts she received in return for, according to her, a less serious indiscretion:

> Daz ich tet, daz was menschlîch:
> sô woltet ir unkristenlîch
> Vil gerne haben getân;
> ir sît ein unreiner man,
> Daz ir durch die minsten gabe zwô
> iuwer êre woldet alsô
> Haben gar verlorn
> sehet, daz ist mir zorn.[60]

[What I did was only human: but you would gladly have done something unchristian; you're an indecent man since you would have forfeited your honor completely for the two least important gifts; see here, that makes me angry.]

According to the narrator, her infidelity differs not only in type of sexual encounter but also in motive. The magic gifts earned through adultery bring success in hunting and fighting. What use, then, are the animals and belt to the woman in her role as wife? It is only by assuming male disguise that she can possibly take advantage of their power. This brings up a curious point that supports the wife's self-proclaimed justification for her behavior. Since she intended to give the gifts to her husband to increase his fame and *êre* (as she indeed does at the conclusion), the exchange takes on new ethical dimensions. In her rebuke, the wife explains her motives:

> einen ritter ich kuste
> Und liez in bî mir slâfen,
> daz ir mit dem wâfen
> Waeret, mit des borten kraft,
> werder in der ritterschaft.[61]

[I kissed a knight and let him sleep with me so that, at arms, by the power of the girdle, you might become worthier in knightly deeds.]

It is not, then, merely the stated distinction between hetero- and homosexual adultery that vindicates the wife but also her purpose. In this "verkehrte Welt," virtue is venal, honor is based on appearances, and a woman can use male disguise to mount a convincing defense of her adultery. Nonetheless, despite the inversion of gender roles, sex, sexual orientation, and traditional morality to criticize courtly society, the narrator's final lesson to his male audience completely vindicates the wife and glorifies the power of female sexuality. Moreover, although he uses the language of *Minnesang*, he suggests that sexual hierarchy should remain inverted:

> Ir man, ich wil iuch lêren,
> vrouwen sult ir êren
> Und sult in undertaenik sîn;
> wand iriu rôten mündelîn
> Und ir wîzen wengelîn
> diu bringent iuch von grôzer pîn.[62]

[You men, I want to teach you this: you should honor all women and you should be subservient to them; because their red mouths and white cheeks can save you from great pain.]

Male disguise serves several familiar functions in *Der Gürtel*. As in the stories of women disguised as minstrels, it enables the woman to find her husband in a strange land. Like the calumniated women, the wife uses a male persona to defend herself against a charge of adultery. And finally, like the Berangier women, she uses male disguise to shame her husband with a sexually explicit trick, thereby forcing him to overlook her illicit affair.

For many women, concealment of the female body hides the sexual (and offending) element of their identity. This is not the case in *Der Gürtel*, where the wife introduces sexuality into her male friendship with her husband. One can find examples of women in male disguise who are propositioned by other women in the saints' lives and in the works to be discussed in the following chapter, but, as far as I can determine, the pseudo-homosexual proposition made to the man by the disguised woman in *Der Gürtel* is unique in medieval literature. Playing a male role similar to that of her seducer, the wife tempts her husband into a homosexual encounter that forces him to acknowledge his own moral infirmity. In the end, female cross dressing in *Der Gürtel* does not concern female as much as male sexuality and male attitudes toward virtue.

Unlike the disguise of the transvestite saints, deviation from societal strictures in this body of literature is neither reactionary nor permanent. Conformity to societal norms tames the potential radicalism of male disguise. This conformity, most evident in the conventional conclusions, also manifests itself in the lack of individual identity for most of the women. With some exceptions, such as Zinevra and Jehane, the women are not named. Identified by the relationship to their husbands, the goal of such women as the wives of Alexander von Mainz and Konrad von Schwaben is preservation of uxorial identity. Only the male disguise that enables these women to reclaim wifely anonymity endows them with a distinct personality (and often with a name).

Male disguise, as a literary device, allows authors to develop nontraditional female characters but, in most cases, foists a male model of fictional heroism onto female characters. Such characters, nonetheless, challenge the concept of biologically determined gender. Several authors comment on the innate "masculine" abilities of the women, revealing the problem at the heart of much of the literature of female disguise: the absence of language and context for portraying female heroism. Because the signifiers of heroism and the imagery for strength, perseverance, and virtue are masculine, the masculinization and, consequentially, the cross dressing of active female protagonists cannot be avoided. The exploits and virtues depicted, however, are obviously attributed to the woman, creating a new type of female protagonist. An authorial uncertainty concerning gender behavior admits this possibility of female heroism, albeit within the universality of the male paradigm of heroism.

Chapter Seven

CROSS DRESSING AND SEXUALITY

S'ot tel vis que qui la veoit
Dire pooit c'est fille ou filz.

[She had such a face that whoever saw her
could say she was either a girl or a boy.]
—*Ovide moralisé*[1]

In several romances of the thirteenth and fourteenth centuries,
disguise not only inverts cultural gender roles but also confuses
or reorients sexuality. A common element in these works is the
dilemma caused when disguised women, usually unintentionally,
arouse the sexual interest of other women. This mistakenly
homoerotic attraction, however, elicits a variety of responses ranging
from rejection to requital of affection. Consequently, sexuality itself
becomes an issue: these works explore, in distinctively frank terms,
the problems of sexual, in addition to cultural, identity that may
arise through cross dressing. Perception of disguised women as
sexually attractive males precipitates a crisis that, in vastly different
ways, always results in relinquishment of male disguise. The problem
of cross dressing and sexual orientation, however, involves both
societal misperception based on appearance and confused self-
perception of the disguised character. The latter element, one not
expressed in other secular disguise literature, takes into account the
psychological difficulties of maintaining disguise.

A classical source for some of the tales may be Ovid's story of
Iphis.[2] Often translated and retold throughout the Middle Ages,[3] it
describes how Iphis, disguised as a boy since birth, develops an
affinity to her cultural maleness that extends to the realm of sexuality.
In love with the girl Ianthe, Iphis prays for, and is granted, sexual
metamorphosis. In medieval variations of this motif, Blanchandine
in *Tristan de Nanteuil* (fourteenth century) and Yde in *Yde et Olive*
(fourteenth century) win the love of princesses while masquerading

as knights and eventually experience a divine change of sex. In the *Roman de Silence* (late thirteenth century), on the other hand, Heldris de Cornuälle's heroine, Silence, who was raised as a man, struggles to reconcile "natural" and constructed sexual identities. Although distinguished by the narrator's thorough consideration of the dichotomy between biological femaleness and cultural maleness, the *Roman de Silence* probably has its origins in an episode from the Merlin legend that is recorded in *L'Estoire de Merlin* (1230), as well as the later English prose *Merlin* (1450/60) and fragmentary German poem *Merlin* (early fourteenth century).[4] In these tales, a woman calling herself Grisandole poses as a young man at the emperor's court until Merlin exposes the sexual transgressions of the court, including Grisandole's gender disguise.

Ovide moralisé, *Yde et Olive*, and the French and English Merlin legends have been available in editions for almost a hundred years, but two of the works, the *Roman de Silence* and *Tristan de Nanteuil*, were first edited in the early 1970s. Lucy Allen Paton, one of the first to study the theme of the disguised woman, traces aspects of the Grisandole legend to Indian sources and documents the motif in a number of Renaissance tales.[5] Unfortunately, two early versions of the story, the *Roman de Silence* and the German *Merlin*, were not available to her. Recently, however, several articles have appeared, most of them concentrating on the *Roman de Silence*. Kate Mason Cooper emphasizes the importance of silence as a leitmotif and discusses the enigmatic language of the romance and its relationship to the dichotomous sexuality of the character.[6] Similarly, Howard Bloch views the *Roman de Silence* as a linguistic hybrid in which intentional ambiguity and, more important, silence itself confuse both the reader and the characters within the fiction.[7] Misunderstanding, misreading, and indeterminacy reflect, according to Bloch, the "perceptual and cognitive impossibility of seeing, reading, hearing, or speaking the silence whose transgression is the premise of the fiction."[8] For the most part, these studies have focused on the role of language in conveying sexual ambiguity. The linguistic aspect of disguise permeates the text of the *Roman de Silence* and, to a lesser extant, *Tristan de Nanteuil*.[9] Silence even defines herself in linguistic terms: "Dont se porpense en lui meïsme / Que Nature li fait sofime: / Por cho que l'-us est encontre us."[10] [He (Silence) thought to himself that *Nature* was speaking in sophistries; because the "-us" (the masculine ending of her name, Silencius) was against natural law ("us").][11] In several texts, the intentional use of enigmatic language to obscure truth illustrates the similarity of purpose in veiling identity and meaning. Some questions that remain, however, relate not so much to the expression of concealed gender as to the effect of this concealment within the fictional narrative.

The stories of Iphis, Yde, Blanchandine, Silence, and Grisandole share several elements. Yde, Blanchandine, and Iphis realize their disguised identities by becoming male; Grisandole and Silence ultimately choose feminine natures; Iphis and Silence share the common experience of male gender training since birth; Yde, Blanchandine, Grisandole, and Silence function as knights in courtly society; nakedness (or fear of it) plays a role in all the stories; and so on. Instead of developing a taxonomy of plots, however, I will focus on representations of the impact of transvestism on the heroine's identity and on societal perception of identity within the context of the narrative, as well as within literary conventions for establishing male or female identity (and sexuality).

The problem of self-perception is perhaps most acute for Silence. At three points in her life—as a child, an adolescent, and a young adult—Silence's feminine sexuality confronts her. Unconcerned about her biological sex until her father discusses it with her sometime before her twelfth birthday, Silence considers herself a boy. She lives in a forest mansion, secluded from the world (a childhood reminiscent of many male heroes of courtly romance), learning sports and knightly activities along with letters. When her father, Cador, the duke of Cornwall, explains the reason for her male disguise (a law against female inheritance), she assures him she is content to remain a male, realizing that her life will be one of deception. Shortly afterward, however, the adolescent girl is assailed by *Nature*, an internal force that admonishes her to adopt the clothing and manners of her true sex. Entering the debate on the other side, *Noreture* (experience or culture) argues in favor of continuing the male activities for which Silence has been raised. Thus, even before entering society, Silence questions her identity. Both *Nature* and Silence lament the concealment of her body, an exquisite and unique work of nature.[12] But, persuaded by *Noreture*, Silence prefers suppression of the body to loss of her accustomed maleness and privilege—a view she expresses in obsessively sexual language, despite

her commitment to disguise and the necessary sexual abstinence
that attends it:

> Que Silences a bien veü
> Que fol consel avoit creü
> Quant onques pensa desuser
> Son bon viel us et refuser,
> Por us de feme maintenir.
> Donques li prent a sovenir
> Des jus c'on siolt es cambres faire
> Dont a oï sovent retraire,
> Et poise dont en son corage
> Tolt l'us de feme a son usage,
> Et voit que miols valt li us d'ome
> Que l'us de feme, c'est la some.
> "Voire," fait il, "a la male eure
> Irai desos, quant sui deseure.
> Deseure sui, s'irai desos.
> Or sui jo moult vallans et pros.
> Nel sui, par foi ains sui honis
> Quant as femes voel estre onis.
> Gel pensai por moi aäsier.
> Trop dure boche ai por baisier,
> Et trop rois bras por acoler.
> On me poroit tost afoler
> Al giu c'on fait desos gordine,
> Car vallés sui et nient mescine,
> Ne voel perdre ma grant honor."[13]

[Silence understood clearly that he had believed foolish advice when
he considered putting off and denying his good old custom to take
up that of a woman. Then he began to remember the games people
play in private, that he had often heard described, and he weighed in
his heart the woman's role against his own, and saw that a man's life
is better than a woman's, all things considered. "Truly," he said, "in
an evil hour will I go underneath, when I am on top. I am on top
now, and I would have to go beneath. Now I am most valorous and
strong, but I wouldn't be any longer; rather, in faith, I'd be shamed if
I wanted to be like the women. I thought of it for my own pleasure.
I have a mouth too hard for kissing, and arms too rough for
embracing. I would quickly be beaten at the game people play under
the covers, for I am a boy, and not a girl at all. I don't want to lose my
great honor, nor exchange it for a lesser one."]

On two levels, the consciousness of characters within the story and the viewpoint of the narrator, the gender hierarchy remains intact, despite the accomplishments of the plot's heroine. Silence herself reflects on women's status as "servitude" (line 2827) and fears the subordinate sex posture she ascribes to women. The narrator also endorses these concepts in several gestures. He explicitly agrees with *Nature's* dictum that women should "va en la cambre a la costure, / Cho violt de nature li us."[14] [Stay in the side-chambers, for nature demands this.] He also praises her parents, who agreed to have Silence raised in this way; it is a worthy investment because "car de mescine avront vallet."[15] [Out of a girl they will get a boy.]

Despite her contempt for the woman's role, Silence eventually plans to acquire a womanly skill in the event that the inheritance law is overturned or she is discovered. She decides to study music but carries out this plan by disguising herself as a male minstrel and apprenticing herself to two successful *jongleurs*. Like her musing on sexual roles, this double male disguise betrays her perception of herself as male; she learns to play an instrument—a sexually ambivalent skill at best—while retaining her male identity. Her reasoning for learning to play again emphasizes her disdain for a woman's life as well as the narrator's critical view of the woman's role in society: if the king should die and the inheritance laws should change, allowing a woman to hold property and making Silence's disguise unnecessary, she tells herself, "Ta harpe et ta viële avras / En lieu de cho que ne savras / Orfrois ne fresials manoier. / Si te porra mains anoier / Se tu iés en un bastonage / Ke tu aiés vials el en grage."[16] [You will have your harp and vielle in place of what you do not know about working orphreys or ribbons. It could well bother you less to be in servitude, for you will at least have other plans.] Although the pull of antinomies is apparent in the desire to prepare for a possible life as a woman, cultural training and trappings continue to dominate her own self-perception.

Later, when Silence arrives at King Ebains's court in her role as the son of the duke of Cornwall, Queen Eufeme provokes Silence's third confrontation with self-perception by trying to seduce her. Silence cites loyalty to the king to justify her rejection, but the encounter leaves her deeply troubled about her secret. The queen thinks Silence might be homosexual (lines 3935-39), but, in fact, the narrator claims it is her heterosexual orientation and female nature which prompt her to reject Eufeme's sexual interest ("Car nel consent pas sa nature").[17] Nonetheless, Silence realizes that she cannot confide her secret and risk undermining her social position: "Ne violt pas dire son covine, / De sa nature verité, / Qu'il perdroit donques s'ireté."[18] [He did not want to tell the secret of his true nature, for then he would lose his inheritance.] Surprisingly perhaps, Eufeme's second seduction attempt, which culminates in a vindictive charge of sexual misconduct against Silence, leads not to the revelation of actual sex but to an intensification of Silence's male identity. Rather than killing Silence as the queen desires, King Ebains sends her to the royal court of France. There, after some initial difficulties caused by a forged letter, Silence is knighted and distinguishes herself at tournaments. The story views maleness as social performance, while femaleness looks much more like a sexed body. An effective athlete and fighter throughout her youth, Silence gains enormous martial prowess by the time of her knighting at age seventeen and a half (line 5132). Thereafter, she appears to be the leading knight at the court of the French king and, indeed, becomes the savior of England at the battle of Chester (line 5186). There, as "the boy from Cornwall,"[19] she saves not only King Ebains but also his entire realm from the rebellious barons. The narrator explains that, despite Silence's feminine nature, *Noreture* made such success possible:

> Kil veïst joster sans mantel
> Et l'escu porter en cantiel
> Et faire donques l'ademise,
> La lance sor le faltre mise,
> Dire peüst que Noreture
> Puet moult ovrer contre Nature,
> Quant ele aprent si et escole
> A tel us feme et tendre et mole.[20]

[Anyone who saw him (Silence) joust without a mantle, carrying the shield on his left arm, and set to the attack, lance on the lance-rest, would say that Nurture can do much against Nature when she teaches and trains a tender, delicate woman in such behavior.]

Away from the sexual threat represented by Eufeme, Silence prospers as a knight, apparently satisfied with leading the life for which she was educated and trained:

> Silences ne se repent rien
> De son usage, ains l'ainme bien.

> Chevaliers est vallans et buens,
> Mellor n'engendra rois ne cuens.
> Ne vos puis dire la moitié
> De si com il a esploitié.
> Ains que li ans trasist a fin
> A bon chevalier et a fin
> Le tienent tolt cil de la terre.[21]

[Silence did not at all regret his habits; indeed, he loved them. He was a fine and valiant knight: no king or count ever sired better. I cannot tell you half of what he accomplished, but before the year drew to an end, everyone in the land considered him a good and fine knight.]

The narrator makes powerful arguments against biological determinism in passages like the one quoted above yet also qualifies descriptions of Silence's knightly prowess (in which the masculine pronoun is used) with references to her femininity. This ambivalence occurs repeatedly; apparently, the narrator never doubts that male and female natures arise from physical sex and cannot be completely or permanently effaced by cultural factors. At one point, we are led to believe that Silence's male training could not have counteracted her female nature were it not God's will. During a battle, Silence prays:

> ...Bials Dex, chaieles,
> Ki m'a[s] jeté de maint anui,
> Done moi vertu viers cestui!
> Cho qu'afoiblie en moi Nature
> Cho puist efforcier T'aventure.
> Mais se Tu viols ne me puet nuire
> Rois, n'amirals o son empire.[22]

[Fair God, for pity's sake, who have delivered me from great trouble, give me strength against this man! That which Nature makes weak in me, may Your Providence strengthen. Unless You wish it, I cannot be harmed by any king, admiral, or whole army.]

Thus, as in hagiographic accounts of female martyrs, the weak woman prevails with the help of God. This condescending view, not expressed elsewhere in the romance, contradicts a basic premise of the plot that society constructs gender roles.[23]

Silence's female body is a source of suspicion throughout the plot, although the romance does not represent a unified view of the nature of sex. It would appear that complexion, not genitalia, mutates. At the beginning of Silence's masculization, the narrator equates corporeity with transvestism: "Li cors n'est mais fors sarpelliere."[24] [The body is nothing but another rough garment.] As many critics have pointed out, emphasis is placed on the creation of the perfect female body for Silence. In a long passage (lines 1795ff.), *Nature* creates the mold for Silence, literally inscribing perfection into it. Nonetheless, the female body, as a sexed body, is a source of irregularity throughout the story, since Silence, although a perfect male knight, is accused of sexual transgression. She is initially thought to be homosexual and soon charged with attempted rape by Queen Eufeme. Sexual irregularity also seemingly taints Silence's lineage, since, as it turns out, Uther Pendragon had sex with Ygraine, one of Silence's forebears, to produce Arthur. With Merlin's help, Uther raped Ygraine by assuming the shape of Duke Gorlaine, her recently deceased husband. The exposure of the good female body at the end of the *Roman de Silence*, moreover, is paralleled by the exposure (and punishment) of the transgressive female body of Eufeme when the fabliau-like closure reveals her depravity through the unclothing of her transvestite male lover.

Although Silence prospers in almost every male endeavor, in the end sexuality shatters her chosen lifestyle when Eufeme's unfulfilled desire leads to sexual revelation. Falsely charged with sexual impropriety, Silence must undertake the task of capturing Merlin to avert her own execution. According to Merlin himself, no man will ever find him (lines 6177-79). Although chosen to ensure Silence's failure and death, the adventure merely serves to reveal her sex, as Merlin's definition of it emphatically shows.[25] However, because this unwanted disclosure forces Silence to accept *Nature* over *Noreture* when compelled to undress publicly, the dilemma of self-perception remains unresolved. Silence accepts *Nature* by learning to play an instrument and rejecting Eufeme, but, in all other matters up to this point, she has followed *Noreture*. After Queen Eufeme is denounced and executed, Silence becomes the new queen. The reaction to her female role is not recorded; in a concluding speech, she explains the reason for her disguise and then merely expresses resignation to fate: "Faites de moi vostre plaisir."[26] [Do with me as you please.] It is as if, by accepting her female status as a passive wife, Silence ceases to contradict *Nature*, becoming, literally, silent.

Shortly before the revelation, the narrator plays with the heroine's name and cultural expectations for women, when the king offers his opinion of women: "Sens de feme gist en taisir. /... Mais entre .m. nen a pas une / Ki gregnor los n'eüst de taire."[27] [A woman's wisdom lies in being silent. ... There is not one in a thousand who would not receive greater praise for being silent.] And indeed, the heroine's greatness lies in the multivalency of being silent—that is, keeping her secret, "being" Silentius for most of the romance, and finally, in "becoming" Silentia (and silent) when exposed as a woman. Yet Silence's antepenultimate statement seems to contradict the silence imposed by her newly exposed femaleness (as well as offering another linguistic conundrum), for she says: "Ne jo n'ai soig mais de taisir."[28] [I no longer want to keep silent.] Unfortunately, the narrative and linguistic confusion leave the consequences of ultimate abandonment of male culture and education unexpressed.

The story and its narrator are concerned with the meanings of signs, especially signs of gender and sex. The playfulness of some of the language, particularly the puns and enigmas of the love talk between Cador and Eufemie as well as the omnipresent bivalent sign of Silence, evokes the semiotic ambiguities of the Tristan romance as written by Thomas and as it survives in Gottfried. Language and signs can be meaningless (as in the announcement of the birth of a son), false (as in the fabricated letter to the King of France), or, as is often the case, multivalent. The audience, however, can generally understand the value of gender signs—although there are exceptions. From the perspective of the gender hierarchy (that is, the hegemony of maleness), the discrepancy between the woman as (passive) body and the male as performance creates gaps in the text, an important example of which is the tropological pun of closure: "A woman's wisdom lies in being silent."[29]

Rather than suppress her feminine nature, Iphis is obsessed with it. As portrayed in the fourteenth-century *Ovide moralisé* (a rendition that adheres closely to Ovid with the exception of an appended religious allegory), Iphis is so completely attuned to her male personality that she perceives her female body as a burden. Sexually attracted to Ianthe, she laments the laws of nature that frustrate her desire:

> Quel vache seult vache requerre,
> Ne quel eque autre eque atoucher?

Les brebis ont le moton cher,
Et la vache dou tor s'acointe.
Ensi veult à male estre jointe
Chasque femele en son endroit.
Nulle femele n'entendroit
Ne de soi joindre n'avroit cure
A femele en non de luxure.[30]

[What cow calls for another cow, what mare touches another mare?
The ewe holds the ram dear, and the cow acquaints herself with the
bull. Thus, each female, in her place, wants to be joined to a male.
No female would ever seek or desire to join herself to a female in the
name of lust.]

Her love for Ianthe is hopeless, she believes, because consummation
is impossible. Although love is requited and the marriage has been
scheduled, Iphis fears the wedding night, when there will be two
brides and no husband. She expresses her own sexual orientation,
however, in the negative formulation of the complaint: "Mes voloirs
ne puet avenir. / Je ne puis malle devinir."[31] [My wish cannot come
true. I cannot become male.] Iphis accepts her male role in society
and desires to reconcile cultural gender with biological sex. Sexual
attraction, not the pull of heterosexual nature or fear of revelation,
induces conflict.

Although Iphis herself does not express it directly, the concept of
male superiority provides the basis for her disguise. Her father
instructed her mother to kill the newborn if it were a girl, since, as
he claims, women are weak and only cause trouble for men: "Fame
est sans force et sans valour. / Par fame est maint home à dolour."[32]
Iphis, therefore, owes her life to the male disguise initiated by her
mother. To live is to be male. Iphis laments that she was ever born,
for not being biologically male still threatens her existence. Possible
discovery does not plague her; she worries more about the sexual
impotency of her female form in union with Ianthe. Without
seriously considering (or understanding) homosexuality, she merely
desires to be transformed into a man.[33] Consequently, frustration
marks her internal conflict of sexual identity. While her sexual
orientation reflects her lifelong disguise and cultural milieu, her
body contradicts this masculine self-perception. The gods finally
grant the only solution to this transsexual dilemma, transforming
Iphis into a biological man.

In *Yde et Olive*, a fourteenth-century continuation of *Huon de Bordeaux*, Yde chooses masculine disguise to escape an incestuous father. Although entering the male world without benefit of male gender conditioning, Ydé (the masculine form of her name) performs in battle like a man, according to the narrator. Throughout the period of disguise, however, the narrator refers to her as "elle" or, more specifically as "Yde la bele" or "Damoisielle Yde," thus emphasizing her femininity.[34] The descriptive emphasis on true sex in the midst of recording the heroine's masculine activities largely replaces the sexual dichotomy expressed in the other romances by the characters' internal debates.

Yde excels in her role as a knight, both in battle and at court. The problem arises when she is perceived as a sexual being. Espoused to King Oton's daughter, Olive, Yde worries about her inability to consummate the marriage: "Ne set comment se porra demener / N'a membre nul qu'a li puist abiter."[35] [She does not know how she should act; she has no member that she can use.] The idea of sexual relations with another woman does not disturb Yde. Although she rejected as unnatural her father's plan to marry her, Yde does not flee Oton's court to avoid marriage to Olive. When she excuses herself from conjugal relations with Olive on the wedding night, she nonetheless accepts Olive's terms without objection. Olive agrees to allow Ydé to do as s/he pleases for fifteen days, on the condition that Ydé kiss and embrace her at night (lines 7146-47). Yde's sexual orientation, although vaguely defined and in the early stages of development, either admits some degree of homosexuality or, more likely, begins to correspond to that of the heterosexual male she pretends to be.

When Yde confesses her true sex, Olive promises, like a loyal wife, to support her and keep her secret. Their relationship under this new understanding is not depicted, since King Oton soon learns the truth from an eavesdropping servant. The threat of nakedness, which exposes the body and the secret, looms when King Oton orders a public bath for his son-in-law. The trial, however, becomes the site of a miracle: an angel announces the sexual transformation of Yde. The reaction to this change is recorded briefly: "Li mot del angle sont mout bien retenu."[36] [The words of the angel were very well received.] In the following ten lines, Ydé and Olive produce an heir, Croissant, who quickly becomes the focus of the story. Thus, from the sketchy details of the narrative, it appears that Yde was attracted to Olive and not at all dissatisfied with the metamorphosis. Although Yde's struggle with sexual orientation receives little attention in the work, her marriage to Olive, her willingness to exchange physical signs of love, and her acceptance of sexual transformation indicate a character whose male disguise influenced sexual orientation and resulted in a permanent (and authentic) male identity.

The massive fourteenth-century epic *Tristan de Nanteuil* includes, among its numerous episodes, the story of Tristan's first love, Blanchandine, whom God metamorphoses into a man. Like Iphis and Silence, Blanchandine does not choose to disguise herself as a man. In her case, it is her husband, Tristan, who suggests the disguise so she can live with him undetected by her pagan father. (As a possible source for Tristan's ploy, it is interesting to note that his grandmother, Aye d'Avignon, temporarily disguised herself as a man to rescue her imprisoned family.)[37] Unlike Iphis and Silence, however, Blanchandine does not suffer a sexual identity crisis. Her male appearance causes difficulties because Clarinde, her cousin and the daughter of a sultan, courts her publicly on several occasions. Blanchandine's heterosexuality, however, allows for no equivocation; on the contrary, her femaleness is stressed in her sexual relationship with Tristan. In one scene, a messenger from the persistent Clarinde comes to Tristan's tent to summon Blanchandin (her masculine name), but Blanchandine is not available immediately because she is making love with Tristan. Even when she believes Tristan has been killed in battle, there is no change in Blanchandine's feelings for Clarinde. Forced to marry Clarinde, Blanchandine delays consummation on the grounds that sexual relations between a Christian and a pagan would be sinful. In fact, Blanchandine is biding time until she can escape the undesired situation. The only emotions she expresses are anxiety (she fears execution if discovered) and sorrow for the death of Tristan. She has no sexual interest in Clarinde.

The crisis comes when the frustrated Clarinde suspects deception and, like King Oton in *Yde et Olive*, prepares a bath to determine her husband's sex. Propitiously saved from this ordeal by the timely appearance of a wild stag rampaging through the palace, Blanchandine escapes and finds herself lost in the woods. Only at this point does she contemplate sexuality. An angel announces that

God has decided to give Blanchandine the choice between remaining a woman or becoming a man. She chooses male transformation, reasoning that she would never want to marry another man and, more important, that with a man's body she can avenge the death of Tristan:

> Veul devenir ungs homs, par quoy aultres n'ara
> A moy la compaignie. Je l'ay voué pieça;
> Sy vengeray Tristan aux paiens par dela.[38]

[I wish to become a man, so another man might not have me as a companion. I have long wished this; in this way, I will avenge Tristan among the pagans.]

This reasoning reflects the author's relative concept of sexual fidelity; to honor the dead husband, the female body must remain inviolate, whereas the male sexual activity that follows her transformation has no moral valence. Even in choosing to change sex, however, it is Blanchandine's female heterosexual fears (not wanting the love of any other man) and her devotion to Tristan, not love for Clarinde, that determine the decision.

While disguised as a man, Blanchandine suffers no conflict of identity. Male disguise is a matter of convenience to facilitate her heterosexual love affair with Tristan. The only hint of sexual conflict comes later, when, as a biological man, Blanchandin meets Tristan, whose death had been mistakenly reported. Tristan embraces Blanchandin, calling him "doulce amye." An embarrassed Blanchandin explains his new sexual state, but Tristan, thinking it a joke, says he desires to sleep with his beloved ("Amie, je doy moult dezirer / Que je puisse o vo corps au vespre reposer").[39] When the situation is made clear, Tristan is beside himself with grief and denounces Clarinde as an unworthy rival. But Blanchandin, who had learned that Tristan was alive moments after the metamorphosis, calms Tristan, claiming that God so willed it. The potential tragedy of the unnecessary sex change fails to overwhelm the characters because Blanchandin remains steadfast in his male role as Clarinde's husband. Blanchandin rues the mistake that destroyed the marriage of Tristan and Blanchandine, but he is no longer emotionally bound or sexually attracted to Tristan. Thus, in male disguise or as a transformed man, Blanchandine/Blanchandin retains heterosexual orientation. At the center of a tale rife with sexual confusion, Blanchandine expresses no sexual ambivalence. It is the reaction of others to appearances that leads to the crisis of transformation and introduces sexual ambiguity.

The basis for societal misperception of sex and sexual orientation in all these works is male dress. Yet, while misunderstanding arises from appearance, the disguised figure also makes a conscious effort to deceive society by adopting male demeanor. To avoid discovery, the heroine not only hides beneath the clothes of the opposite sex but also assumes traditionally male attributes, behavior, and roles. Fictional society, in turn, imposes the curriculum of the traditional male hero on the woman in disguise. When such a course of societal acceptance inevitably brings the hero into the service of an admiring lady, society's skewed perception becomes instrumental in uncovering the truth because it requires that the ideal knight be sexually active. In almost every other way, however, the heroines conform to criteria applied to male heroes of medieval romance.

In addition to their male clothing, the characters' names are also designed to mislead society. Iphis is the exception, but even in her case, the name is not gender specific. When her unsuspecting father names his "son," her mother approves: "La mere se resbaudissoit / Pour le non qui comuns resamble / A malle et à femele ensamble."[40] [The mother rejoiced because the name could apply to either male or female.] On the other hand, Silence's parents actually conspire to find an equivocal name. Yde and Blanchandine adapt their names to conform to their new identities by making only minor modifications in the endings to arrive at acceptable male appellations. Only Avenable makes a radical name change, presenting herself at the emperor's court as Grisandole.[41] Silence, Yde, and Blanchandine hide their female bodies beneath male clothing and their female names behind equally superficial masculine endings. This veneer of masculinity alone suffices to alter the fictional society's perception of them.

Once accepted as males, the women also perform as men. Among the heroines disguised as knights, Silence, having been raised as a boy, is perhaps best prepared for a male role. She draws on her childhood training to perfect her skill in such male activities as jousting and warfare. Her manners are those of a youth trained for service at a court. Society's misperception, in fact, mirrors Silence's own self-understanding under the influence of *Noreture*. Grisandole and Ydé are also credited with deeds of knightly valor. Although not described in detail, Grisandole's male reputation is substantial: "li empereres en auoit fait senescal de toute sa terre car ele estoit de moult grant proece."[42] [The emperor had made her seneschal over his entire land because she had great prowess.] Later, she searches unceasingly for Merlin, bearing many physical hardships before capturing him. Yde's masculine deeds receive more narrative attention: as a squire with a German army, she emerges as the sole survivor in a battle with Spanish troops; she defends herself from a band of robbers; and she successfully defeats the enemies of King Oton of Rome. Only the perception of Blanchandine as a courtly youth is not based on any evidence of knightly or martial deeds. At one point, she arms for battle, but Clarinde insists that Blanchandin withdraw from the troops for fear he might be killed. Blanchandine functions as a knight, therefore, only at court.[43] But courtly society unquestioningly accepts this unproven hero as the new lord of the land when she marries Clarinde.

Despite the false presentation to society, the heroine's femininity is not overlooked. The narrators tend to insert references to the character's feminine nature or to mix masculine and feminine attributes. Disguise and reality are reflected in the double portraits that emerge. As women, all are beautiful: Silence is a wonder of nature; Merlin describes Grisandole as "la plus bele feme et la plus boine de tout vostre terre" [the most beautiful and best woman in all your (the emperor's) land]; Blanchandine is "moult belle"; and Yde, as a young woman of fifteen, surpasses all others in beauty. Through the eyes of fictional society, however, male attributes also accrue to the character. Within the narrative context, faulty perception of name, nature, and appearance—the *nomen, natura,* and *habitus* essential to literary portraiture[44]—causes society to construct idealized portraits of youthful heroes in the tradition of the male ideal of medieval French literature.

Two important studies by Jean Loubier and Alice M. Colby examine representations of men in medieval French romance.[45] According to their surveys, the typical male ideal is noble, young, and beautiful. He usually has blond hair, rosy complexion, fine nose and eyes, and a beautiful neck and beardless chin. Further, he is well built, tall, and exquisitely dressed or armed.[46] In general, the disguised figures in these romances correspond to this portrait. All are noble and none is older than twenty. Silence is perceived as a beautiful youth with a pink and white complexion and blond hair.[47]

Her stylish male clothing is mentioned, and all are struck by the young man's good looks and noble bearing.[48] Blanchandine is caparisoned fashionably in the manner of a knight ("a loy de chevalier") by Tristan. For the most part, however, her maleness is described from Clarinde's perspective; she sees in Blanchandin a handsome knight who is young and beardless ("il estoit moult jeunes, point de barbe n'avoit").[49] In the love scenes with Clarinde, Blanchandine more than once uses her courtly manners to counter the passionate admissions of her cousin. Yde impresses King Oton and the enamored Olive as a handsome youth who is "grant et membru et formé" [tall, well built, and well formed].[50] She dresses "a loi domme mout bien," having purchased shoes, hat, breeches, belt, and sword.[51] Finally, Grisandole's clothing is simply designated as male, but the brief description of her stature and courtly behavior conforms to the ideal for courtly heroes: "Et ele estoit grande et droite et menbrue si se demena en toutes les manieres comme escuiers se demaine sans uilonie."[52] [She was tall and straight and well built and without villainy she practiced all manners as befits a knight.]

Silence, Grisandole, Yde, and Blanchandine are perceived and described according to guidelines for the male paradigm. With the exception of specific items of male clothing, however, none of the general characteristics are sex-specific. Literary portraits of beautiful men and women actually have much in common. Of course, they glean additional praise for more stereotypically male attributes, such as bravery and knightly prowess. But, in bodily terms, the disguised women are not "defeminized" because, most significantly, medieval notions of male and female beauty are compatible. Even in medieval romances without the motif of gender disguise, there exists little difference between masculine and feminine beauty in strictly physical terms. The ideal male hero in courtly romance combines "manly stature and strength with a girlish face."[53]

Descriptions of beauty in courtly epic not only transcend sexual identity but also admit the similarity between the sexes. Beautiful men and women are said to resemble one another in several portraits of celebrated couples in medieval romances. In Chrétien's *Erec et Enide*, the titular characters are paragons of beauty: of Erec, the narrator claims that one could not find a fairer knight in the world; of Enide, that *Nature* used all her skill in creating her.[54] Their resemblance is stressed in the description of them riding toward Arthur's court:

> Si estoient d'une meniere,
> d'unes mors et d'une matiere,
> que nus qui le voir volsist dire
> n'an poïst le meillor eslire
> ne le plus bel ne le plus sage.
> Molt estoient d'igal corage
> et molt avenoient ansanble;
> li uns a l'autre son cuer anble;
> onques deus si beles ymages
> n'asanbla lois ne mariages.[55]

[They were of one character and of one substance, so that no one who wanted to speak truly could have chosen the better one nor the more beautiful nor the wiser. They were very equal in spirit and very well suited to one another. Each of them stole the other's heart; never were two such beautiful figures brought together by law or by marriage.]

In *Le Conte du Graal*, Chrétien also expresses the beauty of Perceval and Blancheflor in similar terms. He describes Blancheflor's golden hair and rosy skin, claiming that God never created such a wonder.[56] A few lines later, one of Blancheflor's knights remarks that Perceval's beauty is without equal.[57] The company declares that the two are a perfect match:

> Mout avient bien delez ma dame,
> et ma dame ausi delez lui.
> ....
> tant est cil biax et cele bele
> c'onques chevaliers ne pucele
> si bien n'avindrent mes ansanble
> que de l'un et de l'autre sanble
> que Dex l'un por l'autre feïst
> por ce qu'ansanble les meïst.[58]

[How well they look; he beside my lady and my lady beside him. He is so handsome and she is so beautiful that never were a knight and maiden better suited. It is as if God made the one for the other, so that he might bring them together.]

Perhaps the most striking description of parallel beauty is that of Floire and Blancheflor.[59] The resemblance of the lovers is described in comparable terms and inspires comment from other characters.

Moreover, their likeness is instrumental to the plot. On four occasions, friendly hosts facilitate Floire's search for his beloved when they comment that his face, form, and behavior remind them of a captive maiden, Blancheflor, who passed by before him. One of the characters even posits that the two are twins:

> Ce m'est avis, quant je le voi,
> Que ce soit Blancheflor la bele;
> Je cuit qu'ele est sa suer jumele,
> Tel vis, tel cors et tel semblant
> Conme ele a voi en cest enfant.
> Bien voi qu'il sont prochain parent
> Au vis et au contenement.[60]

[It seems to me, when I look at him, that he is the beautiful Blancheflor. I believe she is his twin sister. Like her, such a face, such a build, such manner (or appearance) I see in this youth. By their looks and comportment I see clearly that they are closely related.]

Although he plays the role of the male hero and rescuer, the youthful Floire apparently looks like the maiden (the reverse for Blancheflor is not expressed). When found sleeping with Blancheflor in the emir's seraglio, Floire is actually mistaken for a girl:

> Floires en face n'en menton
> N'avoit ne barbe ne grenon;
> N'en la tour n'avoit damoisele
> Qui de visage fust plus bele.[61]

[Floire's face had no beard at all, nor mustache; there was in the tower no maiden who was more beautiful.]

The portrayal of Floire and Blancheflor not only offers further evidence for the epicene ideal of beauty in medieval romance but also illustrates that, in the context of courtly fiction, the body does not always exhibit sexual differences.

Since the vocabulary for portraying beauty differs little for the sexes and, moreover, the heroes and heroines of courtly romance often look alike, we can conclude that the courtly concept of beauty hints at androgyny. Without going so far as to make this claim, Colby presented the evidence for this conclusion by citing stereotypical traits of beauty common to both male and female protagonists.[62] Gender is expressed, first and foremost, by clothing; beauty, however, transcends gender markers. In courtly tales of disguise, a woman passing for a man conforms to the social code, thanks largely to the unisexuality of physical beauty. Of all the genres considered in this study, therefore, courtly romance most easily accommodates gender disguise. The female monks, it was often claimed, were thought to be eunuchs because of their beardlessness and, presumably, their effeminate appearance. Such excuses are unnecessary, however, in a courtly context where youthful beauty is prized.

Despite the parallel perceptions of male and female beauty, gender signifiers, such as dress, name, and activity, determine society's sexual expectations of courtly heroes. The love that unites Erec and Enide and the other complementary beauties of medieval romances is sexual. When, as is inevitable for a hero of courtly romance, a woman falls in love with the newly arrived young knight in disguise, the resulting sexual confusion affects both heroine and society. The conflict of cultural maleness, biological femaleness, and personal sexual orientation may be different for each character, but society reacts similarly to the presence of a handsome stranger at court in all these texts. The disguised woman attains love and honor, both of which are important aspects of the knightly experience in society, by meeting the requirements for knighthood (beauty, manners, and knightly activities). Gender disguise, however, fails in the realm of courtly love because the women infatuated with disguised characters become frustrated. Suited to the role of a man in every other way, the impostor cannot survive when sexual activity is required.

Whether maleness is physically achieved or male disguise is abandoned, these stories end in heterosexual union. The homoerotic undertones and the focus on the confused perception of the characters and society do nothing to challenge the hegemony of heterosexuality. While elsewhere female transvestism signifies asexuality, in the courtly romance it engenders problems of, or obsession with, sexuality. Gender concealment is inevitably challenged by courtly society's focus on heterosexual love and marriage for cross-dressed women perceived as ideal male heroes. Because the denouement in all these works requires resolution of gender concealment and one-sex relationships, sexual transformation serves the narrative as well as the resumption of female identity. The crisis of identity and strain of sexual confrontation are resolved when the traditional marriage motif clarifies sexual ambiguity. Physical metamorphosis offers a slight variation on the typical scheme of disguise, anagnorisis, and union of male and female, but even here traditional notions of sexuality prevail.

Although these characters, like the disguised wives, conform to male models for heroism, the portrayal of the social and psychological difficulties of gender concealment replaces the more typical development of the male prototypes in courtly epic. Whereas the male hero loses his societal status and struggles to regain (and enhance) his reputation or identity in courtly society, the disguised heroine attains the status of the hero at court, conversely, by denying identity. The conflict of culture and nature, the realignment of sexual orientation, and the strain of hiding their sex in the midst of sexual encounters mark important stages in the character's development. In the end, however, she too reaches a higher social plateau, either as a queen (Silence and Grisandole) or male ruler (Iphis, Ydé, and Blanchandin). Fictional society's perception ultimately leads to a sexual crisis and the resolution of the situation necessitating disguise, but the heroine's expression of the personal problems involved in concealing sex often complicates the otherwise simple plot of disguise and discovery.

In general, there is an uneasiness in the portrayal of characters for whom culture, not "nature" (sex), determines gender behavior. The authors may admit that the disguised women perform as well or better than men, but, ultimately, they integrate the characters— either as women or transformed men—into the gender hierarchy by placing them within conventional sexual relationships.

Chapter Eight

CONCLUSIONS

> Hoc autem verbum viriliter, non solum viris,
> sed et feminis credamus esse mandatum.
>
> [We believe, however, that the word "manly"
> is meant not only for men, but also for
> women.]
> —Cassiodorus[1]

The ambiguities of disguise literature invite paradoxical conclusions. Despite generally positive assessments of women in male dress, some form of male domination—cultural, ideological, or linguistic—lies at the root of most stories of gender inversion. The assumption underlying female transvestism, after all, is that maleness is a gender of empowerment. Women in disguise literature are defined by masculine stereotypes and metaphors that equate holiness, courage, or intellectual ability with a "manly spirit," whereas femininity, as an idea, represents weakness and corruption. Nonetheless, disguised women are often said to surpass men, and the basic premise of disguise literature, it would seem, endorses a view that women are hampered only by the demeaning and restricting force of cultural perceptions of gender roles. Most authors, however, do not argue for female superiority. Social norms represent a static construct to be overcome only in the extraordinary instances described. In most cases, including fictional, pseudo-historical, historical, theological, and juridical discourses, the fact that the biological female achieves cultural maleness reveals inconsistencies in medieval views of gender.

If, as Bynum has argued with copious evidence, medieval men "tended to associate a clearly delineated set of social and biological characteristics with each gender,"[2] what can account for the numerous examples in disguise literature that challenge these characteristics? Many male authors not only view female transvestism as a symbolic reversal indicating extraordinary (or, rather, nonfemale) qualities but also take a genuine interest in examining sex roles and the social constructs of gender. According to most of these texts, surprisingly perhaps, societal perception, more than the body itself, determines gender identity. The focus on clothing, which covers the body (sex), or, more specifically, change of clothing, which refashions the body (sex), reveals the impermanence and lability of gender constructs. Yet consistent emphasis on femaleness and resolutions that reestablish conventional sexual and gender order question the possibility of assimilation.

Convention is challenged in the depictions of the effect of cultural gender training on female children, in the attribution of "manly" traits to some women, and in the apparent ease with which women adopt male behavior. Hildegund, Marina, Iphis, and Silence, receive an education that renders them culturally male. The characterization of Zinevra and Jehane seems to admit that "masculine" and "feminine" attributes are not necessarily formed by biological sex. And the examples of Blanchandine and Yde, Jeanne d'Arc, and the wives who rescue husbands undermine both views, since their gender behavior is mixed and, in the end, maleness is neither innate, nor learned, but simply appropriated. The general acceptance of gender traits as teachable, transferable, and assumable is counterbalanced, however, by the overriding concern for exposing the female body, both in hints within the disguise narrative and in the ultimate revelation of closure. In fact, persistent allusions to femaleness (sexual vulnerability, sinfulness, maternal instincts, pregnancy) often confuse the apparent purpose of depicting a woman's attainment of male social status. It is the ambivalence of disguise that invites examination of assumptions about sex and gender. The variety of responses to female transvestism clearly indicates that there were no universal notions of gender behavior as either biological or cultural in the Middle Ages, although there was indeed a general view that male behavior and male characteristics (for men or women) were superior to female.

Because the misogynist underpinnings of most descriptions of female cross dressing do not eradicate the heroic impressions made by transvestite women, there is a tension, one that is unresolved but also omnipresent in this body of literature, between an antifemale ideology and projections of powerful, resourceful women. Combining male and female qualities, the transvestite figure achieves recognition as a talented man yet remains a woman. Accounts of successful women in male disguise allow the possibility that a woman might be wise, courageous, or talented. The approbative presentation of most disguised women runs counter to religious and secular laws, as well as gynophobic anxieties associated with maintaining male dominance. However, since language, especially on the level of metaphor, attributed a moral quality to maleness, the "manly spirit" of cross-dressing women—at least to the mind of the male authors—had positive implications. Within their cultural context, in which the paradigms for saintliness, learnedness, and heroism were male, women as monks, students, rescuers, or knights reflect the absence of models and metaphors for female heroism. The reader or audience is attracted by the sensationalism of disguise and, furthermore, naturally ascribes all accomplishments to a female heroine. Thus, the androcentric premise that necessitates disguise for improvement or empowerment is still qualified by the female body in the male heroic structure. A paradox lies in the willingness to admit female heroism and the inability to move beyond male constructs for describing the exceptional.

Whether consciously presented as challenges to societal constructs or simply created according to male paradigms, the disguised heroine was not meant as a symbol of empowerment for women in general, although there are examples of possible influences. The popular transvestite saints of early eastern Christianity inspired later imitations in medieval Europe, including, perhaps, Hildegund von Schönau. Some have even argued—albeit with slight proof—that Jeanne d'Arc knew of them and was perhaps imitating them when she adopted male clothing.[3] Eleanor of Aquitaine might be said to resemble the calumniated wife of secular literature when she donned male clothing to escape Henry II's wrath.[4] An example from the mid-fifteenth century sounds more like the early stages of the female pope's career: according to Martin of Leibitz (†1464), an excellent student at the University of Kraków was discovered to be a girl.[5] In a male-centered society, women in men's clothing are reflections of male institutions, perceptions, and language, but they are also positive models, not only for men but also for women, whose impressions and values were formed in an androcentric context.

There are limitations to cross-dressed heroism. Many authors, most notably the hagiographers of Hildegund, Jeanne d'Arc's more cautious supporters, and the authors of accounts of the female pope, express uneasiness with women in male roles, despite their praise for the individual heroine. A corollary exists between historicity, perceived or actual, and critical views of cross dressing. Transvestism can be sanctioned or even lauded, if the woman does not challenge male authority or if she disguises herself only temporarily and is situated in a literary setting. If the woman uses male dress to assume power over men, cross dressing is evil. The disguised woman breaks with societal norms in every case, but her transvestism rarely results in negative evaluations unless, like the female pope and Jeanne d'Arc, she also transgresses the bounds of male hegemony. Although several authors appreciate the difficulties experienced by women in an unequal social system and even criticize the sexual hierarchy, none advocates permanent inversion of gender roles or even equality of the sexes, and most show discomfiture with the idea of female cross dressing outside the realm of fiction.

The dissolution of disguise is as important as the disguise itself, since the woman's achievement cannot be assessed until it is recognized. Unclothing the body, the most convincing proof of sex, marks the recognition of numerous characters. The dead female monks are undressed for washing before burial. Eugenia, Zinevra, and the wife in Ritter Alexander bare their breasts to reveal their sex, whereas the circumstances of discovery require the public disrobing of Silence, Grisandole, and the wife in Graf Alexander von Mainz. Jeanne d'Arc's female corpse was displayed to substantiate her sex. The female pope's pregnant female body is exposed in the act of childbirth. And the public baths of Yde and Blanchandine would have revealed their femaleness had miraculous intervention not resulted in sexual metamorphosis. The clothing of the female body in male dress, therefore, is almost always accompanied by its exposure. It is necessary for closure because it results in admiration of patient saints, vindication of faithful wives, societal integration of female knights, and, in the case of the female pope, public humiliation. The woman's body is finally relocated in its cultural place.

What emerges from a study of gender inversion is a series of conflicting understandings of gender roles in medieval society.

Although disguised women are literary and cultural anomalies, the presentation of these characters reveals more about medieval notions of women and gender than idealized portraits of pious women and chivalrous ladies in other medieval literature. Inversion defines female roles, both sexual and social, more clearly than archetypal characterizations. Some indication of traditional female experiences emerges from descriptions of situations escaped, comparisons between the disguised figure and other women, and the presentation of women's concerns. Equally important, however, is the presence of active female protagonists who, precisely because they conform to male ideals, contradict the idea of sex as the determinant for gender behavior. The underlying gender inequity that requires male metaphors and paradigms is balanced, if not outweighed, by the implicit admission that some women, at least, are equal or even superior to men. Redefining the female role, without radically displacing the androcentric archetype of the hero, the crossed-dressed woman compels authors and audiences to confront her as a sexual being, a socially defined gender, an "opposite" sex, and a fellow human.

HAGIOGRAPHIC APPENDIX

The lives of transvestite saints are listed in alphabetical order with approximate date of composition, feast day, and the source used for the summary. Complete references to Greek and Latin versions of the lives can be found in the *Bibliotheca hagiographica graeca* (*BHG*) and *Bibliotheca hagiographica latina antiquae et mediae aetatis* (*BHL*). Bibliographic entry numbers from these sources are listed and the *Bibliotheca hagiographica orientalis* (*BHO*) is cited where applicable.

1. **Agnes of Monçada** (fourteenth century); January 21.
AASS Jan. 2:338.
Agnes was inspired by the preaching of Vincent Ferrer (†1419). After hearing his sermon on virginity and monasticism, she determined to remain celibate and dedicate herself to God. Her parents, however, wanted her to marry. To avoid enforced marriage, she disguised herself as a man and became a hermit. She lived for twenty years in a cave near the monastery of Porta-coelia.

2. **Anastasia Patricia** (sixth century); August 28, March 10.
AASS Mar. 2:40-41 [*BHG*, 79-80e].
Anastasia of Constantinople inflamed the passion of Emperor Justinian and thereby incurred the jealousy of Empress Theodora. To escape further complications, she fled to Alexandria. Outside the city, she built a convent and lived there until Theodora died. Thereafter, when she learned that Justinian was searching for her, she took flight again. Daniel of Skete hid her in a cave, bidding her to stay there, dressed as a man. For twenty years, "Anastasius the Eunuch" lived as a recluse. Only after her death did Daniel reveal her sex.

3. **Angela of Bohemia** (twelfth century); July 6.
AASS July 2:350-59 [*BHL*, 454].
According to legend, Angela was the daughter of Wladislaus II, duke of Bohemia, and the aunt of the more famous St. Agnes

of Bohemia (1205-1282). On her wedding day, she escaped from the bridal chamber, dressed in men's clothes. After several adventures, she arrived in Jerusalem and gave up her disguise to become a nun.

4. Anna/Euphemian (ninth century); October 29.
AASS Oct. 12:913-17 [*BHG*, 2027].

After the deaths of her husband and child, Anna distributed her wealth and left her home in Constantinople. Dressed as a man, she joined the monastery of Mount Olympus under the name Euphemian. One monk suspected her true sex and plagued her with charges. Finally, he pushed Euphemian down a hill to expose "him." When the lower part of her body was revealed, however, by a miracle it appeared so withered that her sex could not be determined. After some peregrinations, she died as a recluse at Constantinople.

5. Antonina (fourth century); May 3, June 9, 10.
AASS May 1:383-86 [*BHG*, 50-50e].

Antonina was a Christian maiden from Constantinople. When she refused to sacrifice to the gods, Festus, the governor, condemned her to serve in a brothel. Her guard, Alexander, exchanged clothes with her to allow her to escape. When Festus discovered the ruse, Alexander was sentenced to death for aiding a Christian. Moments before Alexander's execution, Antonina appeared before the governor, offering her life in exchange for his. Alexander protested that he would rather die for her. In the end, both were martyred.

6. Apollonaris/Dorotheus (sixth century); January 5.
AASS Jan.1:257-61 [*BHG*, 148].

On a pilgrimage to Jerusalem, Apollonaris, daughter of Emperor Anthemius, secretly abandoned her servants to become a recluse in a mosquito-ridden swamp. Later, after having been disfigured beyond recognition by bites and hardships, she joined the monastery of Macarius of Alexandria under the name Dorotheus. A few years later, Anthemius's other daughter became possessed by the devil and was sent to Macarius to be cured. Macarius commended her to Dorotheus, who healed her after praying with her in his cell for a few days. Soon after she returned home, the devil caused her to swell up as if pregnant, and forced her to say that Dorotheus was responsible. When Dorotheus was brought before the emperor, she secretly revealed her actual sex. Cleared of the charges yet maintaining her male disguise, she returned to the monastery. At her death, the monks were astounded when they discovered her sex.

7. **Athanasia** (fifth century); October 9.

AASS Oct. 4:997-1001 [*BHG*, 120-23i; *BHO*, 59].

Grieved by the deaths of their children, Andronikos and Athanasia of Antioch decided to leave the secular world and devote themselves to God. After several years, both set out on a pilgrimage although neither knew the intent of the other. They met by chance and traveled together. In the clothes of a pilgrim and tanned from her journey, Athanasia was not recognized by Andronikos, although she knew him. When the time came to part, Andronikos begged his travel companion to stay with him. They lived in the same cell, praying together but otherwise under the rule of silence. When Athanasia died, a letter found in her hand revealed her identity. Andronikos died soon afterward.

8. **Callisthene** (fourth century); October 4.

AASS Oct. 2:407-11.

Callisthene and her family were persecuted by Emperor Maximianus because she had rejected his advances. After her father, St. Audactus, was murdered, she cut her hair and disguised herself as a man to escape further revenge. She left Ephesus and went to Nicomedia, where she lived as a man. Although her exact activity is not described, it appears that she practiced medicine. Later, she went to Thrace, where she healed a young girl of an eye disease. When the happy parents offered their daughter in marriage, Callisthene revealed her sex.

9. **Charitine** (?fourth century).

Acts of Philip, in *Acta apostolorum apocrypha*, 2:19-20.

Charitine, the daughter of Nikokeides of Azotus, encouraged her father to offer hospitality to the apostle Philip. While in their house, Philip cured Charitine of an eye disease. The whole family was converted. Charitine then put on men's clothing and followed the apostle. No reason is given for her transvestism and no further mention is made of her.

10. **Christina of Markyate** (ca. 1096-1160).

From MS. Cotton Tiberius E. I. Edited and translated by C.H. Talbot in *The Life of Christina of Markyate* (Oxford: Clarendon, 1959), pp. 34-193.

Forced into marriage by her parents and a corrupt bishop, Christina managed to elude consummation despite cruel tricks meant to aid her bridegroom but tantamount to planned rape. Finally, she devised a means of escape with the help of a male companion. Dressed in men's clothing, she left her house but was recognized by her sister. After misleading the sister, she went on until she came to the place where her companion waited with horses for the flight. When she showed some embarrassment at mounting the horse, the friend admonished her to act like a man: "Quid sexum feminei veneris? Virilem animum indue et more viri in equum ascende" (p. 92). ["Why do you honor your feminine sex? Put on a manly spirit and mount the horse like a man."] Later, she lived as a female recluse with the hermits Alfwen of Flamstead and Roger of Markyate.

11. **Domna** (fourth century); September 30, December 3, 28, 30. *Passio Indes et Domnae*, PG 116:1037-81 [*BHG*, 822z-23a; *BHO*, 457].

Raised as a pagan in the court of Galerius Maximianus (ruled 305-311), Domna participated in services to the twelve gods at Nicomedia until she was fourteen. She was converted after reading the *Acts of the Apostles* and the letters of Paul. Her brother Indes was also baptized and soon afterward suffered martyrdom. Domna and other Christians had gone into hiding, but when Domna learned of her brother's death, she disguised herself as a man and went in search of his body. While she was burying him, some of Galerius's soldiers found her and beheaded her.

12. **Eugenia/Eugenius** (sixth or seventh century); December 24, 25. *AASS* Sept. 3:761-62 [*BHG*, 607w-08b; *BHL*, 2666-70; *BHO*, 281-84].

Eugenia was the daughter of Philip, proconsul of Egypt under Commodus. After she had read the teachings of Paul and the story of Thecla and had heard Christians singing psalms, she and two of her servants, Prothus and Hyacinthus, were converted. To escape from the palace, she disguised herself as a man and, together with her servants, joined a monastery. Although the abbot Helenus had a divine revelation as to her sex, he let her live as a monk at the monastery. A local woman, Melanthia, conceived a passionate desire for the young monk and tried to seduce him. Eugenius rejected her advances, but the spurned woman took revenge by charging "him" with trying to seduce her. Eugenius was brought before the court of Philip. After suffering false accusations and public scorn, she dramatically uncovered her breasts to prove her innocence. She also revealed her relation to the judge. Eugenia's family was converted, but her father and brothers were soon killed in new persecutions. Eugenia and her mother traveled to Rome, where they too were martyred.

13. **Euphrosyne/Smaragdus** (fifth century); February 11, September 25.
AASS Feb. 2:535-44 [*BHG*, 625-26m; *BHL*, 2722-26; *BHO*, 288-91].

Paphnutius of Alexandria wanted Euphrosyne, his only daughter, to marry a wealthy nobleman, but she wished to remain celibate. After consulting a priest about the dilemma between filial obedience and religious vocation, Euphrosyne left her father's home. Since she knew her father would search the convents, she cut her hair and disguised herself as a monk. Presenting herself as a eunuch named Smaragdus, she entered a monastery near her father's house. Her beauty so distracted the monks that the abbot ordered Smaragdus to remain in his cell. When Paphnutius came to the abbot for consolation, he was sent to the cell of the pious young eunuch. For over thirty years, Euphrosyne comforted her father about the loss of his daughter. On her deathbed, she revealed her identity to her father, asking that he might bury her himself. Paphnutius lived out his life in his daughter's cell.

14. **Euphrosyne junior/Johannes** (ca. 854-923); November 8.
AASS Nov. 3:861-77 [*BHG*, 627].

To avoid an unwanted marriage, Euphrosyne put on men's clothing and fled from her bridegroom. She hid for three months in the desert, living on bread and water. Pursued by her betrothed, she went to the coast and boarded a ship under the alias Johannes. Soon afterward she joined a monastery and lived an exemplary life as a monk for many years. When the abbot died, she was elected to replace him, but she secretly left the monastery and went again into the desert. She lived as a hermit for ten years before resuming her female identity and returning to Constantinople. There she lived as a celebrated wise woman and holy ascetic.

15. **Eusebia/Xena or Hospita** (fifth century); January 24, 30.
AASS Jan. 3:212-16 [*BHG*, 633-34m].

Moments before her marriage, Eusebia escaped with two of her servants. Dressed as men, the three traveled to Mylas in Caria, where she gave up her male disguise and established a church and a house for holy women.

16. **Glaphyra** (fourth century); January 13, April 26.
AASS Jan. 2:53-54.

Glaphyra was an attendant to Constantia, sister of Constantine and wife of Licinius. (Licinius shared power with Constantine until 324.) Licinius made sexual advances toward Glaphyra, but she spurned him because she was a Christian and had

taken the vow of chastity. On Constantia's advice, Glaphyra fled
to Amasia, disguised as a man. Licinius discovered her whereabouts
and ordered her and Bishop Basileus, who was harboring her, to
be thrown in chains and returned. Glaphyra died before this could
be carried out; Basileus was martyred.

17. **Hilaria/Hilarion** (sixth century); January 16, November 27.
For a translation of the Coptic life, see *Three Coptic Legends: Hilaria,
   Archellites, The Seven Sleepers*, translated by James Drescher
   (Cairo: L'Institute Français d'Archéologie Oriental, 1947)
   [*BHO*, 379].
   Hilaria was the daughter of Emperor Zeno. While traveling,
she escaped from her party and received baptism. Disguised as a
man, she entered the monastery of Daniel of Skete. When her sister
became possessed by an evil spirit, Hilaria exorcised it by praying
with her sister and embracing her. When her sister reported the odd
conduct of the monk, Zeno summoned Hilarion to his court. After
revealing her identity to her father to clear herself of sexual
suspicion, Hilaria returned to her life as a monk.

18. **Hildegard** (†783); April 30.
AASS Apr.3:797-811 [*BHL*, 3934-35.]
   Hildegard of Swabia, the wife of Charlemagne, is regarded
as "Blessed" by the Roman Catholic Church. According to some
accounts of her life, she was forced to disguise herself as a man in
order to escape execution when falsely accused of adultery. She
became a famous doctor and eventually cured her accuser of an eye
disease. When he confessed, she was vindicated and regained her
position as Charlemagne's wife. This episode in her life, although
fictitious, has much in common with the calumniated wives in
disguise discussed in Chapter 6.

19. **Hildegund von Schönau** (†1188); April 20.
[*BHL*, 3936-40]. See Chapter 3.

20. **Hugolina of Vercelli** (ca. 1300); August 8.
AASS Aug. 2:395-98.
   Hugolina fled an incestuous father by disguising herself as a
man. She lived forty-seven years as a recluse in a closed cell so that
no one might see her. At her death, her confessor revealed her story.

21. **Jachelina** (?early thirteenth century).

Speculum magnum exemplorum omnibus christicolis salubriter inspiciendum ut exemplis discant disciplinam (Strasbourg: [Georg Husner], 1490), dist. 5, cap. 65.

The "comes apuliae" in Rome tried to force his sister Jachelina to marry. To avoid this, Jachelina dressed as a man ("assumpto virili habitu") and fled. Her brother pursued her as far as the sea. There, he watched in horror as she hurled herself from the cliffs in order to escape. He vowed that he would build a monastery, if only she could be saved. Miraculously, she walked out of the sea unharmed. Later, she lived as a male hermit in the desert, eating only bread and water. According to the fifteenth-century report, Innocent III (†1216) recognized her holiness.

22. **Juana de la Cruz** (1481-1534); May 3.

AASS May 1:364. For a full account, see Antonio Daza, *Historia, vida, y milagros, extasis, y revelaciones de la Iuana de la Cruz* (Madrid: Sanchez, 1613). Translated into English in *The History ... of the Blessed Virgin, Sister Joane* (1625). *English Recusant Literature* (London: Scolar, 1977), vol. 35.

Juana was born in Azana, Spain. As a child, she determined to dedicate herself to a religious life. When she reached marriageable age, she fled from her home in male disguise. After reaching the monastery of St. Maria of the Cross, she gave up her disguise and became a leader in the Third Order of the Franciscans.

23. **Margareta Reparata/Pelagius** (n.d.); May 7.

AASS July 4:287 [*BHL*, 5323].

The legend of Margareta from Jacobus de Voragine's *Legenda aurea* (cap. 151) combines elements from the legends of Pelagia (also called Margarita on account of her pearls) and Marina. Disguised as a man, Margareta left her bridal chamber on the night of her marriage. Under the name Pelagius, she joined a monastery. Later, when a young girl who lived near the monastery became pregnant, she accused Pelagius of seducing her. Without a trial, Pelagius was banished from the monastery and forced to live in a cave. After suffering in silence for many years, she felt death approaching and wrote her story on a shell, requesting that women might bury her.

24. **Mariamne** (?fourth century).

Acts of Philip, Acta apostolorum apocrypha, 2:37.

Often called "Equal of the Apostles," Mariamne was the sister of the apostle Philip. She confided in the resurrected Jesus Christ that her brother was worried about his assignment to convert

Greeks. Jesus told her to dress as a man in order to go with Philip
on his mission. The subsequent account of Mariamne's adventures
with Philip does not refer to any disguise.

25. **Marina/Marinus** (fifth or sixth century); July 17, February 8, 12.
AASS July 4:286-87 [*BHG*, 1163-63e; *BHL*, 5528-30; *BHO*,690-97].
   When her mother died, Marina's father, Eugenius, left her
with relatives and entered a monastery. After a time, he confessed
to the abbot that he missed his child. Assuming the child was a boy,
the abbot advised Eugenius to bring him to the monastery. Marina
was dressed as a boy and brought up in the monastery as Marinus.
Her father's final wish was for her to keep her femaleness concealed.
It happened that Marinus was responsible for gathering wood for
the monastery, a duty that often required her to spend the night at
an inn. When the innkeeper's daughter became pregnant, she said
she had been seduced by Marinus. The abbot confronted Marinus
with the charges, but she merely said, "peccavi pater." Presuming
her guilty, he exiled her from the monastery. She lived outside the
gates begging food for "her child" and suffering patiently for five
years. Finally, the monks felt sorry for Marinus and allowed him
to return. But after only a few days, Marinus died. The abbot
remarked that God had punished this grievous sinner by not even
allowing him to finish his penance before death. Soon afterward,
when the monks discovered her sex, the abbot regretted his
hardheartedness and buried the saint with great solemnity. The
woman who falsely accused Marina became possessed and could be
cured only when she confessed her sin before the saint's grave.

26. **Matrona/Babylas** (fifth or sixth century); November 7, 8, 9.
AASS Nov.3:786-813 [*BHG*, 1221-23].
   Because she spent too much time in church, Matrona's
husband finally forbade her to go out of the house. Matrona escaped
by cutting her hair and disguising herself as a man. Under the name
Babylas, she became a monk at the monastery of St. Bassianus, but
her true sex was revealed to the abbot in a dream, and he advised
her to go to a convent in Emesa. She spent much of her life moving
from place to place to evade her husband's pursuit. After his death,
she returned to Constantinople and died at the age of one hundred.

27. **Natalia** (fourth century); December 1, August 26.
AASS Sept. 3:218-30. See also Voragine, *Legenda aurea*, cap. 134.
   [*BHG*, 27-29; *BHL*, 3744; *BHO*, 370].
   Natalia was the Christian wife of Hadrian, an imperial guard
in Nicomedia. When her husband was imprisoned for defending

some Christians, she attended to him in jail. She instructed him as a catechumen, for he had not yet been baptized. Emperor Maximianus wanted to thwart her activity, so he forbade women to visit prisoners. Natalia cut her hair and disguised herself as a man in order to maintain contact with her husband. Her boldness inspired other women to do the same. After Hadrian's execution, she traveled to Byzantium, hoping to receive martyrdom, but died on the way.

28. **Papula of Gaul** (ca. 500); January 31.
Gregory of Tours, *Gloria confessorum*, cap. 16. See *Gregorii Turonensis opera*, edited by Wilhelm Arndt and Bruno Krusch in *Monumenta Germaniae Historica: Scriptores Rerum Merovingicarum*, 1:756-57. [*BHL*, 6452].

Against the wishes of her parents, Papula wanted to join a convent. After a childhood of abuse and beatings for her religious zeal, she cut her hair and dressed as a man to escape from her parents. She traveled to Tours, where she entered a monastery as a "vir inter viros." When the abbot died, the monks chose Papula to succeed him because she was the most virtuous monk in the order. She ruled for thirty years. Three days before her death, she told the monks the truth and asked to be buried by women. The hagiographer claims that many miracles occurred at her tomb.

29. **Pelagia of Antioch/Pelagius** (fifth century); May 8, October 8.
AASS Oct. 4:248-68 [*BHG*, 1478-79m; *BHL*, 6605-11; *BHO*, 919].

Pelagia was a courtesan in Antioch until Bishop Nonnus (Veronus) converted her. A few days after her baptism, she secretly left Antioch, disguised as a male hermit. For the next several decades, she lived in a cave on Mount Olivet, known to pilgrims as the eunuch Pelagius. Jacobus Diaconus, the author of her life, claims to have been present when her sex was discovered after death.

30. **Susanna/John** (fourth century); September 20, December 15.
AASS Sept.6:151-60 [*BHG*, 1673-1673b].

Susanna was the daughter of a pagan priest of Eleutheropolis and a Jewish mother. When she converted to Christianity at fifteen, she shaved her head and put on men's clothes. So disguised, she entered a monastery under the name John. Later, when she rejected a woman's amorous advances, the woman accused John of rape. Susanna/John was brought before the abbot and the bishop to answer the charge. She said she did not think she had harmed the woman, but nonetheless asked for forgiveness for her own sins. The bishop assumed she was guilty and ordered her stripped of her monk's habit. Susanna begged him to wait until she had told the truth to four virgins. When her innocence was made known, the monks wanted to stone the evil woman who had calumniated her, but Susanna prevented it. Since she could no longer remain with the monks, Susanna became an abbess in Eleutheropolis and later died as a martyr.

31. **Thecla** (second century); September 23.
Acts of Paul and Thecla, Acta apostolorum apocrypha, 1:235-72. [*BHG*, 1710-22; *BHL*, 8020-25; *BHO*, 1152-56].

Thecla was the daughter of a pagan family in Iconium. Having heard Paul preach on virginity, she determined to become a Christian and follow him. Her bridegroom and family were displeased with her conversion, and, when they could not persuade her to give up the new religion, they asked the prefect to condemn Thecla to death. Saved from the pyre by a miraculous rainstorm, Thecla sought out Paul. She traveled with him but was not baptized. In Antioch, the Roman prefect Alexander was attracted to her and tried to seize her in the marketplace. In an effort to escape his embrace, she tore his robes and dashed his crown to pieces. For her impudence, she was condemned to be thrown to wild animals. During her trials, she baptized herself in the circus trench. A cloud covered her nakedness and she escaped death. Thereafter, she cut her hair, put on men's garb, and returned to Paul's entourage. After learning that she had been baptized, Paul allowed her to preach in male clothing. She returned to Iconium but failed to convert her mother. Some lives say she became a female hermit and later escaped violation by disappearing into a rock.

32. **Theodora and Didymus** (fourth century); April 6, 28, May 27.
AASS Apr. 3:578-81 [*BHG*, 1742; *BHL*, 8072-73].

Like Antonina, Theodora was condemned to serve in a brothel after she refused to sacrifice to the gods. Didymus exchanged clothes with her to help her escape. Later, both Theodora and Didymus were martyred.

33. **Theodora of Alexandria/Theodorus** (fifth or sixth century); September 11.
AASS Sept. 3:788-97 [*BHG*, 1727-30; *BHL*, 8070-71; *BHO*, 1158-59].

Theodora, a married noblewoman of Alexandria, was pursued by a suitor. She succumbed but later felt guilty about the adultery. Disguised as a man, she left her husband and went to a monastery to live under the name Theodorus. Her husband was told in a dream that he would see her at a certain crossroads on a particular day. He went there but saw only a monk pulling a wagon of wood. The monk was Theodora. She recognized her husband and blessed him. Later, a woman claimed that Theodorus was the father of her child. Without a trial, Theodora and "her child" were banished. After several years, during which the devil tormented her, she was permitted to return to the abbey. One day, the abbot had a dream that revealed Theodora's true sex. He rushed to her cell but found she had just died. Miraculously, her husband was led to her cell at the same time. Praising her patience and endurance, they buried her with great solemnity. Her husband remained as a monk in her cell until his own death.

34. **Anonymous disguised recluse**, recorded in Joannis Moschius, *Pratum spirituale*, 170; *PG* 87:3036-37.

On a walk to Mount Sinai, two monks from the monastery of Sampson discovered the cave of a hermit. When they entered, they found a man who had died only moments before. While burying the holy man, they discovered, to their great surprise, that he was a woman. They praised God for leading them to such a wonder.

NOTES

1. The idea of the "manly spirit" *(animus virilis)*, a major theme in this book, occurs in numerous descriptions of cross-dressing women (e.g., the lives of St. Eugenia and Christina of Markyate, Palladius's *Lausiac History*, the biographies of Hildegund).

2. Magnus Hirschfeld, *Die Transvestiten: Eine Untersuchung über den erotischen Verkleidungstrieb mit umfangreichem casuistischen und historischen Material* (Berlin: Pulvermacher, 1910). By disassociating transvestism from homosexuality, Hirschfeld modified Richard von Krafft-Ebing's earlier study of cross dressing as homoerotic "fetish." See Richard von Krafft-Ebing, *Psychopathia Sexualis, eine klinisch-forensische Studie* (Stuttgart: Enke, 1886).

3. Havelock Ellis, *Studies in the Psychology of Sex* (New York: Random House, [1936]), esp. vol. 2.

4. Rudolf M. Dekker and Lotte C. van de Pol, *The Tradition of Female Transvestism in Early Modern Europe* (New York: St. Martin's, 1989).

5. Ibid., p. 2.

6. Julie Wheelwright, *Amazons and Military Maids: Women Who Dressed as Men in the Pursuit of Life, Liberty, and Happiness* (London: Pandora, 1989). Jessica Amanda Salmonson, *The Encyclopedia of Amazons: Women Warriors from Antiquity to the Modern Era* (New York: Paragon, 1991), provides an even broader survey of fighting woman in literature and history.

7. Dekker and van de Pol, *The Tradition of Female Transvestism,* pp. 102-3.

8. Marjorie Garber, *Vested Interests: Cross Dressing and Cultural Anxiety* (New York: Routledge, 1992). Although Garber's study surpasses it in girth, Peter Ackroyd's *Dressing Up: Transvestism and Drag, the History of an Obsession* (New York: Simon and Schuster, 1979) covers much of the same material in a very competent survey.

9. Garber, *Vested Interests,* p. 7.

10. See Ursula K. Heise, "Transvestism and the Stage Controversy in Spain and England, 1580-1680," *Theatre Journal* 44 (1992):357-74;

Vincent Oscar Freeburg, *Disguise Plots in Elizabethan Drama* (New York: Columbia University Press, 1915); Carmen Bravo-Villasante, *La mujer vestida de hombre en el teatro español: siglos XVI-XVII* (Madrid: Sociedad General Español de Libreria, 1976); and John D. Lyons, *A Theater of Disguise: Studies in French Baroque Drama (1630-1660)* (Columbia, S.C.: French Literature Publications, 1978).

11. Phyllis Rackin, "Androgyny, Mimesis, and the Marriage of the Boy Heroine on the English Renaissance Stage," *PMLA* 102 (1987):29-41.

12. David Price, "When Women Would Rule: Reversal of Gender Hierarchy in Sixteenth-Century German Drama," *Daphnis* 20 (1991):147-66.

13. Kristina Straub, "The Guilty Pleasures of Female Theatrical Cross Dressing and the Autobiography of Charlotte Clarke," in *Body Guards: The Cultural Politics of Gender Ambiguity,* edited by Julia Epstein and Kristina Straub (New York: Routledge, 1991), pp. 142-66.

14. Susan Gubar, "Blessings in Disguise: Cross-Dressing and Re-Dressing for Female Modernists," *Massachusetts Review* 22 (1981):479.

15. Estelle C. Jelinek, "Disguise Autobiographies: Women Masquerading as Men," *Women's Studies International Forum* 10 (1987):53-62.

16. John Anson, "The Female Transvestite in Early Monasticism: The Origin and Development of a Motif," *Viator* 5 (1974):1-32.

17. Michèle Perret, "Travesties et transsexuelles: Yde, Silence, Grisandole, Blanchandine," *Romance Notes* 25 (1985):328-40.

18. Vern L. Bullough, "Transvestites in the Middle Ages," *Journal of American Sociology* 79 (1974):1381-94.

19. See, for example, *Feminist Approaches to the Body in Medieval Literature,* edited by Linda Lomperis and Sarah Stanbury (Philadelphia: University of Pennsylvania Press, 1993) and *ReImagining Women: Representations of Women in Culture,* edited by Shirley Neuman and Glennis Stephenson (Toronto: University of Toronto Press, 1993).

20. Other works on social phenomena in the Middle Ages, such as *A History of Private Life,* edited by Philippe Ariès and Georges Duby (Cambridge: Harvard University Press, 1987), esp. vol. 2, and John Boswell, *Christianity, Social Tolerance, and Homosexuality* (Chicago: University of Chicago Press, 1980), have made similar use of the combined records of history and the arts.

21. See Diana Fuss, *Essentially Speaking* (New York: Routledge, 1989), pp. 97-112, for a description of the debate between the essentialist and constructivist camps of feminist criticism.

22. Thomas Laqueur, *Making Sex: Body and Gender from the Greeks to Freud* (Cambridge: Harvard University Press, 1990), pp. 11-12.

23. Ibid., p. 22.

24. Michel Foucault, *The History of Sexuality,* translated by Robert Hurley (New York: Vintage, 1990), 1:92-97 et passim; Mikhail Bakhtin,

Rabelais and His World, translated by H. Iswolsky (Cambridge: MIT Press, 1968), esp. pp. 3-20 and 109; and Julia Kristeva, *Desire in Language*, edited by Leon S. Roudiez; translated by T. Gora, A. Jardine, and Leon S. Roudiez (New York: Columbia University Press, 1980), pp. 65 and 79.

25. Peter Stallybrass and Allon White, *The Politics and Poetics of Transgression* (London: Methuen, 1986).

26. See Stith Thompson, *Motif-Index of Folklore-Literature* (Bloomington: Indiana University Press, 1955), esp. entries K1800-2999.

27. See *Die deutsche Märendichtung des 15. Jahrhunderts*, edited by Hanns Fischer (Munich: Beck, 1966), pp. 178-87.

28. For information on this legend, see Eugene F. Rice, *St. Jerome in the Renaissance* (Baltimore: Johns Hopkins University Press, 1985), p. 28. Rice reproduces a depiction of the scene from the Limbourg *Book of Hours* in fig. 17.

29. A few examples of this type can be found in Guillaume de Blois, *Alda* (twelfth century), edited by Carl Lohmeyer (Leipzig: Teubner, 1892); Ludovico Ariosto, *Orlando Furioso*, edited by Cesare Segre (Milan: Mondadori, 1982), cantos 22 and 25; and Bonaventure des Périers, *Les Nouvelles récréations et joyeux devis* (no. 62), edited by Louis Lacour (Paris: Librairie des Bibliophiles, 1874). In each tale, a young man dresses like a woman to gain access to his beloved, or in one case to a cloister. In later tales of Achilles, the hero dresses as a girl not only to escape military service but also to woo a woman. The Spanish hero Agesilan of Colchos follows the same pattern, disguising himself as a female minstrel to seduce an Amazon princess. For later examples, see Winfried Schleiner, "Male Cross-Dressing and Transvestism in Renaissance Romances," *Sixteenth Century Journal* 19 (1988):605-19.

30. Ulrich von Liechtenstein, *Frauendienst*, edited by Reinhold Bechstein (Leipzig: Brockhaus, 1888), esp. 1:177-313.

31. Among the disguised heroes of medieval epic are Tristan, Huon de Bordeaux, Charlemagne, and King Horn. In religious literature, the stories of St. Abraham and St. Paphnutius come to mind, both of whom posed as clients at brothels in order to convert prostitutes. For the saints' stories, see Hrotsvitha von Gandersheim, *Opera*, edited by Helene Homeyer (Munich: Schöningh, 1970), pp. 298-349. For a collection of essays on the general theme of disguise and dissembling within gender in medieval literature, see *Masques et déguisements dans la littérature médiévale*, edited by Marie-Louise Ollier (Montreal: Vrin, 1988).

32. Bullough, "Transvestites in the Middle Ages," p. 1383. A more recent work by Vern Bullough and Bonnie Bullough, *Cross Dressing, Sex, and Gender* (Philadelphia: University of Pennsylvania Press, 1993), explores some of the same issues in a broader historical context.

33. See Charles Joseph Hefele, *Histoire des conciles* (Paris: Letouzey et Ané, 1907), 1:1038; the decrees of Burchard of Worms in *Patrologia Latina*

140, col. 805; and *Decretum Gratiani emendatum et notationibus...Gregorii XIII,* edited by Justus Henning Boehmer in *Patrologia Latina* 187, col. 165. The *Patrologia Latina* is henceforth abbreviated as *PL.*

34. See *Straßburger Zunft- und Polizei-Verordnungen des 14. und 15. Jahrhunderts,* edited by Johann Brucker and G. Wethly (Strasbourg: Trübner, 1889), p. 293. See also Liselotte Constance Eisenbart, *Kleiderordnungen der deutschen Städte zwischen 1350 und 1700: Ein Beitrag zur Kulturgeschichte des deutschen Bürgertums* (Göttingen: Musterschmidt, 1962).

35. See Price, "When Women Would Rule," pp. 165-66, Jonathan Dollimore, *Sexual Dissidence* (Oxford: Clarendon, 1991), pp. 297-98, and Valerie R. Lucas, "Hic Mulier: The Female Transvestite in Early Modern England," *Renaissance and Reformation/Renaissance et Reforme* 12 (1988):65-84.

NOTES TO CHAPTER TWO

1. From Meister Eckhart, *Predigten,* edited by Josef Quint, *Meister Eckhart: Die deutschen und lateinischen Werke* (Stuttgart: Kohlhammer, 1958), 1:337. Translations throughout this study are mine unless otherwise noted.

2. Hermann Usener, "Legenden der heiligen Pelagia," in *Vorträge und Aufsätze* (Leipzig: Teubner, 1907), pp. 191-215, was the first to recognize the transvestite saint as a distinct hagiographic type.

3. Although all the women discussed are considered holy and included in collections of saints' legends, not all enjoy the official status of saint. Regardless of the absence of papal canonization, however, many of the women have been venerated locally as saints.

4. See the hagiographic appendix for sources, dates, and summaries of their lives.

5. Usener, "Legenden der heiligen Pelagia," pp. 210-15, claims that the mixture of carnal pleasure and ascetic chastity in the life of Pelagia, as well as the blurring of gender distinction, links the saint to the goddess. There is some evidence that the epithet "Pelagia" was applied to Aphrodite, and the latinized form of Pelagia is Marina—the name of another transvestite saint.

6. Ludwig Radermacher, *Hippolytos und Thekla: Studien zur Geschichte von Legende und Kultus* (Vienna: Hölder, 1916), esp. pp. 89-92 and 251-69. Also see Rosa Söder, *Die apokryphen Apostelgeschichten und die romanhafte Literatur der Antike* (Stuttgart, 1932; reprint, Stuttgart: Kohlhammer, 1969).

7. Evelyne Patlagean, "L'Histoire de la femme déguisée en moine et l'évolution de la sainteté féminine à Byzance," *Studi Medievali* 17

(1976):597-623. For a survey of the different views of gender within the "Gnostic" movement, see Michael A. Williams, "Variety in Gnostic Perspectives on Gender," in *Images of the Feminine in Gnosticism*, edited by Karen King (Philadelphia: Fortress, 1988), pp. 2-22.

8. Other studies of the Byzantine transvestite saints that bear mentioning are Marie Delcourt, *Hermaphrodite: Myths and Rites of the Bisexual Figure in Classical Antiquity*, translated by Jennifer Nicholson (London: Studio Books, 1961), especially the chapter entitled "Female Saints in Masculine Clothing," pp. 84-102, and Khalifa A. Bennasser, "Gender and Sanctity in Early Byzantine Monasticism: A Study in the Phenomenon of Female Ascetics in Male Monastic Habit" (Diss., Rutgers University, 1984), which includes a brief description of the phenomenon followed by a translation of the Life of St. Matrona.

9. Bibliographies of the Latin versions of many of these *vitae* can be found in *Bibliotheca hagiographica latina antiquae et mediae aetatis*, edited by Socii Bollandiani (Brussels: Société des Bollandistes, 1898-1901). Entry numbers for each saint appear in the hagiographic appendix.

10. *Vitae Patrum, liber primus*, edited by Heribert Rosweyd, *PL* 73:101-708.

11. Bede, *Martyrologium poeticum* and *Martyrologia*, edited by Smith and Giles, *PL* 94:603-6 and 797-1148; Hrabanus Maurus, *Martyrologium*, edited by John McCulloh, *Corpus Christianorum, Continuatio Mediaevalis* 44 (Turnhout: Brepols, 1969); Ado, *Martyrologium*, edited by Heribert Rosweyd, *PL* 123:139-436; Notker, *Martyrologium*, *PL* 131:1029-1164; and Flodard, *De triumphis Christi*, *PL* 135:491-886. [The *Corpus Christianorum* series are hereafter cited as *CCSL* for *Series Latina* or *CCCM* for *Continuatio Mediaevalis*.]

12. Aldhelm, *De laudibus virginitatis* and the poetic *De laudibus virginum*, edited by Rudolf Ehwald, *Aldhelmi opera* (Berlin: Weidmann, 1919), pp. 211-471.

13. Vincent de Beauvais, *Speculum historiale*, vol. 4 of *Speculum quadruplex sive speculum maius* (Duaci, 1624; reprint, Graz: Akademische Druck- und Verlagsanstalt, 1965); Jacobus de Voragine, *Legenda aurea*, edited by Th. Graesse (Breslau: Zeller, 1890; reprint, Osnabrück: Zeller, 1969); Petrus de Natalibus, *Catalogus sanctorum et gestorum eorum ex diversis voluminibus collectus*, edited by Antonio Verlo (Vicenza: Henricus de Sancto Ursio, 12 December 1493). For the most part, I have used the versions recorded in the Bollandists' collection of Greek and Latin saints' lives: *Acta Sanctorum quotquot toto orbe coluntur, vel a catholicis scriptoribus celebrantur*, edited by Joannes Bollandus et al. (Paris: Palmé [etc.], 1863-1940). Hereafter cited as *AASS*.

14. *Das altenglische Martyrologium*, edited by Günter Kotzor (Munich: Bayerische Akademie der Wissenschaften, 1981), includes the lives of Eugenia, Natalia, Pelagia, and Thecla. *Aelfric's Lives of the Saints*,

edited by Walter W. Skeat, *Early English Text Society*, nos. 76, 82, 94, 114 (London: Trübner, 1881-1900), includes the lives of Eugenia, Euphrosyne, and Thecla.

15. For overviews of some of the vernacular versions, see Werner Williams-Krapp, "Euphrosyne" in *Die deutsche Literatur des Mittelalters: Verfasserlexikon*, edited by Kurt Ruh et al. (Berlin: de Gruyter, 1977-), 2:641-42; *Vie et office de sainte Marine*, edited by Leon Clugnet (Paris: Picard, 1905); and Séminaire d'Histoire des Textes (Paris), *Pelagie la pénitente: metamorphoses d'une légende*, 2 vols. (Paris: Etudes Augustiniennes, 1981-84.

16. See *Legenda aurea: sept siècles de diffusion*, edited by Brenda Dunn-Lardeau (Montreal: Bellarmin, 1986). The *Legenda aurea* was printed at least one hundred and fifty-six times before 1500, more often than the Bible.

17. Radermacher, *Hippolytus und Thekla*, pp. 83-92, and Zoja Pavlovskis, "The Life of St. Pelagia the Harlot: Hagiographic Adaptation of Pagan Romance," *Classical Folio* 30 (1976):138-49.

18. Christine de Pizan, "The *Livre de la cité des dames* of Christine de Pizan: A Critical Edition," edited by Maureen Cheney Curnow (Diss., Vanderbilt University, 1975), and Jacopo Filippo da Bergamo Foresti, *De claris scelerisque mulieribus*, edited by Albertus de Placentia and Augustinus de Casali Mairori (Ferrara: Laurentius de Rubeis, 1497). It is worth noting that Christine de Pizan's *Livre de la mutacion de fortune*, edited by Suzanne Solente (Paris: Picard, 1959-66), begins with the actual transformation of the female narrator into a man.

19. See Christine de Pizan, *Livre de la cité des dames*, edited by Curnow, pp. 1012-18 and 1024-26.

20. *AASS*, Apr. 3: 892.

21. Caroline Walker Bynum, *Holy Feast and Holy Fast* (Berkeley: University of California Press, 1987), p. 291. Bynum makes a similar argument in "Women's Stories, Women's Symbols: A Critique of Victor Turner's Theory of Liminality," *Anthropology and the Study of Religion*, edited by Robert L. Moore and Frank E. Reynolds (Chicago: Center for the Scientific Study of Religion, 1984), pp. 105-24.

22. *Passio Sanctarum Perpetuae et Felicitatis*, edited by Cornelius Ioannes Maria Ioseph Van Beek (Noviomagi [Nijmegen]: Dekker & Van de Vegt, 1936), p. 35.

23. Anson, "The Transvestite in Early Monasticism," p. 30.

24. *The Gospel According to Thomas*, edited and translated by A. Guillaumont et al. (New York: Harper, 1959), pp. 56-57. For a discussion of this passage, see Elizabeth Castelli, "'I Will Make Mary Male': Pieties of the Body and Gender Transformation of Christian Women in Late Antiquity," in *Body Guards*, edited by Julia Epstein and Kristina Straub, pp. 29-49. Castelli discusses the figures of Mary Magdalene and Perpetua,

whose symbolic and prophetic maleness transcends biological gender constructs, to demonstrate the instability of gender identity.

25. Augustine, *Confessionum libri XIII*, edited by Lucas Verheijen, *CCSL* 27:137 (lib. IX, cap. 4): "matre adhaerente nobis muliebri habitu, virili fide, anili securitate, materna caritate, christiana pietate" [with my mother accompanying us, with womanly dress, manly faith, an old woman's composure, maternal love, and Christian piety].

26. Ambrose, *Expositio Evangelii secundum Lucam*, edited by M. Adriaen, *CCSL* 14:392.

27. See Kerstin Aspergren, *The Male Woman: A Feminine Ideal in the Early Church* (Stockholm: Almqvist and Wiksell, 1990), pp. 115-39 and Gillian Cloke, *This Female Man of God: Women and Spiritual Power in the Patristic Age 350-450* (New York: Routledge, 1994).

28. Basil of Caesarea, *Ascetica*, PG 31:625: "καὶ πολλαὶ γυναῖκες ἠρίστευσαν ἀνδρῶν οὐκ ἔλαττον." [And many women are better than men, not worse.]

29. Palladius, *Historia Lausiaca*, edited by Cuthbert Butler (Cambridge: Cambridge University Press, 1898), 2:4: "ἄθλους μεγάλων ἀνδρῶν καὶ ἀνδρειοτέρων τῆς φύσεως γυναικῶν διὰ τὴν εἰς Χριστὸν ἐλπίδα ἐνσημάνας ἐν τῷ βιβλίῳ τούτῳ" [In this book are athletic contests of great men, and also of women—like men in spirit, on account of their hope in Christ]. See also p. 128: "Ἀναγκαῖον δέ ἐστι καὶ γυναικῶν ἀνδρείων μνημονεῦσαι ἐν τῷ βιβλίῳ, αἷς καὶ ὁ Θεὸς τὰ ἴσα τοῖς ἀνδράσι τῶν ἄθλων ἐχαρίσατο." [In this book, I must also remember the manly women to whom God gave struggles equal to those of men.]

30. Translation quoted from *The Desert Christian: Sayings of the Desert Fathers*, translated by Benedicta Ward (New York: Macmillan, 1980), p. 230.

31. Horace, *Epistles* 1.9.28.

32. See Joan Cadden, *Meanings of Sex Differences in the Middle Ages: Medicine, Science, and Culture* (Cambridge: Cambridge University Press, 1993), pp. 13-39.

33. Similar military metaphors can be found in Romans 13:12, 2 Corinthians 10:4, and 1 Thessalonians 5:8.

34. The authorities on this are numerous: Jerome, Tertullian, and Augustine are only a few examples of Christian authors who faulted womankind for the sin of Eve. For some assessments of the church's view of women, see Elizabeth Clark, *Women in the Early Church* (Wilmington: Glazier, 1983), and Vern L. Bullough, *The Subordinate Sex: A History of Attitudes Towards Women* (Urbana: University of Illinois Press, 1973).

35. Although these legends are early examples of this use of disguise (fourth century), the simple ruse can be found in the literature of all ages and nationalities. See Thompson, *Motif Index of Folklore-Literature*, entries K520-538 and R152.1-3.

36. *AASS*, Apr. 3:580.

37. Among the many nonhagiographic sources that refer to the concept of the "animus virilis" are Cassiodorus, *Expositio psalmorum*, edited by M. Adriaen, *CCSL* 97:241-2, and the *Speculum virginum*, edited by Jutta Seyfarth, *CCCM* 5:105-6 and 349.

38. Jerome, *Commentarius in Epistolam ad Ephesios*, *PL* 26:533:"Sin autem Christo magis voluerit servire quam saeculo, mulier esse cessabit, et dicetur vir, quia omnes in perfectum virum cupimus occurrere." [If, however, she should desire to serve Christ more than the world, she will cease to be called a woman and will be called a man, since we wish everyone to attain the state of the perfected male.]

39. Jerome, *Epistolae*, *PL* 22:413 (XXII, cap. 27).

40. See Peter Brown, *The Body and Society: Men, Women and Sexual Renunciation in Early Christianity* (New York: Columbia University Press, 1988), esp. pp. 33-64, for a study of the rise of this movement. Brown, however, does not discuss the transvestite saints in this context.

41. Quoted from Voragine, *Legenda aurea*, edited by Graesse, p. 603.

42. *AASS*, Feb. 2:541.

43. *AASS*, Oct. 4:266.

44. See *Acta apostolorum apocrypha*, edited by Richard Lipsius and Maximilian Bonnet (Leipzig, 1891-1903; reprint, Darmstadt: Wissenschaftliche Buchgesellschaft, 1959), 1:235-72.

45. One wonders if the *Acts* themselves do not contain thinly veiled criticism (or satire) of Paul, the apostle who discusses the necessity of veils and long hair for women (1 Corinthians 11) and forbids them to speak in church (1 Corinthians 14).

46. *Acta apostolorum apocrypha*, 2:20.

47. That the Pauline theology of baptism influenced early baptismal ceremonies is obvious in the works of Cyril of Jerusalem (†387), Ambrose, John Chrysostom (†407), and Theodore of Mopsuestia (†428). See Hugh M. Riley, *Christian Initiation* (Washington, D.C.: Catholic University Press, 1974), esp. pp. 413-51.

48. See Jean Daniélou, "Die Symbolik des Taufritus," *Liturgie und Mönchtum* 3 (1949):45-68.

49. Konrad Zwierzina, "Der Pelagiatypus der fabulosen Märtyrerlegende," *Nachrichten von der Gesellschaft der Wissenschaften zu Göttingen* (Berlin: Weidmann, 1928), pp. 144-46, and Anson, "The Transvestite in Early Monasticism," pp. 6-7.

50. *Acta apostolorum apocrypha*, 1:253-54.

51. For early interpretations of nakedness and baptism, see Riley, *Christian Initiation*, pp. 180-89.

52. *Acta apostolorum apocrypha*, 1:260.

53. See Daniélou, "Die Symbolik des Taufritus," pp. 58-59.

54. Iconography does not depict Thecla in male dress at this point in her life, probably because she became a major figure in debates on whether or not women could preach. Also, the last episode of her life, a Daphne-like flight from a potential rape, clearly marks her as female. See Claudia Nauerth and Rüdiger Warns, *Thekla: Ihre Bilder in der frühchristlichen Kunst* (Wiesbaden: Harrassowitz, 1981).

55. *Acta apostolorum apocrypha*, 2:37.

56. For even more variations on the name, see Agnes B. C. Dunbar, *A Dictionary of Saintly Women* (London: Bell, 1905), 2:302-3. Gregory the Great, *Dialogorum libri IV, PL* 77:340-41 (IV, cap. 13), mentions a certain Galla who grew a beard after her husband's death, apparently as a consequence of rejecting her "passionate nature" when she refused a second husband and became a nun instead.

57. The image of a bearded girl on a cross probably explains the origin of this legend. Apparently, it is based on a misunderstanding of some crucifixes, particularly the much-copied Volto Santo crucifix that depicted a bearded Christ in a long, flowing robe. See Jean Gessler, *La Légende de sainte Wilgeforte ou Ontcommer: la vierge miraculeusement barbue* (Brussels: Editions Universelle, 1938), and Gustav Schurer and Joseph M. Ritz, *Sankt Kümmernis und Volto Santo: Studien und Bilder* (Düsseldorf: Schwann, [1934]).

58. See Dunbar, *A Dictionary of Saintly Women*, 1:291; 2:82, 119-20, and 192-93. Jane Tibbetts Schulenburg, "The Heroics of Virginity: Brides of Christ and Sacrificial Mutilation," in *Women in the Middle Ages and the Renaissance*, edited by Mary Beth Rose (Syracuse: Syracuse University Press, 1986), pp. 29-72, discusses numerous historical cases of self-mutilation, particularly the cutting off of the nose.

59. From the English translation in James Drescher, *Three Coptic Legends* (Cairo: L'Institute Français d'Archéologie Oriental, 1942), p. 77.

60. *AASS*, Feb. 2:540.

61. *AASS*, Jan. 1:259-60.

62. *AASS*, Feb. 2:539.

63. See, for example, Rutebeuf's *Frère Denis* (thirteenth century), edited by Raymond Eichmann and John Duval in *The French Fabliau: B.N. MS. 837* (New York: Garland, 1985), pp. 247-59, and Poncellet's tale (no. 60) in *Les Cent nouvelles nouvelles* (ca. 1456-67), edited by Franklin P. Sweetser (Geneva: Droz, 1966), pp. 373-77, where women dressed as monks enter monasteries and engage in surreptitious sexual relations with monks.

64. *AASS*, Jul. 4:286.

65. *AASS*, Oct. 4:262. She is called "prima mimarum Antiochae" and "prima choreutriarum pantomimarum." Although this might offer new evidence for dramatic performances in the fifth century, we should assume that these are merely terms implying low moral character, for Pelagia later is referred to as "meretrix."

66. See Sigmund Freud, "Fetischismus" in *Gesammelte Werke*, edited by Anna Freud et al. (London: Imago, 1940-52), 14:317, and, more recently, Jeffrey J. Andresen, "Rapunzel: The Symbolism of the Cutting of Hair," *Journal of the American Psychoanalytic Association* 28 (1980):69-88, and Armado R. Favazza, "Normal and Deviant Self-Mutilation," *Transcultural Psychiatric Research Review* 26 (1989):113-27.

67. Jerome, *Epistolae, PL* 22:413 (XXII, 27).

68. See Methodius's *Convivium decem virginum* (ca. 270/90), in *Le Banquet*, edited by Herbert Musurillo; translated by Victor-Henry Debidour (Paris: Cerf, 1963), p. 52.

69. Voragine, *Legenda aurea*, p. 398.

70. *Chrestomathie de l'ancien français*, edited by Karl Bartsch, revised by Leo Wiese (New York: Hafner, 1969), p. 207 (no. 59).

71. For a collection of essays on women mystics, see *Frauenmystik im Mittelalter*, edited by Peter Dinzelbacher and Dieter R. Bauer (Ostfildern bei Stuttgart: Schwabenverlag, 1985).

72. The play will appear in a forthcoming edition of the Wolfenbüttel MS Blackenburg 9 currently being prepared by Alan E. Knight. See also Pedro Calderón de la Barca, *El Josef de las mujeres*, vol. 3 of *Las comedias de D. Pedro Calderón de la Barca*, edited by Juan Jorge Keil (Leipzig: Fleischer, 1829), pp. 248-70.

NOTES TO CHAPTER THREE

1. [Engelhard von Langheim], "Vitae und Miracula aus Kloster Ebrach," edited by Joseph Schwarzer, *Neues Archiv der Gesellschaft für ältere deutsche Geschichtskunde*, 6 (1881):516.

2. An account by Engelhard von Langheim (1188), a poetic version by an anonymous monk of Windberg (1188-91), a short anonymous prose life, based largely on the poem (ca. 1200-20), a chapter in Caesarius of Heisterbach's *Dialogus miraculorum* (1220), and a lengthy account by an unnamed fellow novice (after 1191).

3. In addition to the contemporaneous accounts of her life, Hildegund appears among the saints included in the earliest *menologia* of the order, the *Kalendarium Cisterciense*, and the works of such historians as Nicolas Ménard, Arnold Wion, Henriquez Chrysostomus, Johannes Trithemius, and Angelius Manrique. See *A Benedictine Bibliography*, edited by Oliver L. Kaspner (Collegeville, Minn.: St. John's Abbey Press, 1962), for bibliographic citations.

4. The so-called *Exempelbuch für die Nonnen von Wechterswinkel*. For a description of the work, see Bruno Griesser, "Engelhard von Langheim und sein Exempelbuch für die Nonnen von Wechterswinkel," *Cistercienser-Chronik* 70 (1963):55-73. For the edition, see note 1.

5. [Engelhard von Langheim], "Vitae und Miracula," p. 520: "Nulli tamen feminarum similia suaserim, quia multis par fortitudo, sed dispar est fortuna, et eodem belli discrimine sepe cadit fortior, quo vincit infirmior." [To no woman do I recommend a similar course, since many have equal strength, yet fortune is varied. The stronger often falls in battle, while the weaker conquers.]

6. "Vita Hildegundis metrica und andere Verse," edited by W. Wattenbach, *Neues Archiv der Gesellschaft für ältere deutsche Geschichtskunde*, 6 (1881):533-36.

7. Hugo von Trimberg, *Registrum multorum auctorum*, edited by Karl Langosch (Berlin, 1942; reprint, Nendeln/Liechtenstein: Kraus, 1969), pp. 191-92.

8. "Vita Hildegundis metrica," p. 533.

9. Royal Library of Brussels, codex 7503-18, 131ᵛ - 132ᵛ. For the text, see *Catalogus codicum hagiographicorum bibliothecae regiae Bruxellensis*, edited by Hagiographi Bollandiani (Brussels: Polleunis, Ceuterick & De Smet, 1886-89), 1/2:92-95.

10. Andrea Liebers, *"Eine Frau war dieser Mann": Die Geschichte der Hildegund von Schönau* (Zürich: eFeF Verlag, 1989), found the text in the University Library of Heidelberg (Cod. Sal. X 1, fol. 151ᵛ - 152ᵛ). According to Liebers, the manuscript was written for liturgical or homiletic purposes in the Cistercian abbey of Salem. She offers a critical edition of the text based on the two existing manuscripts on pp. 184-90.

11. As noted by F.J. Worstbrock, "Hildegund von Schönau," in *Die deutsche Literatur des Mittelalters: Verfasserlexikon*, 4:4-8. For example, lines 87, 90, 98, 146, and 147 of the poem are quoted directly in the prose account. In fact, most of the Brussels/Heidelberg account is a rephrasing of the poem.

12. Caesarius of Heisterbach, *Dialogus miraculorum* (Dist. 1, cap. XL), edited by Joseph Strange (Cologne: Lempertz, 1851), 1:46-53.

13. Compare, for example, *Catalogus codicum hagiographicorum*, 1/ 2:94, lines 4-6 and 34-36 (Liebers, p. 189), with Caesarius *Dialogus miraculorum*, p. 49, lines 17-18 and p. 52, lines 3-6. I cite the text from the *Catalogus codicum hagiographicorum* because it is more widely available in libraries than is Liebers's edition. References to the new edition, however, are included in parentheses.

14. The text was edited by Daniel Papebroch in the *AASS*, Apr. 2:778-88. Meinrad Schaab, *Die Zisterzienserabtei Schönau im Odenwald* (Heidelberg: Winter, 1963), p. 43, says the author's name was Berthold, but he cites no evidence for this claim.

15. *AASS*, Apr. 2:784 and 787. The death of Schönau's abbot, Gottfried (1191), and founding of the Cistercian monastery at Bebenhausen (1190) are mentioned as events of the not too recent past.

16. Her confessor was the prior Diepold. According to Schaab, *Die Zisterzienserabtei Schönau*, p. 37, he later became abbot at Schönau.

17. See *AASS*, Apr. 2:781.

18. In his account, the fellow novice says her father died at sea before reaching the Holy Land. See ibid., p. 781.

19. *Catalogus codicum hagiographicorum*, 1/2:93 (Liebers, p. 186). She may mean that she begged from the students at the school, but a similar statement in the "Vita Hildegundis metrica" (line 34) also implies that she learned something during this period: "Panis et ignoti sermonis colligo micas." [I collected scraps of bread and (scraps of) unknown words.] Caesarius, *Dialogus miraculorum*, p. 48, claims that she attended school: "Mendicando tamen scholas in eadem civitate anno uno frequentavit." [By begging, however, she attended the school in this same city for one year.] It was common for medieval students to beg.

20. *AASS*, Apr. 2:784.

21. Philipp of Heinsberg (1167-1191) was then archbishop of Cologne and Lucius III (†1185) was pope. The message concerned the controversy between the church and Friedrich I over the consecration of the bishop of Trier. Here again, the fellow novice's account differs in the details. See ibid., p. 782.

22. The fellow novice claims that the shepherds ran off at that moment to protect their flocks from some threatening wolves. See ibid., p. 783.

23. In the Brussels/Heidelberg version and Caesarius's *Dialogus miraculorum*, it is said that an old woman, who claimed to be a relative, came forward with the information. The fellow novice also reveals the name but says the abbess of the monastery at Neuss was the source.

24. Joseph Schwarzer, W. Wattenbach, and Daniel Papebroch include little introductory material and no analysis of the texts they edit. Bruno Griesser, "Engelhard von Langheim und sein Exempelbuch," pp. 58 and 71, and Hans D. Oppel, "Die exemplarischen Mirakel des Engelhard von Langheim" (Diss., Würzburg, 1976), pp. 83-85, mention Hildegund in passing in their studies of Engelhard von Langheim, and Ernst Pfeiffer, "Die Pilgerfahrt der heiligen Hildegund von Schönau," *Cistercienser-Chronik* 47 (1935):198-200, synopsizes the story. In *Eine Frau war dieser Mann*, Liebers retells and partially translates the lives; her purpose is to present the bizarre tale to a general audience within a historical framework of short essays that characterize the twelfth and thirteenth centuries. Maximilian Huffschmid and Richard Benz describe some sixteenth-century renderings of Hildegund's story but do not discuss the hagiobiographical accounts. See Maximilian Huffschmid, "Beiträge zur Geschichte der Cisterzienserabtei Schönau," *Zeitschrift für die Geschichte des Oberrheins* 6 (1891):430-33, and Richard Benz, *Heidelberg: Schicksal und Geist* (Konstanz: Thorbecke, 1961), pp. 13-14 and plate 3. The drawings are also included in the exhibition

catalog *Die Zisterzienser: Ordensleben zwischen Ideal und Wirklichkeit*, edited by K. Elm et al. (Cologne: Rheinland-Verlag, 1981), pp. 424-426, 431.

25. [Engelhard von Langheim], "Vitae und Miracula," p. 516. See also "Vita Hildegundis metrica," line 9: "Hic vir erat pro veste viri, sub veste puella." [He was a man according to his male dress, but under his clothes, a girl.]

26. Quoted from Caesarius, *Dialogus miraculorum*, p. 52. Similar statements occur in other accounts. See, for example, Engelhard ("Vitae und Miracula," p. 517), who quotes Hildegund's claim, "Invenietis in me, quod miremini." [You will find in me something that will astound you.] In the "Vita Hildegundis metrica," line 135, she says: "Materies vobis migrans parebo stuporis." [Going from you, I shall seem to you a thing of wonderment.] And the Brussels/Heidelberg version (*Catalogus codicum hagiographicorum*, 1/2:94; Liebers, p. 189) quotes her as saying: "Et cum migravero, apparebit in me unde stupeatis et Deo, bonorum omnium largitori, gratias agere debeatis." [And when I pass away, there will appear in me something at which you will be astounded and you ought to give thanks to God, giver of all good.]

27. [Engelhard von Langheim], "Vitae und Miracula," p. 520. Engelhard goes on to criticize the "womanly" infirmity of most men, who, he says, should find in Hildegund an example for spiritual fortitude.

28. "Vita Hildegundis metrica," lines 12-14.

29. *Catalogus codicum hagiographicorum*, 1/2:95 (Liebers, p. 190).

30. Caesarius, *Dialogus miraculorum*, p. 53: "Tanta est fortitudo mentis in quibusdam feminis, ut merito laudetur." [So great is the fortitude of mind in certain women that it is worthy of praise.]

31. *AASS*, Apr. 2:784: "quod femina viros opus virtutem faciens praevenit et praecellit." [Because a woman doing a deed, she excelled at virtue/manliness and outdid men.]

32. [Engelhard von Langheim], "Vitae und Miracula," p. 520: "magnum aliquid de illo futurum sperarent." [They hoped something great would come from him.]

33. "Vita Hildegundis metrica," line 3.

34. *Catalogus codicum hagiographicorum*, 1/2:92 (Liebers, p. 185).

35. *AASS*, Apr. 2:787. He claims she miraculously appeared to him at Bebenhausen when he was seriously ill, assuring him he would recover.

36. Caesarius, *Dialogus miraculorum*, p. 52.

37. *AASS*, Apr. 2:787. An amusing scene precedes this announcement when Gottfried changes the gender of the pronouns used to describe the dead. Only those monks who understood Latin well, we are told, began to whisper and murmur among themselves.

38. Herbert Thurston, "The Story of Hildegund: Maiden and Monk," *The Month* 127 (1916):156, suggested this interpretation but did not develop it beyond a single sentence.

39. See *The French Fabliau*, edited by Raymond Eichmann, pp. 247-59. Although *Frère Denise* is the earliest example I can find of this satirical theme (and obviously postdates Hildegund), the presence of a woman in a male monastery would lend itself to such a bawdy interpretation.

40. This story enjoyed great popularity in France, Italy, and Germany from Rutebeuf's time to well into the Renaissance. See, for example, no. 60 in *Les Cent nouvelles nouvelles* (1461), edited by Franklin P. Sweetser, pp. 371-77; no. 31 in Marguerite de Navarre, *L'Heptaméron* (1558), edited by Michel François (Paris: Garnier, 1981); "Von keuschen mönchen historia" in Hans Wilhelm Kirchhof's *Wendunmuth* (1563), edited by Hermann Österley (Tübingen: Laupp, 1869), pp. 515-17; and no. 75 in Celio Malespini's *Ducento novelle* (Venice, 1609).

41. See Heinrich Cornelius Agrippa von Nettesheim, *De incertitudine et vanitate omnium scientium et artium* ([Antwerp, 1531]), cap. 63: "Palamque videmus ubicunque sunt magnifica ista templa, et sacerdotum monachorumque collegia, ut plurimum in proximo esse lupanaria, quin et plurimae monalium et vestalium ac beguinarum domus privatae quaedam meretricularum fornices sunt, quas etiam monachos et religiosos (ne diffametur eorum castitas) nonnunquam sub monachali cuculla ac virili veste in monasteriis aluisse scimus." [Clearly, we see that wherever there are magnificent churches and colleges of priests and monks, there are many brothels in close proximity, indeed, many houses of nuns and virgins and beguines are certain private brothels of prostitutes, whom we also know that monks and religious (lest their chastity be defamed) sometimes keep in monasteries under a monkish cowl and manly clothes.]

42. See Bernard of Clairvaux, *De gradibus humilitatis et superbiae*, in *Sancti Bernardi opera*, edited by Jean Leclercq and H.M. Rochais (Rome: Editiones Cisterciensis, 1957-77), 3:38-45. Quotation is from p. 45.

43. Ibid., p. 46: "Monachus enim, qui sui negligens, alios curiose circumspicit, dum quosdam suspicit superiores, quosdam despicit inferiores, et in aliis quidem videt quod invidet, in aliis quod irridet." [For the monk who neglects himself and looks at another with curiosity suspects some as superior, despises some as inferior, and in some he sees what he envies, in others what he ridicules.]

44. For a discussion of sinful *curiositas*, see Richard Newhauser, "The Sin of Curiosity and the Cistercians," in *Erudition at God's Service*, edited by John R. Sommerfeldt (Kalamazoo: Cistercian Publications, 1987), pp. 71-95.

45. [Engelhard von Langheim], "Vitae und Miracula," p. 517.

46. Ibid., p. 517. The prior Diepold was her confessor, but he, too, was apparently unaware of her sex.

47. *AASS*, Apr. 2:786.

48. Ibid., p. 786.

49. Ibid., p. 787.

50. Caesarius, *Dialogus miraculorum*, p. 50.

51. Ibid., p. 51.

52. *AASS*, Apr. 2:786

53. [Engelhard von Langheim], "Vitae und Miracula," p. 516.

54. Caesarius, *Dialogus miraculorum*, p. 51.

55. See [Engelhard von Langheim], "Vitae und Miracula," p. 520 and *Catalogus codicum hagiographicorum*, 1/2:92 (Liebers, p. 185).

56. *AASS*, Apr. 2:785. The admission of struggles with temptation is acceptable in saints' lives, provided that the saint overcomes the tormenters.

57. Ibid., p. 784.

58. This "inclusa sancta" is also mentioned in the Brussels/ Heidelberg version, the "Vita Hildegundis metrica," and in Engelhard's account as the person who recommended Joseph to the monks at Schönau.

59. *AASS*, Apr. 2:786.

60. See Bynum, *Holy Feast and Holy Fast*, p. 214, where she cites Albertus Magnus's observation that holy women cease to menstruate. For a discussion of menstruation in the Middle Ages, see Charles Wood, "The Doctor's Dilemma: Sin, Salvation and the Menstrual Cycle in Medieval Thought," *Speculum* 56 (1981):710-27.

61. *Three Coptic Legends*, translated by James Drescher, p. 75.

NOTES TO CHAPTER FOUR

1. Jean Chapelain, *La Pucelle ou la France délivrée* (Paris: Libraire Marpon & Flammarion, 1656). Cited from Ingvald Raknem, *Joan of Arc in History, Legend and Literature* (Oslo: Universitetsforgaget, 1971), p. 270, note 8.

2. Edward Hall, *The Union of the Two Noble and Illustre Families of Lancastre and York* (London: Richard Grafton, 1548), p. cxiii^v.

3. In the final list of charges, Jeanne was also accused of attempting suicide when she tried to escape by leaping from the tower at Beaurevoir. See *Procès de condamnation et de réhabilitation de Jeanne d'Arc dite La Pucelle*, compiled and edited by Jules Quicherat (Paris: Renouard, 1841- 49), 1:416. This work is hereafter cited as *Procès*.

4. Ibid., 1:55.

5. Ibid., 2:446.

6. From the testimonies of Johannes Pasquerel and Jean d'Aulon; see ibid., 3:102 and 209-10. The quote is from Pasquerel's account.

7. See the testimonies of Jean, Duc d'Alençon, Haimond de Macy, and Jean d'Aulon; ibid., 3: 89, 100, 121, 219.

8. The image is from a manuscript in the Biblothèque Nationale; it is reproduced often, as, for example, on the cover of Charles Wood, *Joan*

of Arc and Richard III: Sex, Saints, and Government in the Middle Ages (New York: Oxford University Press, 1988).

9. Ibid., 3:391-92. They advised Charles to follow Paul's dictate: "Probate spiritus, si ex Deo sunt." [Test the spirit (to see) if it is from God.]

10. Ibid., 5:119.

11. Ibid., 1:94.

12. For references to the Poitiers investigation, see ibid., 1:71, 75, 94; 3:4, 17, 22, 93, 209, and 391 (résumé). The "résumé des conclusions" (1429) testifies that all interrogations and outside investigations have found nothing to contradict her good character and Christian life. Charles also received the advice he desired: they recommended that he send the maid to Orléans. If she could conquer the English as she claimed, she should be accepted as sent from God.

13. *Saint Joan of Orleans: Scenes from the Fifteenth-Century "Mystère du Siège d'Orléans,"* edited by Paul Studer; translated by Joan Evans (Oxford: Clarendon, 1926), p. 86.

14. *Procès*, 4:509-10.

15. Ibid., 4:211. According to the *Chronique de la Pucelle*, she gave a similar response at Auxerre, but in that instance she cited preservation of virginity as the chief reason before adding that it would be difficult to fight in women's clothing. See ibid., 4:250-51.

16. See the account of Radulphus Silvestris, ibid., 1:372.

17. See, for example, the testimonies of Jean de Nouillonpont and Bertrand de Poulengy, ibid., 2:438 and 457.

18. Ibid., 3:411-21. See also Dorothy G. Wayman, "The Chancellor and Jeanne d'Arc," *Franciscan Studies* 17 (1957):273-305, for the text and a discussion of the attribution. Her contention that it is the work of Jean Gerson has been challenged by Georges Peyronnet, "Gerson, Charles VII et Jeanne d'Arc: La Propagande au service de la guerre," *Revue d'Histoire Ecclesiastique* 84 (1989):339-58.

19. *Procès*, 3:415.

20. Ibid., 3:417.

21. Ibid., 3:412.

22. Ibid., 3:412: "Ubi autem de equo descendit, solitum habitum reassumens, fit simplicissima, negotiorum saecularium quasi innocens agnus imperita." [Yet when she dismounts from the horse, putting on her customary clothes again, she becomes very simple, innocent of worldly matters just like an inexperienced lamb.]

23. Ibid., p. 3:420: "Et talem personam indecens videtur transformare in virum saecularem armorum. Non enim sic legitur de Esther et Judith, licet ornarent se cultu solemniori muliebri tamen, ut gratius placerent his, cum quibus agere conceperunt." [And it seems indecent for such a person (one destined for a divine mission) to transform herself into a worldly man of arms. For thus it is not written of Esther and Judith, although they

adorned themselves with customary feminine ornament in order to be more pleasing to those with whom they intended to deal.]

24. Ibid., 3:299-302.

25. If it is indeed the work of Gerson, it was written before his death on 12 July 1429, and may even predate *De quadam puella*.

26. *Procès*, 3:440.

27. Thomas Aquinas, *Summa theologiae*, edited by the Blackfriars (New York: McGraw-Hill, 1964–), 2, 2, 169. For the reference in the *Sibylla Francica*, see *Procès*, 3:440.

28. Ibid., 3:441.

29. See *Procès en nullité de la condamnation de Jeanne d'Arc*, edited by Pierre Duparc (Paris: Klincksieck, 1977-89), vol. 2 , pp. 206-8, 248-49, 262-63, 327-28, and 457-75. The treatises of Jean de Montigny and Robert Ciboule, ibid., 280-82 and 377-80, also excuse Jeanne's cross dressing. For a discussion of these defenses in the broader context of fifteenth-century perceptions of Jeanne d'Arc, see Jane Marie Pinzino, "Devil or Angel? Fifteenth-Century Verdicts on Joan of Arc" (Diss., University of Pennsylvania, 1996).

30. Ibid., 3:405.

31. Ibid., 5:48.

32. Christine de Pizan, *Ditié de Jehanne d'Arc*, edited and translated by Angus J. Kennedy and Kenneth Varty (Oxford: Society for the Study of Mediaeval Languages and Literatures, 1977).

33. Christine de Pizan recounts the stories of five transvestite heroines, St. Marina, St. Natalia, St. Euphrosyne, Semiramis, and Zinevra, in her *Livre de la cité des dames*.

34. This prophecy appears only in documents postdating Jeanne's appearance. It is recorded in Mathieu Thomassin's *Registre delphinal* (1456) and the *Scotichronicon* of Walter Bower (ca. 1437); see *Procès*, 4:305 and 481. The same prophecy is attributed to Bede in the rehabilitation proceedings (ibid., 3:338).

35. See *The First Biography of Joan of Arc with the Chronicle Record of a Contemporary Account*, translated by Daniel Rankin and Claire Quintal (Pittsburgh: University of Pittsburgh, 1964), p. 120, for this translation of the letter from Bibliothèque National MS. 23018. The letter is also recorded, with slight variation, in Enguerran de Monstrelet's chronicle (see *Procès*, 4:382).

36. *Procès*, 5:136.

37. Ibid., 1:265 and 447.

38. Ibid., 1:496-97.

39. Ibid., 4:464.

40. Ibid., 1:418. See also 1:89, 203, 209, 276, 304, 436, and 471 for more references to sorcery.

41. From the testimonies of Jean Toutmouillé, Thomas Marie, Guillaume Manchon, and Jean Riquier; ibid., 2:3, 344, 373, and 3:189, respectively.

42. William Shakespeare, *Henry VI, Part I*, esp. act V, scene 3.

43. *Procès*, 1:3.

44. Ibid., 1:432-33.

45. See ibid., 1:38-193, esp. 1:68, 74, 132-33, 161, 176, and 192.

46. Ibid., 1:74.

47. Ibid., 1:193.

48. Ibid., 1:164-65.

49. Ibid., 1:227-28.

50. Ibid., 1:177.

51. Ibid., 1:74: "Interrogata an praeceperit sibi assumere vestem virilem: respondit quod de veste parvum est, et est de minori."

52. She even demanded to be taken to the pope in a public declaration immediately preceding her abjuration. See ibid., 1:445: "Je m'en raporte à Dieu et à nostre saint père le Pape."

53. *Decretum Gratiani emendatum et notationibus ... Gregorii XIII, PL* 187:165. The statement is based on bk. 6, can. 13 of the decrees of the Council of Gangra; see Hefele, *Histoire des conciles*, 1:1038.

54. See *Medieval Handbooks of Penance*, translated by John T. McNeill and Helena M. Gamer (New York: Columbia University Press, 1938), p. 293, and Robert of Flamborough, *Liber poenitentialis*, edited by J.J. Francis Firth (Toronto: Pontifical Institute of Mediaeval Studies, 1971), p. 264. In both cases, the cross dressing in question seems to be in the context of a carnival celebration.

55. *Procès*, 1:436-437.

56. Ibid., 1:86: "Qualiter loqueretur Anglicum, cum non sit de parte Anglicorum?"

57. See, for example, ibid., 1:249-50, and 366. The faculty of the University of Paris passed a similar judgment on Jeanne's visions; see ibid., p. 414: "vel sunt ficta mendacia, seductoria et perniciosa, vel praedictae apparitiones et revelationes sunt superstitiosae, a malignis spiritibus et diabolicis, Belial, Satan et Behemmoth, procedentes." [Either they are evil, seductive, and pernicious lies or the proclaimed visions and revelations are superstitions coming from the evil and diabolic spirits, Belial, Satan, and Behemoth.]

58. Ibid., 1:447. I quote only part of a statement almost two pages in length. Witnesses at the rehabilitation trial claimed that Jeanne signed a document of only a few lines, whereas the abjuration statement included in the trial record is a detailed rejection of every position that Jeanne had maintained throughout her year-long imprisonment. See Frances Gies, *Joan of Arc: The Legend and the Reality* (New York: Harper & Row, 1981), pp. 213-14.

59. *Procès*, 1:455.

60. Ibid., 1:455.

61. Anne Llewellyn Barstow, *Joan of Arc* (New York: Mellen, 1986), p. 217.

62. See *Procès*, 3:149. Jeanne had been led to believe that if she abjured she would be taken to a women's church prison. Actually, as a defendant in an ecclesiastical court, she should have been kept in such a prison from the start. The English, however, feared she might escaped (as she had twice attempted already). After her relapse, Jeanne herself promised she would obey the church if they would place her in a women's prison (see 1:456).

63. See testimonies of Isambert de la Pierre, Pierre Cusquel, Manchon, and Martin Ladvenu; ibid., 2:5 and 306; 3:147-48, and 168.

64. Ibid., 3:168 and 2:365. See also Bardinus de Petra's testimony, ibid., 2:305.

65. Several rehabilitation witnesses attest to seeing Jeanne's feet manacled to her bed in prison. See ibid., 2:18; 3:131, 140, and 161.

66. Marina Warner, *Joan of Arc: The Image of Female Heroism* (London: Weidenfeld and Nicolson, 1981), p. 106, and Barstow, *Joan of Arc*, p. 117.

67. *Procès*, 3:102.

68. Ibid., 3:108.

69. According to the testimony of Jean Massieu, the Duchess of Bedford gave strict orders that Jeanne not be violated in prison (see ibid., 3:155). Manchon claims that even her bitter enemy, the Earl of Warwick, once saved her from rape and replaced the offending guards (ibid., 3:147-48).

70. Ibid., 1:457-58: "Item dit que de paour du feu, elle a dit ce qu'elle a dit. [...] et que ce qui estoit en la cédule de l'abjuracion, elle ne l'entendoit point." [That she had said what she had said from fear of fire. ... and she did not understand what was in the schedule of abjuration.]

71. Ibid., 1:458.

72. Ibid., 1:176.

73. Ibid., 1:177.

74. For Massieu's testimony, see ibid., 3:157-58. See also 4:517, for Pius II's description of the forced relapse.

75. Ibid., 2:376.

76. Ibid., 2:300-309.

77. Ibid., 2:306.

78. See ibid., 2:42, where this defense appears in the statement of Theodorus de Leliis.

79. See the *Sibylla Francica* and the treatise for the rehabilitation by Theodorus de Leliis, a canon lawyer, ibid., 3:440-41 and 2:42, and the rehabilitation documents cited in note 29. More recently, Warner, *Joan of*

Arc, pp. 151-55, and Andrien Harmand, *Jeanne d'Arc, ses costumes, son armure* (Paris: Leroux, 1929), p. 12, have compared Jeanne's transvestism with that of the female monks, though neither cites the rehabilitation documents nor the *Sibylla Francica*.

80. *Procès*, 1:66: "Interrogata si bene voluisset se esse marem, quando debebat venire ad Franciam: respondit quod alias ipsa ad hoc responderat." [Asked if she had wished to be male when she was ordered to come to France, she responded that she had answered this elsewhere.] She may be referring to the Poitiers trial, which she mentions later in this interrogation session.

81. Warner, *Joan of Arc*, pp. 139-58.

NOTES TO CHAPTER FIVE

1. Giovanni Boccaccio, *De casibus virorum illustrium*, edited by Pier Giorgio Ricci and Vittorio Zaccaria (Milan: Mondadori, 1983), p. 774. Boccaccio also included the papess in his *De mulieribus claris*, edited by Vittorio Zaccaria (Milan: Mondadori, 1967), pp. 414-16.

2. David Blondel, *Familier esclaircissement de la question si une femme a este assise au siege papal de Rome entre Leon IV et Benoit III* (Amsterdam: Blaeu, 1647).

3. Johannes Wolf, *Lectionum memorabilium et reconditarum centenarii XVI* (Lauingen: Rheinmichel, 1600), p. 225-31. Wolf also cites Rudolphus Flaviacensis (ca. 900-925), but no extant texts support this claim. Other early authors Wolf wrongly credited with the story were Marianus Scotus (1028-1082?), Sigebertus Gemblacensis (twelfth century?), Otto von Freising (†1158), and Gottfried Witerbiensis (twelfth century).

4. See Johannes Joseph Ignaz von Döllinger, *Die Papstfabeln des Mittelalters* (Stuttgart: Cotta, 1890), pp. 7-18. Döllinger, whose work follows the findings of earlier investigations by Florimond de Raemond (1587) and David Blondel (1647), posits that the proliferation of the myth in the thirteenth-century chronicles of the mendicant orders was a direct consequence of the rift between Pope Boniface VIII (1294-1303) and the orders, particularly the Dominicans.

5. Fedor von Zobeltitz, "Die Päpstin Johanna: Ein Beitrag zur Kuriositätenlitteratur," *Zeitschrift für Bücherfreunde* 2 (1898):279-90; 437-39, presents a useful overview of the literature on the papess, but his purpose is not to discuss or interpret the works.

6. See *Chronicon universalis Mettensis*, edited by Georg Waitz, in *Monumenta Germaniae Historica: Scriptores* (*MGH*), 24:502-26. Waitz does not credit the work to Mailly. The attribution was made a few years before this edition by Ludwig Weiland in "Die Chronik des Predigermönches

Johannes von Mailly," *Archiv der Gesellschaft für ältere deutsche Geschichte* 12 (1874):469-73, more on the basis of a hypothesis by Döllinger than any textual evidence. Waitz tried to rectify this rash attribution in "Über kleine Chroniken des dreizehnten Jahrhunderts," *Neues Archiv der Gesellschaft für ältere deutsche Geschichtskunde* 3 (1878):49-76, but most scholarship on the female pope continues to attribute the chronicle to Mailly.

7. *Chronica minor auctore minorita Erphordiensi*, edited by O. Holder-Egger in *MGH: Scriptores*, 24:172-213. The passage about the papess from Stephen de Bourbon's work is included in *Scriptores ordinis praedicatorum*, edited by Jacob Quetif and Jacob Echard (Paris: Ballard and Simart, 1719), 1:397.

8. Edited by Ludwig Weiland in *MGH: Scriptores*, 22:377-482.

9. Döllinger, *Papstfabeln*, pp. 10-14.

10. *MGH: Scriptores*, 22:428. One manuscript copy of the *Chronicon* adds that she survived and lived out her days as a penitent. According to this version, her son later became a bishop.

11. *Chronica minor auctore minorita Erphordiensi*, p. 184.

12. *Flores temporum*, edited by O. Holder-Egger in *MGH: Scriptores*, 24:226-50. The alliterative verse appears on p. 243.

13. See Döllinger, *Die Papstfabeln*, pp. 38-42, where he suggests that such seats can be found in Roman baths. This one was particularly prized for the unusual color of the marble. Cesare D'Onofrio, *Mille anni de leggenda: una donna sul trono di Pietro* (Rome: Romana Società Editrice, 1978), pp. 124-59, however, offers conclusive evidence that the chair was used in ancient Rome by women in childbirth. The practice of receiving the keys while seated on this pre-Christian artifact was abandoned in the sixteenth century.

14. J. Bignami-Odier, "Les Visions de Robert d'Uzès O. P.," *Archivum fratrum praedicatorum* 25 (1955):274.

15. In Felix Hemmerlin's *De nobilitate et rusticitate dialogus* ([Strasbourg: Johann Prüss, ca. 1493-1500]), p. 99: "Ut electus summus pontifex ibidem [i.e., the throne] collocaretur: et per duos de clero fide dignos eius testiculi, tamquam testes, testimonium de suo sexu virili praebentes, debite tangerentur. Et dum invenirentur illaesi, clamabant tangentur alta voce dicentes: 'Testiculos habet!' Et reclamabant clerus et populus, 'Deo gratias!'"

16. William of Ockham, *Opus nonaginta dierum*, edited by J. G. Sikes et al. in *Opera politica* (Manchester: University of Manchester Press, 1940-63), 2: 854 [cap. 124].

17. Jean Gerson, *Apparavit gratio Dei* in *Oeuvres complétes*, edited by Palémon Glorieux (Paris: Desclee, 1960-71), 5:87.

18. Jan Hus, *Documenta Mag. Joannis Hus*, edited by Francis Palacky (1869; reprint, Osnabrück: Biblio-Verlag, 1966), p. 178.

19. See ibid., pp. 61, 178, 229, and 291, and Jan Hus, *Tractatus de Ecclesia*, edited by S. Harrison Thomson (Cambridge: Heffer, 1956), pp. 48, 103, 107, 141, 223.

20. As early as the mid-fifteenth century, Enea Sylvio Piccolomini (Pope Pius II from 1448-1464) fretted about how to answer critics who confronted the papacy with this scandalous affair. See *Der Briefwechsel des Eneas Silvius Piccolomini*, edited by Rudolf Wolkan (Vienna: Hölder, 1918), 3/1:40.

21. Martin Luther, *Werke: Kritische Gesammtausgabe: Tischreden*, vol. 5 (Weimar: Böhlau, 1967), no. 6447. See also no. 6452 and *Wider das Papsttum zu Rom, vom Teufel gestiftet* in *Werke*, 54:287.

22. Jean Calvin, *Vera christianae pacificationis et ecclesiae reformandae ratio* in *Opera quae supersunt omnia*, edited by Guilielmus Baum et al. (Braunschweig C. A. Schwetschke, 1868), p. 633.

23. John Foxe, *Papa Confutatus* (London: Thomas Dawson, 1580), 37ᵛ. English from the 1580 translation by James Beer, *The Pope Confuted: The Holy and Apostolique Church Confuting the Pope* (London: Thomas Dawson, 1580), p. 40.

24. For a survey of attitudes concerning the female pope in the Reformation, see Valerie R. Hotchkiss, "The Legend of the Female Pope in the Reformation," *Acta Conventus Neo-Latini Hafniensis: Proceedings of the Eighth International Congress of Neo-Latin Studies* (Binghamton: MRTS, 1994), pp. 495-505.

25. See Johannes Aventinus [Johann Turmair], *Annalium Boiorum liber septem* (Ingolstadt: Weissenhorn, 1554), p. 474. A similar view is expressed in E.R. Chamberlin, *The Bad Popes* (New York: Dial, 1969), pp. 25-39. According to Chamberlin, in the mid-ninth century Theodora and her daughter Marozia of the house of Theophylact were enormously influential in papal affairs. Some scholars have therefore attributed the origins of the legend to this period when powerful women were indeed running the papacy, though not actually sitting on the throne.

26. See Battista Platina, *Historia de vitis pontificum romanorum*, edited by Onofrio Panvinio (Cologne: Maternus Cholinus, 1568), pp. 134-37.

27. Ibid., p. 136.

28. Available to me only in the later edition *L'Anti-Christ et L'Anti-Papesse* (Paris: l'Angelier, 1599). For more information on the work of Raemond, see Barbara Sher Tinsley, "Pope Joan Polemic in Early Modern France: The Use and Disabuse of Myth," *Sixteenth Century Journal* 18 (1987):381-97.

29. David Blondel, *Familier esclaircissement de la question si une femme a este assise au siege papal de Rome entre Leon IV et Benoit III*. I used the Latin translation, *De Ioanna papissa* (Amsterdam: Bleau, 1657).

30. An exception is the late nineteenth-century author and papal critic Emmanuel Royidis, who wrote treatises defending the historicity of the female pope, as well as a romantic novel about her. See Royidis, *Pope Joan: A Historical Study*, translated by Charles Hastings Collette (London: Redway, 1886). His novel *Papissa Joanna* (Athens, 1886) has been translated by Lawrence Durrell, *Pope Joan* (New York: Dutton, 1960).

31. Boccaccio, *De mulieribus claris*, pp. 414-16.

32. Ibid., p. 416.

33. Ibid., p. 416.

34. Ibid., p. 416.

35. Hans Sachs, "Der Babst mit dem Kind," in Karl Drescher, "Hans Sachs und Boccaccio," *Zeitschrift für vergleichende Litteraturgeschichte* 7 (1894):407-16.

36. Ibid., p. 416.

37. Dietrich Schernberg, *Ein schön Spiel von Frau Jutten: nach dem Eislebener Druck von 1565*, edited by Manfred Lemmer (Berlin: Schmidt, 1971).

38. Ibid., p. 98.

39. Richard Haage, *Dietrich Schernberg und sein Spiel von Frau Jutten* (Marburg: Universitäts-Buchdruckerei, 1981), p. 31.

40. Schernberg, *Ein schön Spiel von Frau Jutten*, p. 17: "Aus Legendenspielen, aus Fastnachts- Weltgerichts-, Oster-, und Passionsspielen nahm er, was ihm für seine Zwecke brauchbar schien, kleine Szenen, Motive, Einzelwendungen oder ganze Sätze, und hat alles zu einem neuen Werk zusammengeschweißt."

41. Rosemary Pardoe and Darroll Pardoe, *The Female Pope: The Mystery of Pope Joan* (Wellingborough: Aquarian, 1988), pp. 26, 34, 83-84, mention Schernberg's play in passing several times but they give the incorrect date for the work and include only a brief summary.

42. See Haage, *Dietrich Schernberg und sein Spiel von Frau Jutten*, pp. 22-24.

43. Michael rescues souls from hell in other medieval dramas; see *Das Redentiner Osterspiel*, edited by Willy Krogmann (Leipzig: Hirzel, 1937), lines 669-82; *Das Alsfelder Passionsspiel*, edited by R. Froning, in *Das Drama des Mittelalters* (Stuttgart: Deutsche Verlagsgesellschaft, 1891), lines 6621ff.; and *Das Künzelsauer Fronleichnamsspiel vom Jahr 1479*, edited by Albert Schumann (Ohringen: Hohenlohesche Buchhandlung, 1925), lines 193-96.

44. Schernberg, *Ein schön Spiel von Frau Jutten*, lines 143-46.

45. She thanks her teacher in Paris in God's name (line 386), she prays to God that she and Clericus might obtain positions with the pope (line 436), and as pope she praises God (lines 679-81) and, most significant, promises to forgive all sinners by the power invested in her "durch den barmhertzigen Gott" (line 689). Until Gabriel gives her the choice between

a shameful death or everlasting torment for her offense, Jutta does not exhibit a clear understanding that what she did was wrong.

46. Schernberg, *Ein schön Spiel von Frau Jutten*, lines 897-98.

47. Ibid., after line 216.

48. See Maximilian Josef Rudwin, *Der Teufel in den deutschen geistlichen Spielen des Mittelalters und der Reformationszeit* (Göttingen: Vandenhoeck und Ruprecht, 1915).

49. Schernberg, *Ein schön Spiel von Frau Jutten*, lines 863-66.

50. Ibid., lines 879-80.

51. See ibid., lines 989-94:

> Wenn Gott hat mir die laub gegeben /
> Das ich dir sol nemen dein leben /
> Darumb / das du hast wider jhn gethan /
> Vnd hast gegangen wie ein Man /
> Vnde hast solch vngefug in der Christenheit getrieben /
> Vnd bist nicht ein Weibsbild geblieben.

> [God has given me permission to take your life because you have sinned against him and gone about as a man, and have perpetrated such mischief throughout Christianity, and did not remain a female.]

52. On the harrowing of hell in the Middle Ages, see Norbert H. Ott, *Rechtspraxis und Heilsgeschichte* (Munich: Artemis, 1983).

NOTES TO CHAPTER SIX

1. First told in the *Chronica Regia Coloniensis*, edited by Georg Waitz, *MGH: Scriptores Rerum Germanicorum*, 30:77 [under the year 1140]. The legend became popular in accounts of other sieges as well. For an overview of its dissemination in European folklore, see Jan de Vries, *Die Märchen von klugen Rätsellösern* (Helsinki: Suomalainen Tiedeakatemia, 1928), pp. 278-83.

2. For examples of the motif in folklore, see Thompson, *Motif-Index*, entries H923.1, R152, R152.2, T211.1, and T215.6-7.

3. The story is recorded in Herodotus, IV, 146. In Latin, the tale is included in Valerius Maximus (first century), *Facta et dicta memorabilia*, IV.6.3. Medieval retellings of the story appear in such popular works as Boccaccio's *De mulieribus claris*, cap. 31, and Christine de Pizan's *Livre de la cité des dames*, II.24.1.

4. See Thompson, *Motif-Index*, entries K521.4.1, R152.1, and R152.3, and Ernst Heinrich Rehermann, *Das Predigtexempel bei protestantischen Theologen des 16. und 17. Jahrhunderts* (Göttingen: Schwarz, 1977), pp. 163, 292, 374, 410, and 416. A historical case was recorded in 1645 when James,

Lord Ogilvy, escaped from prison the night before his scheduled execution by changing clothes with his sister Margaret during her final visit. When the trick was discovered, Margaret was not prosecuted. Eventually, Lord Ogilvy himself was pardoned. See Rosalind K. Marshall, *Virgins and Viragos* (London: Collins, 1983), pp. 161-62.

5. Texts in *Die deutsche Märendichtung des 15. Jahrhunderts*, pp. 330-37, and *Deutsche Dichtung im Mittelalter*, edited by Karl Goedeke and Hermann Oesterley (Dresden: Ehlermann, 1871), pp. 565-68. *Ritter Alexander* comes from the 1490 imprint of *Des pfaffen geschicht und histori vom Kalenberg. Auch von dem aller schönsten ritter Alexander unnd von seiner schonen frauwen* ([Heidelberg]: Heinrich Knoblochtzer, 1490). *Der Ritter auß Steyermarck*, attributed to Martin Meyer, is also known as *Triumnitas*.

6. *Deutsche Dichtung im Mittelalter*, p. 598.

7. *Die deutsche Märendichtung*, p. 336.

8. Ibid., p. 337. Wives are also addressed at the conclusion of *Der Ritter auß Steyermarck*; see *Deutsche Dichtung im Mittelalter*, p. 568: "Nempt ein Beyspiel bey diesem Weib, / sie hat jn trew beweret, / Gott gnad ewig jhr Seel und Leib, / sie hats zum besten kehret, / ein sach die unleidenlich was." [Learn from the example of this woman, she held her faith to him. May God always honor her soul and body; she turned things for the best in a situation that was unbearable.]

9. *Aucassin et Nicolette: chantefable du XIIIe siècle*, edited by Mario Roques (Paris: Champion, 1982).

10. The first modern edition of *Ysaÿe le Triste* appeared only recently: *Ysaÿe le Triste: Roman arthurien du moyen âge tardif*, edited by André Giacchetti (Rouen: Publications de l'Université de Rouen, 1989). Also available in the sixteenth-century edition, *Sensuit l'histoire de Ysaie le triste, filz Tristan de leonnois jadis chevalier de la table ronde: et de la royne Izeut de Cornouaille* (Paris: Philippe le Noir, [1530?]). A detailed synopsis can be found in Julius Zeidler, "Der Prosaroman *Ysaye le Triste*," *Zeitschrift für romanische Philologie* 25 (1901):175-214, 472-88, and 641-68. The lengthy, rambling adventure concerns second- and third-generation Arthurian knights. Although Marthe is a major character, her travels in disguise are a minor episode in the adventure.

11. Among the many adaptations of the story are a German ballad, *Der Graf von Rom* (ca.1550); a Low German *Volksbuch*, *Florentina de ghetrouwe* (1621); Latin plays by Jakob Bidermann (before 1639) and Paul Aler (1701); and German dramatizations (now lost) by Heinrich Knaust (1550) and Clemens Stephani (1584). See Johannes Bolte, "Deutsche Märchen aus dem Nachlasse der Brüder Grimm," *Zeitschrift des Vereins für Volkskunde* 26 (1916):19-33, for information on numerous other versions. Recent revivals of the story appear in the collection *Die Frau, die auszog, ihren Mann zu erlösen: Europäische Frauenmärchen*, edited by Sigrid Früh (Frankfurt: Fischer, 1985). According to the compiler, the stories were

collected in an effort to counterbalance the conservative view of women found in traditional fairy tales.

12. The text is printed in Bolte, "Deutsche Märchen," pp. 33-42.

13. Ibid., p. 41.

14. Ibid.

15. For bibliographic references, see Friedrich Schanze, "Der Graf von Rom," in *Die deutsche Literatur des Mittelalters: Verfasserlexikon*, 3:209-12.

16. Neither account can be historically documented. See Reinhold Röhricht, *Die Deutschen im Heiligen Lande* (Innsbruck: Wagner'sche Universitäts-Buchhandlung, 1894), pp. 136-37. Röhricht cites another tale of disguise, set in the twelfth century, about the bride of Konrad Bayer of Boppard, who armed herself as a knight to follow him. Unfortunately, Konrad assumed he was being pursued by a hostile knight and turned to fight, killing the woman. Röhricht offers no historical sources for this information.

17. For an overview of the popularity of the motif in French medieval literature, see Glynnis M. Cropp, "The Disguise of the Jongleur," *AUMLA: Journal of the Australasian Universities Language and Literature Association* 65 (1986):36-47, where many of the examples cited are discussed.

18. For plot summaries of Spielmannsepen, see Walter Johannes Schröder, *Spielmannsepik* (Stuttgart: Metzler, 1962). The motif of abduction in disguise can also be found in German literature in the heroic epic *Kudrun* (ca. 1240), where the minstrel Horant, disguised as a merchant, uses his musical skill to win Hilde for King Hetel. See *Kudrun*, edited by Karl Bartsch and Karl Stackmann (Wiesbaden: Brockhaus, 1965).

19. *König Rother*, edited by Theodor Frings and Joachim Kuhnt (Bonn: Schroeder, 1922).

20. *Salman und Morolf*, edited by Alfred Karnein (Tübingen: Niemeyer, 1979). See also *Der Münchener Oswald*, edited by Michael Curschmann (Tübingen: Niemeyer, 1974), a late twelfth-century religious *Spielmannsepos* in which Oswald uses disguise (as a goldsmith) in an elaborate plan to capture Pamige, the daughter of a heathen king. (It should be noted that Pamige later dresses as a knight to make her escape, but the disguise motif is not developed.)

21. Christine de Pizan, *Livre de la cité des dames*, pp. 913-23.

22. For bibliographic references to several pre-1500 editions, see Ferdinand Geldner, *Die deutschen Inkunabel-Drucker* (Stuttgart: Hiersemann, 1968), 1:180-82, and 247.

23. Hans Sachs, *Fraw Genura* in Hans Sachs, edited by Adalbert von Keller, *Bibliothek des litterarischen Vereins Stuttgart*, 140 (Tübingen: Laupp, 1879), pp. 40-63. Sach's play, however, is little more than an awkward

reproduction of the essential elements of the tale. Original to Sachs are the seven moral lessons adduced at the end.

24. Boccaccio, *Decameron*, edited by Vittore Branca (Milan: Mondadori, 1985), pp. 194-208. For Boccaccio's possible sources, see Marcus Landau, *Die Quellen des Dekameron* (Stuttgart: Scheible, 1884), pp. 135-45. The subsequent popularity of the tale of Zinevra is well documented in A.C. Lee, *The Decameron: Its Sources and Analogues* (New York: Haskell House, 1966), pp. 42-57.

25. Boccaccio, *Decameron*, p. 195. Translations quoted from *The Decameron*, translated by Mark Musa and Peter Bondannella (New York: Norton, 1982), pp. 140-52.

26. Ibid., p. 197.

27. Boccaccio, *Decameron*, p. 195.

28. False testimony of adultery based on the observation of body marks is common in stories of calumniated women; it occurs in *Le Roman de Violette*, *Le Roman du Comte de Poitiers*, and, as we will see, in *Le Conte du Roi Flore et de la belle Jehane*.

29. *Le Conte du Roi Flore et de la belle Jehane*, edited by Moland and d'Héricault in *Nouvelles françoises en prose du XIIIe siècle* (Paris: Jannet, 1856), pp. 83-157.

30. The rash wager is a common motif in folklore. For other examples, see Thompson, *Motif-Index*, entries N0-N25, and G. Paris, "Le Cycle de la Gageure," *Romania* 32 (1903):481-551. See also Roberta L. Krueger, "Double Jeopardy: The Appropriation of Woman in Four Old French Romances of the 'Cycle de la Gageure,'" in *Seeking the Woman in Late Medieval and Renaissance Writings: Essays in Feminist Contextual Criticism*, edited by Sheila Fisher and Janet E. Halley (Knoxville: University of Tennessee, 1989), pp. 21-50.

31. *Flore et Jehane*, p. 110.

32. This view was variously based on the authority of the Bible (esp. Genesis 3:16, Ephesians 5:22-24, Colossians 3:18) and Aristotle. The courtly knight of medieval love poetry likens himself to a slave, but in practice wives were legally subject to their husbands throughout medieval Europe.

33. *Flore et Jehane*, pp. 101-02. The servant claims that Raoul is a "chevalier biel et preu et sage [...] et est molt rices hom, et est plus biaus ke ne soit li couars fallis [Robiert] ki vous a laisie." [A knight fair and brave and wise [...] he is a very rich man and much more handsome than the coward who left you.] To fulfill a vow of pilgrimage, Robiert had left Jehane before the marriage could be consummated.

34. Ibid., p. 129. One of the few scholars to treat *Flore et Jehane*, Sheila Delany, "*Flore et Jehane*: A Case Study of the Bourgeois Woman in Medieval Life and Letters," *Science and Society* 45 (1981):272-87, argues that Jehane's business ventures illustrate that the opportunities for women in the Middle Ages were not as limited as they became in subsequent periods. Whether

or not the argument about women's positions in medieval society is valid, its application to Jehane is inappropriate since Jehane achieves success in business while disguised as a man.

35. *Flore et Jehane*, p. 130.

36. Ibid.

37. Wolfram von Eschenbach, *Willehalm*, edited by Werner Schröder (Berlin: de Gruyter, 1978), bk. IV.

38. *Kudrun*, p. 254.

39. *Flore et Jehane*, pp. 147-48.

40. Ibid., p. 152.

41. Ibid., p. 154.

42. *Le Roman du Comte d'Artois*, edited by Jean-Charles Seigneuret (Geneva: Droz, 1966).

43. *Riddarsögur*, edited by E. Bjarni Vilhjálmsson (Reykjavík: Islendingasagnaútgáfan, 1949-54), 2:137-94 (esp. pp. 160-68). A German synopsis is available in Jürg Glauser, *Isländische Märchensagen* (Basel: Helbing und Lichtenhahn, 1983), p. 271.

44. See Natalie Zemon Davis, "Women on Top," in *Society and Culture in Early Modern France* (Stanford: Stanford University Press, 1975), pp. 124-52, for a discussion of this type of comic and festive inversion.

45. Both texts were edited by Anatole de Montaiglon and Gaston Raynaud in *Recueil général et complet de fabliaux des XIIIe et XIVe siècles* (Paris: Librairie des Bibliophiles, 1872-90), 3:253-62 and 4:51-66. The relation between the two French versions has been discussed in Jean Rychner, *Contribution à l'étude des fabliaux* (Neuchâtel: Faculté des Lettres, 1960), 1:63-67, and Roy J. Pearcy, "Relations between the D and A Versions of 'Bérenger au long cul,'" *Romance Notes* 14 (1972):173-78.

46. *Recueil général et complet de fabliaux*, 3:259. The same choice is offered in the anonymous version; see ibid., 4:63-64.

47. The image of women in fabliaux is discussed in Raymond Eichmann, "The Anti-Feminism of the Fabliaux," *Authors and Philosophers: French Literature Series* 6 (1979):26-34.

48. *Ritter Beringer*, in *Maeren-Dichtung*, edited by Thomas Cramer (Munich: Wilhelm Fink, 1979), 1:71-81.

49. Ibid., line 290.

50. Ibid., lines 425-27, 432.

51. A.L. Stiefel, "Ritter Beringer und seine Quelle," *Zeitschrift für deutsches Altertum* 39 (1895):429.

52. *Ritter Beringer*, line 433.

53. Hans Folz, *Die Reimpaarsprüche*, edited by Hanns Fischer (Munich: Beck, 1961), pp. 4-6.

54. See Folz's portrayal of a lascivious princess in "Die halbe Birne"; ibid., pp. 22-28.

55. *Der Gürtel*, in *Gesammtabenteuer*, edited by Friedrich von der Hagen, 1:455-78. The work is also called *Der Borte*.

56. See Otto Richard Meyer, "Das Quellenverhältnis der 'Borten,'" *Zeitschrift für deutsches Altertum* 59 (1922):36-46, for a discussion of the possible sources. Ovid's version of the story appears in *Metamorphosis*, VII, lines 661-862.

57. In an interesting variation on the narrator's prologue, the poem itself speaks, naming its audience in line 7: "Man sol mich hovischen liuten lesen." [One ought to read me to courtly people.]

58. The trade of sexual favors for a magic belt calls to mind the later *Sir Gawain and the Green Knight* but I have not found any references to Dietrich von der Glezze's *Der Gürtel* in standard works on the analogues and sources of the Middle English poem, such as Elisabeth Brewer, *Sir Gawain and the Green Knight: Sources and Analogues*, 2d ed (Woodbridge: Brewer, 1992).

59. The woman claims to be a knight in female disguise, using the ruse to persuade an innkeeper to purchase male clothing and knightly accoutrements for her (see lines 471-90).

60. *Der Gürtel*, lines 795-801.

61. Ibid., lines 786-90.

62. Ibid., lines 869-74.

NOTES TO CHAPTER SEVEN

1. *Ovide moralisé*, edited by C. de Boer (Amsterdam: Noord-Hollandische Uitgeversmaatschappij, 1930), 3:291.

2. Ovid, *Metamorphoses*, 9:666-797.

3. See Franco Munari, *Ovid im Mittelalter* (Zürich: Artemis, 1960). For the discussion of Iphis, I will use the early fourteenth-century poem *Ovide moralisé*, edited by de Boer.

4. *L'Estoire de Merlin* is discussed below. The English and German works are available in the following editions: *Merlin or The Early History of King Arthur*, edited by Henry B. Wheately (London: Paul, 1898); and *Der rheinische Merlin: Text, Übersetzung, Untersuchungen der Merlin- und Lüthild-Fragmente*, edited by Hartmut Beckers (Paderborn: Schöningh, 1991), esp. pp. 40-46.

5. Lucy Allen Paton, "The Story of Grisandole: A Study in the Legend of Merlin," *PMLA* 22 (1902):234-76.

6. Kate Mason Cooper, "Elle and L: Sexualized Textuality in *Le Roman de Silence*," *Romance Notes* 25 (1985):341-60.

7. Howard Bloch, "Silence and Holes: The *Roman de Silence* and the Art of the Trouvère," *Yale French Studies* 70 (1986):81-99.

8. Ibid., p. 98.

9. Keith V. Sinclair, *Tristan de Nanteuil: Thematic Infrastructure and Literary Creation* (Tübingen: Niemeyer, 1983), pp. 38-42 and 98-105, discusses the language and motifs of disguise and gender change, comparing *Tristan de Nanteuil* with the *Roman de Silence* and *Yde et Olive*.

10. *Le Roman de Silence*, lines 2539-41. The edition by Lewis Thorpe is cited throughout.

11. Translations are cited according to Heldris de Cornuälle, *Le Roman de Silence*, translated by Regina Psaki (New York: Garland, 1991).

12. Over a hundred and sixty lines (1795-1958) are devoted to describing *Nature's* creation of Silence's ideal feminine form. In his description of Silence as *Nature's* finest work, Heldris draws on a common topos for *descriptio formosae*. See lines 2587-624, for *Noreture's* argument in favor of maleness.

13. *Le Roman de Silence*, lines 2627-52.

14. Ibid., lines 2528-29.

15. Ibid., line 2209.

16. Ibid., lines 2867-72.

17. Ibid., line 3824. Her femininity is stressed at several other points in the seduction scenes with phrases like "li vallés qui est mescine" (line 3785). See also lines 3763, 3871, 3954.

18. Ibid., line 3872-75.

19. Ibid., line 5572.

20. Ibid., lines 5149-56.

21. Ibid., lines 5177-85.

22. Ibid., lines 5604-10.

23. This devaluing of female heroism contradicts the argument of Kathleen C. Brahney, "When Silence Was Golden: Female Personae in the *Roman de Silence*," in *The Spirit of the Court: Selected Proceedings of the Fourth Congress of the International Courtly Literature Society*, edited by Glyn S. Burgess and Robert A. Taylor (Cambridge: Brewer, 1985), pp. 52-61, who explores the possibility that Heldris de Cornuälle was actually a woman who wrote "her own fantasy—the tale of what a great thirteenth-century heroine could do if she only had the encouragement and opportunity to do so." For a discussion of female heroism in the *Roman de Silence*, see Anita Benaim Lasry, "The Ideal Heroine in Medieval Romances: Quest for a Paradigm," *Kentucky Romance Quarterly* 32 (1985):227-43.

24. *Le Roman de Silence*, line 1843.

25. The task of capturing Merlin is doubly apt within the context of the narrative: not only will the successful capture reveal the heroine's true sexual identity, but it also affords Silence revenge for the wrong (a sexual transgression) perpetrated by Merlin against her ancestor Ygraine.

26. *Le Roman de Silence*, line 6628.

27. Ibid., lines 6397 and 6404-05.

28. Ibid., line 6627.

29. Ibid., line 6398.

30. *Ovide moralisé*, lines 2943-42.

31. Ibid., lines 2961-62.

32. Ibid., lines 2791-92.

33. In this view, I differ from Boswell, *Christianity, Social Tolerance, and Homosexuality*, pp. 152 and 237, who sees Ovid's Iphis and Ianthe as examples of lesbianism. Certainly, Iphis discusses lesbianism at some length, but she considers homosexual relations impossible.

34. See Perret, "Travesties et transsexuelles," pp. 332-33, on the mixture of masculine activity and feminine description. Although primarily concerned with the language used to dissimulate sex, Perret also concludes that the two solutions—conformity to apparent sex or resumption of actual sex—represent sexual polarities in which either cultural experience or nature dominates.

35. *Esclarmonde, Clarisse et Floret, Yde et Olive: Drei Fortsetzungen der Chanson von Huon de Bordeaux*, edited by Max Schweigel (Marburg: Elwert, 1889), lines 7065-06.

36. Ibid., lines 7246-47.

37. See *Tristan de Nanteuil, chanson de geste inédite*, edited by Keith V. Sinclair (Assen: Van Gorcum, 1971), lines 1730-2621 and 4273-335.

38. Ibid., lines 16171-73.

39. Ibid., lines 17572-73. This scene with homosexual undertones echoes an earlier scene that occurred soon after Blanchandine assumed male disguise (lines 12824-26). Presenting the new "knight" to his compatriots (who know the truth), Tristan says he is looking forward to sleeping with this knight to learn new love games. They laugh at his mock homosexuality.

40. *Ovide moralisé*, lines 2878-80.

41. Although the episode begins at court, we are told that her father has lost his lands and the family has been separated. Perhaps the loss of familial and social status explains the drastic name change. Neither Avenable nor Grisandole, however, is a gender distinctive name.

42. *L'Estoire de Merlin*, edited by H. Oskar Sommer (Washington, D.C.: Carnegie Institution, 1908), p. 282.

43. Her eloquence and manners, especially in the delicate exchanges with the enamored Clarinde, are impeccably courtly in tone; see *Tristan de Nanteuil*, lines 12999-13099, 13361-64, and 13496-504. Blanchandine does take up a sword when the wild stag rushes through the palace, yet her intention is not to pursue the beast but rather to use the opportunity to escape forced disrobing. After metamorphosis, however, Blanchandin becomes a famous warrior.

44. See Henrik Specht, "The Beautiful, the Handsome, and the Ugly: Some Aspects of the Art of Character Portrayal in Medieval Literature,"

Studia Neophilologica 56 (1984):129-46, for a discussion of the guidelines, including *nomen*, *natura*, and *habitus*, for character description as outlined in Cicero's *De inventione* and the works of several medieval rhetoricians.

45. Jean Loubier, *Das Ideal der männlichen Schönheit bei den altfranzösischen Dichtern des XII. und XIII. Jahrhunderts* (Halle: Kaemmerer, 1890), and Alice M. Colby, *The Portrait in Twelfth-Century French Literature* (Geneva: Droz, 1965), esp. pp. 104-12.

46. Colby, *The Portrait in Twelfth-Century French Literature*, pp. 104-12.

47. These are common topoi for beautiful men and women in French medieval literature. See ibid., pp. 30-32 and 43-45, for dozens of examples; Atys, Narcissus, Hector, Blancheflor, Sordamors, and Philomena are among the male and female beauties with blond hair and rosy and white complexions.

48. See *Le Roman de Silence*, lines 4417-56. Because of her beauty and nobility, the King of France hesitates to carry out the execution of Silence as ordered in the false message she is carrying.

49. *Tristan de Nanteuil*, line 12972. Facial hair is rarely mentioned in descriptions of male beauty in medieval French romance; in fact, a beard is often a sign of ugliness. See Colby, *The Portrait in Twelfth-Century French Romance*, pp. 81 and 93.

50. *Yde et Olive*, line 6806.

51. Ibid., lines 6597 and 6549-51.

52. *L'Estoire de Merlin*, p. 282. Both heroes and heroines of medieval romance are typically tall in stature. See Colby, *The Portrait in Twelfth-Century French Romance*, pp. 26-28.

53. Sally North, "The Ideal Knight as Presented in Some French Narrative Poems," in *The Ideals and Practice of Medieval Knighthood*, edited by Christopher Harper-Bill (Woodbridge: Boydell, 1986), p. 123.

54. Chrétien de Troyes, *Erec et Enide*, edited by Mario Roques (Paris: Champion, 1973), lines 85-88 and 411-23.

55. Ibid., 1495-1504. Translation is taken from Chrétien de Troyes, *Erec and Enide*, translated by Carleton W. Carroll (New York: Garland, 1987), p. 66.

56. Chrétien de Troyes, *Le Conte du Graal*, edited by Félix Lecoy (Paris: Champion, 1972), 1, lines 1824-27.

57. Ibid., lines 1862-63.

58. Ibid., lines 1864-72. A similar description of parallel beauty and resemblance appears in Wolfram's *Willehalm*, bk. VI, 274, where a brother and sister, Gyburc and Rennewart, are likened to one another.

59. The earliest extant version of the story is the French *Floire et Blancheflor* (ca. 1155-70), but throughout the Middle Ages the story was translated and retold in almost every European language, making it one of the most popular medieval romances. For a survey of the numerous

versions, see J. Reinhold, *Floire et Blancheflor: étude de littérature comparée* (Paris: Larose, 1906), pp. 16-49. I have used Margaret M. Pelan's edition, *Floire et Blancheflor* (Paris: Société d'Edition, 1956).

60. *Floire et Blancheflor*, lines 1542-48. For the other examples, see lines 1096-1101, 1273-79, and 1347-56.

61. Ibid., lines 2384-87. Later, when the emir investigates reports of a stranger in Blancheflor's bed, he is uncertain about the sex of the bedfellow until he pulls back the sheets (lines 2431-35).

62. Colby, *The Portrait in Twelfth-Century French Literature*, pp. 25-72.

NOTES TO CHAPTER EIGHT

1. Cassiodorus, *Expositio psalmorum, CCSL* 97:241-42.

2. Bynum, *Holy Feast and Holy Fast,* p. 282.

3. See Delcourt, *Hermaphrodite,* p. 98, and Warner, *Joan of Arc,* pp. 151-55.

4. The disguise failed, and she was imprisoned for fifteen years for trying to overthrow her husband. See Bonnie S. Anderson and Judith P. Zinsser, *A History of Their Own* (New York: Harper and Row, 1988), 1:302.

5. For the details of this case, see Michael H. Shank, "A Female University Student in Late Medieval Kraków," *Signs* 12 (1987):373-80.

BIBLIOGRAPHY

TEXTS

Acta apostolorum apocrypha. Edited by Richard Lipsius and Maximilian Bonnet. Leipzig, 1891-1903; reprint, Darmstadt: Wissenschaftliche Buchgesellschaft, 1959.

Acta Sanctorum quotquot toto orbe coluntur, vel a catholicis scriptoribus celebrantur. Edited by Joannes Bollandus et al. Paris: Palmé [etc., etc.], 1863-1940.

Ado. *Martyrologium.* Edited by Heribert Rosweyd. *PL* 123:139-436.

Aelfric. *Aelfric's Lives of the Saints.* Edited by Walter W. Skeat. Early English Text Society, nos. 76, 82, 94 and 114. London: Trübner, 1881-1900.

Aldhelm. *Aldhelmi Opera.* Edited by Rudolf Ehwald. *Monumenta Germaniae Historica: Auctorum Antiquissimi,* 15. Berlin: Weidmann, 1919.

Das Alsfelder Passionspiel. Edited by R. Froning. In *Das Drama des Mittelalters.* Stuttgart: Deutsche Verlagsgesellschaft, 1891.

Das altenglische Martyrologium. Edited by Günter Kotzor. Munich: Bayerische Akademie der Wissenschaften, 1981.

Ambrose. *Expositio Evangelii secundum Lucam.* Edited by M. Adriaen. *CCSL* 14:1-400.

Aquinas, Thomas. *Summa theologiae.* Edited by Blackfriars. New York: McGraw-Hill, 1964- .

Ariosto, Ludovico. *Orlando Furioso.* Edited by Cesare Segre. Milan: Mondadori, 1982.

Augustine. *Confessionum libri XIII.* Edited by Lucas Verheijen. *CCSL* 27.

Aucassin et Nicolette: Chantefable du XIIIe siècle. Edited by Mario Roques. Paris: Champion, 1982.

Aventinus, Johannes [Johann Turmair]. *Annalium Boiorum libri septem.* Ingolstadt: Weissenhorn, 1554.

Basil of Caesarea. *Ascetica. PG* 31:619-26.

Bede. *Martyrologium poeticum* and *Martyrologia.* Edited by Smith and Giles. *PL* 94.

Bernard of Clairvaux. *Sancti Bernardi opera.* Edited by Jean Leclercq and H.M. Rochais. Rome: Editiones Cisterciensis, 1957-77.

Bibliotheca hagiographica graeca. 3rd ed. François Halkin. Brussels: Société des Bollandistes, 1957.

Bibliotheca hagiographica latina antiquae et mediae aetatis. Edited by Socii Bollandiani. Brussels: Société des Bollandistes, 1898-1901.

Bibliotheca hagiographica orientalis. Edited by Socii Bollandiani. Brussels: Société des Bollandistes, 1910.

Boccaccio, Giovanni. *De casibus virorum illustrium.* Edited by Pier Giorgio Ricci and Vittore Zaccaria. Milan: Mondadori, 1983.

—————. *De mulieribus claris.* Edited by Vittore Zaccaria. Milan: Mondadori, 1967.

—————. *Decameron.* Edited by Vittore Branca. Milan: Mondadori, 1985.

—————. *The Decameron.* Translated by Mark Musa and Peter Bondannella. New York: Norton, 1982.

Bonaventure des Périers. *Le Nouvelles récréations et joyeux devis.* Edited by Louis Lacour. Paris: Librairie des Bibliophiles, 1874.

Burchard of Worms. *Opera omnia. PL* 140.

Caesarius of Heisterbach. *Dialogus miraculorum.* Edited by J. Strange. Cologne: Lempertz, 1851.

Calderón de la Barca, Pedro. *Las comedias de D. Pedro Calderón de la Barca.* Edited by Juan Jorge Keil. Leipzig: Fleischer, 1829.

Calvin, Jean. *Opera quae supersunt omnia.* Edited by Guilielmus Baum et al. Braunschweig: C.A. Schwetschke, 1868.

Cassiodorus. *Expositio psalmorum.* Edited by M. Adriaen, *CCSL* 97.

Catalogus codicum hagiographicorum bibliothecae regiae Bruxellensis. Edited by Hagiographi Bollandiani. Brussels: Polleunis, Ceuterick, et De Smet, 1886-89.

Les Cent nouvelles nouvelles. Edited by Franklin P. Sweetser. Geneva: Droz, 1966.

Chapelain, Jean. *La Pucelle ou la France délivrée.* Paris: Libraire Marpon & Flammarion, 1656.

Chrestomathie de l'ancien français (VIIIe - XVe siècles). Edited by Karl Bartsch and Leo Wiese. New York: Hafner, 1969.

Chrétien de Troyes. *Le Conte du Graal.* Edited by Félix Lecoy. Paris: Champion, 1972.

—————. *Erec et Enide.* Edited by Mario Roques. Paris: Champion, 1973.

—————. *Erec and Enide.* Translated by Carleton W. Carroll. Introduction by William W. Kibler. New York: Garland, 1987.

Christine de Pizan. *Ditié de Jehanne d'Arc.* Edited and translated by Angus J. Kennedy and Kenneth Varty. Oxford: Society for the Study of Mediaeval Languages and Literature, 1977.

—————. "The *Livre de la cité des dames* of Christine de Pisan: A Critical Edition." Edited by Maureen Cheney Curnow. Ph.D. diss., Vanderbilt University, 1975.

—————. *Livre de la mutacion de fortune.* Edited by Suzanne Solente. Paris: Picard, 1959-66.

Chronica minor auctore minorita Erphordiensi. Edited by Oswald Holder-Egger. *Monumenta Germaniae Historica: Scriptores,* 24:172-213. Hannover, 1879; reprint, Stuttgart: Hiersemann, 1975.

Chronica Regia Coloniensis. Edited by George Waitz. *MGH: Scriptores Rerum Germanicorum,* 30. Hannover, 1879; reprint, Stuttgart: Hiersemann, 1975.

Chronicon universalis Mettensis. Edited by Georg Waitz. *Monumenta Germaniae Historica: Scriptores,* 24:502-26. Hannover, 1879; reprint, Stuttgart: Hiersemann, 1975.

Daza, Antonio. *Historia, vida, y milagros, extasis, y revelaciones de la Iuana de la Cruz.* Madrid: Sanchez, 1613.

—————. *The History ... of the Blessed Virgin, Sister Joane (1625).* English Recusant Literature, 335. London: Scolar, 1977.

Decretum Gratiani emendatum et notationibus...Gregorii XIII. Edited by Justus Henning Boehmer. *PL* 187.

The Desert Christian: Sayings of the Desert Fathers. Translated by Benedicta Ward. New York: Macmillan, 1980.

Deutsche Dichtung im Mittelalter. Edited by Karl Goedeke and Hermann Oesterley. Dresden: Ehlermann, 1871.

Die deutsche Märendichtung des 15. Jahrhunderts. Edited by Hanns Fischer. Munich: Beck, 1966.

Eckhart, Meister. *Meister Eckhart: Die deutschen und lateinischen Werke.* Edited by Albert Zimmermann, Loris Sturlese, Josef Quint et al. Stuttgart: Kohlhammer, 1958.

[Engelhard von Langheim]. "Vitae und Miracula aus Kloster Ebrach." Edited by Joseph Schwarzer. *Neues Archiv der Gesellschaft für ältere deutsche Geschichtskunde* 6 (1881):515-29.

Esclarmonde, Clarissa et Floret, Yde et Olive: Drei Fortsetzungen der Chanson von Huon de Bordeaux. Edited by Max Schweigel. Marburg: Elwert, 1889.

L'Estoire de Merlin. Edited by H. Oskar Sommer. Washington, D.C.: Carnegie Institution, 1908.

The First Biography of Joan of Arc with the Chronicle Record of a Contemporary Account. Translated by Daniel Rankin and Claire Quintal. Pittsburgh: University of Pittsburgh, 1964.

Flodard. *De triumphis Christi. PL* 135:491-886.

Floire et Blancheflor. Edited by Margaret M. Pelan. Paris: Société d'Edition, 1956.

Flores temporum. Edited by O. Holder-Egger. *Monumenta Germanicae Historica: Scriptores,* 24:226-50. Hannover, 1879; reprint, Stuttgart: Hiersemann, 1975.

Folz, Hans. *Die Reimpaarsprüche.* Edited by Hanns Fischer. Munich: Beck, 1961.

Foresti, Jacopo Filippo da Bergamo. *De claris scelerisque mulierbus.* Edited by Albertus de Placentia and Augustinus de Casali Mairori. Ferrara: Laurentius de Rubeis, 1497.

Foxe, John. *Papa Confutatus.* London: Thomas Dawson, 1580.

——————. *The Pope Confuted: The Holy and Apostolique Church Confuting the Pope.* Translated by James Beer. London: Thomas Dawson, 1580.

Die Frau, die auszog, ihren Mann zu erlösen: Europäische Frauenmärchen. Edited by Sigrid Früh. Frankfurt: Fischer, 1985.

The French Fabliaux: B.N. MS. 837. Edited and translated by Raymond Eichmann and John Duval. New York: Garland, 1985.

Gerbert de Montreuil. *Le Roman de la Violette ou Gerart de Nevers.* Edited by Douglas Labaree Buffum. Paris: Société des Anciens Textes Français, 1928.

Gerson, Jean. *Oeuvres complétes.* Edited by Palémon Glorieux. Paris: Desclée, 1960-71.

Gesammtabenteuer: Hundert altdeutsche Erzählungen. Edited by Friedrich von der Hagen. Stuttgart: Cotta, 1850.

The Gospel According to Thomas. Edited and translated by A. Guillaumont et al. New York: Harper, 1959.

Gregory of Tours. *Gloria confessorum.* Edited by Wilhelm Arndt and Bruno Krusch. *Monumenta Germaniae Historica: Scriptores Rerum Merovingicarum,* 1:744-820. Berlin: Weidmann, 1885.

Gregory the Great. *Dialogorum libri IV. PL* 77.

Guillaume de Blois. *Guilelmi Blesensis Aldae Comoedia.* Edited by Carl Lohmeyer. Leipzig: Teubner, 1892.

Hall, Edward. *The Union of the Two Noble and Illustre Families of Lancastre and York.* London: Richard Grafton, 1548.

Heldris de Cornuälle. *Le Roman de Silence.* Edited by Lewis Thorpe. Cambridge: Heffer, 1972.

——————. *Le Roman de Silence.* Translated by Regina Psaki. New York: Garland, 1991.

Hemmerlin, Felix. *De nobilitate et rusticitate dialogus.* [Strassburg: Johann Prüss, ca. 1493-1500].

Hrabanus Maurus. *Martyrologium*. Edited by John McCulloh. *CCCM* 44.

Hrotsvitha von Gandersheim. *Opera*. Edited by Helene Homeyer. Munich: Schöningh, 1970.

Hugo von Trimberg. *Das "Registrum multorum auctorum" des Hugo von Trimberg*. Edited by Karl Langosch. Berlin, 1942; reprint, Nendeln/Liechtenstein: Kraus, 1969.

Hus, Jan. *Tractatus de Ecclesia*. Edited by S. Harrison Thomson. Cambridge: Heffer, 1956.

—————. *Documenta Mag. Joannis Hus*. Edited by Francis Palacky. 1869; reprint, Osnabrück: Biblio-Verlag, 1966.

Jerome. *Commentarius in Epistolam ad Ephasios*. Edited by Valtarsi and Maffei. *PL* 26.

—————. *Epistolae*. *PL* 22.

Kirchhof, Hans Wilhelm. *Wendunmuth*. Edited by Hermann Österley. *Bibliothek des litterarischen Vereins*, 95-99. Tübingen: Laupp, 1869.

König Rother. Edited by Theodor Frings and Joachim Kuhnt. Bonn: Schroeder, 1922.

Kudrun. Edited by Karl Bartsch and Karl Stackmann. Wiesbaden: Brockhaus, 1965.

Das Künzelsauer Fronleichnamsspiel vom Jahre 1479. Edited by Albert Schumann. Ohringen: Hohenlohesche Buchhandlung, 1925.

The Life of Christina of Markyate. Edited and translated by C.H. Talbot. Oxford: Clarendon, 1959.

Luther, Martin. *D. Martin Luthers Werke: Kritische Gesammtausgabe*. Weimar: Böhlau, 1883- .

Maeren-Dichtung. Edited by Thomas Cramer. Munich: Fink, 1979.

Malespini, Celio. *Ducento novelle*. Venice, 1609.

Marguerite de Navarre. *L'Heptaméron*. Edited by Michel François. Paris: Garnier, 1981.

Martinus Polonus. *Chronicon pontificum et imperatorum*. Edited by Ludwig Weiland. *Monumenta Germaniae Historica: Scriptores*, 22:377-482. Hannover, 1872; reprint, Stuttgart: Hiersemann, 1976.

Medieval Handbooks of Penance. Translated by John T. McNeill and Helena M. Gamer. New York: Columbia University Press, 1938.

Merlin or The Early History of King Arthur. Edited by Henry B. Wheately. London: Paul, 1898.

Methodius. *Le Banquet*. Edited by Herbert Musurillo; translated by Victor-Henry Debidour. Paris: Cerf, 1963.

Miracles de nostre dames par personnages. Edited by Gaston Paris and Ulysse Robert. Paris: Didot, 1876-93.

Moschius, Joannis. *Pratum spirituale*. Edited by Heribert Rosweyd. *PG* 87/3:2847-112.

Der Münchener Oswald. Edited by Michael Curschmann. Tübingen: Niemeyer, 1974.

Natalibus, Petrus de. *Catalogus sanctorum et gestorum eorum ex diversis voluminibus collectus*. [Edited by Antonio Verlo.] Vicenza: Henricus de Sancto Ursio, 12 December 1493.

Nettesheim, Heinrich Cornelius Agrippa von. *De incertitudine et vanitate omnium scientium et artium*. [Antwerp, 1531].

Notker. *Martyrologium*. *PL* 131:1029-164.

Nouvelles françoises en prose du XIIIe siècle. Edited by L. Moland and C. d'Hericault. Paris: Jannet, 1856.

Ovide moralisé. Edited by C. de Boer. Amsterdam: Noord-Hollandische Uitgeversmaatschappij, 1930.

Palladius. *Historia Lausiaca*. Edited by Cuthbert Butler. Cambridge: Cambridge University Press, 1898.

Passio Sanctarum Perpetuae et Felicitatis. Edited by Cornelius Ioannes Maria Ioseph Van Beek. Nijmegen: Dekker & Van de Vegt, 1936.

Des pfaffen geschicht und histori vom Kalenberg. Auch von dem aller schönsten ritter Alexander unnd von seiner schonen frauwen. [Heidelberg]: Heinrich Knoblochzer, 1490.

Piccolomini, Enea Silvio. *Der Briefwechsel des Eneas Silvius Piccolomini*. Edited by Rudolf Wolkan. Vienna: Hölder, 1918.

Platina, Battista. *Historia de vitis pontificum romanorum*. Edited by Onofrio Panvinio. Cologne: Maternus Cholinus, 1568.

Procès de condamnation et de réhabilitation de Jeanne d'Arc dite La Pucelle. 5 vols. Compiled and edited by Jules Quicherat. Paris: Renouard, 1841-49.

Procès en nullité de la condemnation de Jeanne d'Arc. 5 vols. Edited by Pierre Duparc. Paris: Klincksieck, 1977-89.

Recueil géneral et complet des fabliaux des XIIIe et XIVe siècles. Edited by Anatole de Montaiglon and Gaston Raynaud. Paris: Librairie des Bibliophiles, 1872-90.

Das Redentiner Osterspiel. Edited by Willy Krogmann. Leipzig: Hirzel, 1937.

Der rheinische Merlin: Text, Übersetzung, Untersuchungen der Merlin- und Lüthild-Fragmente. Edited by Hartmut Beckers. Paderborn: Schöningh, 1991.

Riddarsögur. Edited by E. Bjarni Vilhjálmsson. Reykjavík: Islendingasagnaútgáfen, 1949-54.

Robert of Flamborough. *Liber poenitentialis*. Edited by J.J. Francis Firth. Toronto: Pontifical Institute of Mediaeval Studies, 1971.

Le Roman de Galerent. Edited by Anatole Boucherie. Paris: Maisonneuve et Leclerc, 1888.

Le Roman du Comte d'Artois. Edited by Jean-Charles Seigneuret. Geneva: Droz, 1966.

Royidis, Emmanuel. *Pope Joan.* Translated by Lawrence Durrell. New York: Dutton, 1960.

Sachs, Hans. *Fraw Genura.* In *Hans Sachs.* Edited by Adalbert von Keller, vol. 12:40-63. *Bibliothek des litterarischen Vereins Stuttgart,* 140. Tübingen: Laupp, 1879.

——————. "Der Babst mit dem Kind." (Meisterlied, 29 March 1532). Printed in Karl Drescher, "Hans Sachs und Boccaccio." *Zeitschrift für vergleichende Litteraturgeschichte* 7 (1894):407–16.

Saint Joan of Orleans: Scenes from the Fifteenth-Century "Mystère du Siège d'Orléans." Edited by Paul Studer, translated by Joan Evans. Oxford: Clarendon, 1926.

Salman und Morolf. Edited by Alfred Karnein. Tübingen: Niemeyer, 1979.

Schernberg. Dietrich. *Ein schön Spiel von Frau Jutten: nach dem Eislebener Druck von 1565.* Edited by Manfred Lemmer. Berlin: Schmidt, 1971.

Scriptores ordinis praedicatorum. Edited by Jacob Quetif and Jacob Echard. Paris: Christophor Ballard and Nicolaus Simart, 1719.

Sensuit l'histoire de Ysaie le triste, filz Tristan de leonnois jadis chevalier de la table ronde: et de la royne Izeut de Cornouaille. Paris: Philippe le Noir, [1530?].

Speculum magnum exemplorum omnibus christicolis salubriter inspiciendum ut exemplis discant disciplinam. Strasbourg: [Georg Husner], 1490.

Speculum virginum. Edited by Jutta Seyfarth. *CCCM* 5.

Straßburger Zunft- und Polizei-Verordnungen des 14. und 15. Jahrhunderts. Edited by Johann Brucker and G. Wethly. Strasbourg: Trübner, 1889.

Three Coptic Legends: Hilaria, Archellites, The Seven Sleepers. Edited and translated by James Drescher. *Supplément aux annales du service des antiquités de l'Egypte,* 4. Cairo: L'Institute Français d'Archéologie Oriental, 1947.

Tristan de Nanteuil, chanson de geste inédite. Edited by Keith V. Sinclair. Assen: Van Gorcum, 1971.

Ulrich von Liechtenstein. *Frauendienst.* Edited by Reinhold Bechstein. Leipzig: Brockhaus, 1888.

Valerius Maximus. *Factorum et dictorum memorabilium libri novem.* Edited by Carl Kempf. Berlin, 1854; reprint, Hildesheim: Olms, 1976.

Vie et office de Sainte Marine. Edited by Leon Clugnet. Paris: Picard, 1905.

Vincent de Beauvais. *Speculum quadruplex sive speculum maius.* Duaci, 1624; reprint, Graz: Akademische Druck- und Verlagsanstalt, 1965.

"Vita Hildegundis metrica." Edited by W. Wattenbach. *Neues Archiv der Gesellschaft für ältere deutsche Geschichtskunde 6* (1881):533-36.

Vitae Patrum. Edited by Heribert Rosweyde. *PL* 73.

Voragine, Jacobus de. *Legenda aurea.* Edited by Th. Graesse. Breslau, 1890; reprint, Osnabrück: Zeller, 1969.

The Vulgate Version of the Arthurian Romances. Edited by H. Oskar Sommer. Washington, D.C.: Carnegie Institute, 1908.

William of Ockham. *Opera politica.* Edited by J. G. Sikes et al. Manchester: Manchester University Press, 1940-63.

Wolf, Johannes. *Lectionum memorabilium et reconditarum centenarii XVI.* Lauingen: Rheinmichel, 1600.

Wolfram von Eschenbach. *Willehalm.* Edited by Werner Schröder. Berlin: de Gruyter, 1978.

Ysäye le Triste: Roman arthurien du moyen âge tardif. Edited by André Giacchetti. Rouen: Publications de l'Université de Rouen, 1989.

SECONDARY LITERATURE

Ackroyd, Peter. *Dressing Up: Transvestism and Drag, the History of an Obsession.* New York: Simon and Schuster, 1979.

Anderson, Bonnie S., and Judith P. Zinnser. *A History of Their Own: Women in Europe from Prehistory to the Present.* New York: Harper & Row, 1988.

Andresen, Jeffrey J. "Rapunzel: The Symbolism of the Cutting of Hair." *Journal of the American Psychoanalytic Association* 28 (1980):69-88.

Anson, John. "The Female Transvestite in Early Monasticism: The Origin and Development of a Motif." *Viator* 5 (1974):1-32.

Aspergren, Kerstin. *The Male Woman: A Feminine Ideal in the Early Church.* Stockholm: Almqvist and Wiksell, 1990.

Bakhtin Mikhail. *Rabelais and his World.* Translated by H. Iswolsky. Cambridge: MIT Press, 1968.

Barstow, Anne Llewellyn. *Joan of Arc.* New York: Mellen, 1986.

A Benedictine Bibliography. Compiled by Oliver L. Kaspner. Collegeville, Minn.: St. John's Abbey Press, 1962.

Bennasser, Khalifa A. "Gender and Sanctity in Early Byzantine Monasticism: A Study in the Phenomenon of Female Ascetics in Male Monastic Habit." Ph.D. diss., Rutgers University, 1984.

Benz, Richard Edmund. *Heidelberg: Schicksal und Geist*. Konstanz: Thorbecke, [1961].

Bignami-Odier, J. "Les Visions de Robert d'Uzès O. P." *Archivum Fratrum Praedicatorum* 25 (1955):258-310.

Bloch, Howard. "Silence and Holes: The *Roman de Silence* and the Art of the Trouvère." *Yale French Studies* 70 (1986):81-99.

Blondel, David. *Familier esclaircissement de la question si une femme a este assise au siege papal de Rome entre Leon IV et Benoit III*. Amsterdam: Blaeu, 1647.

—————. [Latin translation]. *De Ioanna papissa: sive famosae quaestionis, an foemina ulla inter Leonum IV, et Benedictum III, Romanos Pontifices, media sederit ἀνάκρισις*. Amsterdam: Blaeu, 1657.

Body Guards: The Cultural Politics of Gender Ambiguity. Edited by Julia Epstein and Kristina Straub. New York: Routledge, 1991.

Bolte, Johannes. "Deutsche Märchen aus dem Nachlasse der Brüder Grimm." *Zeitschrift des Vereins für Volkskunde* 26 (1916):19-33.

Boswell, John. *Christianity, Social Tolerance, and Homosexuality*. Chicago: University of Chicago Press, 1980.

Bravo-Villasante, Carmen. *La mujer vestida de hombre en el teatro español: siglos XVI-XVII*. Madrid: Sociedad General Español de Libreria, 1976.

Brewer, Elisabeth. *Sir Gawain and the Green Knight: Sources and Analogues*. 2d ed. Woodbridge: Brewer, 1992.

Brown, Peter. *The Body and Society: Men, Women and Sexual Renunciation in Early Christianity*. New York: Columbia University Press, 1988.

Bullough, Vern L. *The Subordinate Sex: A History of Attitudes Towards Women*. Urbana: University of Illinois Press, 1973.

—————. "Transvestites in the Middle Ages." *Journal of American Sociology* 79 (1974):1381-94.

Bullough, Vern L., and Bonnie Bullough. *Cross Dressing, Sex, and Gender*. Philadelphia: University of Pennsylvania Press, 1993.

Bynum, Caroline Walker. *Holy Feast and Holy Fast*. Berkeley: University of California Press, 1987.

—————. "Women's Stories, Women's Symbols: A Critique of Victor Turner's Theory of Liminality." In *Anthropology and the Study of Religion*, edited by Robert L. Moore and Frank

E. Reynolds. Chicago: Center for the Scientific Study of
Religion, 1984, pp. 105-24.

Cadden, Joan. *Meanings of Sex Difference in the Middle Ages:
Medicine, Science, and Culture*. Cambridge: Cambridge
University Press, 1993.

Chamberlin, E.R. *The Bad Popes*. New York: Dial, 1969.

Clark, Elizabeth. *Women in the Early Church*. Wilmington: Glazier,
1983.

Cloke, Gillian. *This Female Man of God: Women and Spiritual Power
in the Patristic Age, 350-450*. New York: Routledge, 1994.

Colby, Alice M. *The Portrait in Twelfth-Century French Literature*.
Geneva: Droz, 1965.

Cooper, Kate Mason. "Elle and L: Sexualized Textuality in *Le
Roman de Silence*." *Romance Notes* 25 (1985):341-60.

Cropp, Glynnis M. "The Disguise of the Jongleur." *AUMLA:
Journal of the Australasian Universities Language and Literature
Association* 65 (1986):36-47.

Daniélou, Jean. "Die Symbolik des Taufritus." *Liturgie und
Mönchtum* 3 (1949):45-8.

Davis, Natalie Zemon. "Women on Top." In *Society and Culture
in Early Modern France*. Stanford: California University Press,
1975, pp. 124-152.

Dekker, Rudolf M., and Lotte C. van de Pol. *The Tradition of Female
Transvestism in Early Modern Europe*. New York: St. Martins,
1989.

Delany, Sheila. "*Flore et Jehane*: A Case Study of the Bourgeois
Woman in Medieval Life and Letters." *Science and Society* 45
(1981):272-87.

Delcourt, Marie. *Hermaphrodite: Myths and Rites of the Bisexual
Figure in Classical Antiquity*. Translated by Jennifer
Nicholson. London: Studio Books, 1961.

Döllinger, Johannes Joseph Ignaz von. *Die Papstfabeln des
Mittelalters: Ein Beitrag zur Kirchengeschichte*. 2nd ed.
Stuttgart: Cotta, 1890.

Dollimore, Jonathan. *Sexual Dissidence*. Oxford: Clarendon, 1991.

D'Onofrio, Cesare. *Mille anni di leggenda: una donna sul trono de
Pietro*. Rome: Romana Societá Editrice, 1978.

Dunbar, Agnes B.C. *A Dictionary of Saintly Women*. London: Bell,
1904-05.

Eichmann, Raymond. "The Anti-Feminism of the Fabliaux."
Authors and Philosophers: French Literatures Series 6 (1979):26-
34.

Eisenbart, Constance. *Kleiderordnungen der deutschen Städte zwischen 1350 und 1700: Ein Beitrag zur Kulturgeschichte des deutschen Bürgertums.* Göttingen: Musterschmidt, 1962.

Ellis, Havelock. *Studies in the Psychology of Sex.* New York: Random House, [1936].

Erudition at God's Service. Edited by John R. Sommerfeldt. Kalamazoo: Cistercian Publications, 1987.

Favazza, Armado R. "Normal and Deviant Self-Mutilation." *Transcultural Psychiatric Research Review* 26 (1989):113-27.

Feminist Approaches to the Body in Medieval Literature. Edited by Linda Lomperis and Sarah Stanbury. Philadelphia: University of Pennsylvania Press, 1993.

Foucault, Michel. *The History of Sexuality.* Translated by Robert Hurley. New York: Vintage, 1990.

Frauenmystik im Mittelalter. Edited by Peter Dinzelbacher and Dieter R. Bauer. Ostfildern bei Stuttgart: Schwabenverlag, 1985.

Freeburg, Vincent Oscar. *Disguise Plots in Elizabethan Drama.* New York: Columbia University Press, 1915.

Freud, Sigmund. *Gesammelte Werke.* Edited by Anna Freud et al. London: Imago, 1940-52.

Fuss, Diana. *Essentially Speaking.* New York: Routledge, 1989.

Garber, Marjorie. *Vested Interests: Cross Dressing and Cultural Anxiety.* New York: Routledge, 1992.

Geldner, Ferdinand. *Die deutschen Inkunabel-Drucker.* Stuttgart: Hiersemann, 1968.

Gessler, Jean. *La Légende de sainte Wilgeforte ou Ontcommer: la vierge miraculeusement barbue.* Brussels: Editions Universelle, 1938.

Gies, Frances. *Joan of Arc: The Legend and the Reality.* New York: Harper & Row, 1981.

Glauser, Jürg. *Isländische Märchensagen.* Basel: Helbing und Lichtenhahn, 1983.

Griesser, Bruno. "Engelhard von Langheim und sein Exempelbuch für die Nonnen von Wechterswinkel." *Cistercienser-Chronik* 70 (1963):55-73.

Gubar, Susan. "Blessings in Disguise: Cross-Dressing and Re-Dressing for Female Modernists." *Massachusetts Review* 22 (1981):477-507.

Haage, Richard. *Dietrich Schernberg und sein Spiel von Frau Jutten.* Marburg: Universitäts-Buchdruckerei, 1891.

Harmand, Andrien. *Jeanne d'Arc, ses costumes, son armure.* Paris: Leroux, 1929.

Hefele, Charles Joseph. *Histoire des conciles.* Paris: Letouzey et Ané, 1907.

Heise, Ursula K. "Transvestism and the Stage Controversy in Spain and England, 1580-1680." *Theatre Journal* 44 (1992):357-74.

Hirschfeld, Magnus. *Die Transvestiten: Eine Untersuchung über den erotischen Verkleidungstrieb mit umfangreichem casuistischen und historischen Material.* Berlin: Pulvermacher, 1910.

A History of Private Life. Vol. 2. Edited by Philippe Ariès and Georges Duby. Cambridge: Harvard University Press, 1987.

Hotchkiss, Valerie R. "The Legend of the Female Pope in the Reformation." *Acta Conventus Neo-Latini Hafniensis: Proceedings of the Eighth International Congress of Neo-Latin Studies.* Binghamton: MRTS, 1994, pp. 495-505.

Huffschmid, Maximilian. "Beiträge zur Geschichte der Cisterzienserabtei Schönau bei Heidelberg." *Zeitschrift für die Geschichte des Oberrheins* 6 (1891):416-49.

The Ideals and Practice of Medieval Knighthood. Edited by Christopher Harper-Bill. Woodbridge: Boydell, 1986.

Images of the Feminine in Gnosticism. Edited by Karen King. Philadelphia: Fortress, 1988.

Jelinek, Estelle C. "Disguise Autobiographies: Women Masquerading as Men." *Women's Studies International Forum* 10 (1987):53-62.

Krafft-Ebing, Richard von. *Psychopathia Sexualis, eine klinisch-forensische Studie.* Stuttgart: Enke, 1886.

Krappe, Alexander Haggerty. "*Tristan de Nanteuil.*" *Romania* 61 (1935):65-71.

Kristeva, Julia. *Desire in Language.* Edited by Leon S. Roudiez, translated by T. Gora, A. Jardine, and Leon S. Roudiez. New York: Columbia University Press, 1980.

Landau, Marcus. *Die Quellen des Dekameron.* Stuttgart: Scheible, 1884.

Laqueur, Thomas. *Making Sex: Body and Gender from the Greeks to Freud.* Cambridge: Harvard University Press, 1990.

Lasry, Anita Benaim. "The Ideal Heroine in Medieval Romances: Quest for a Paradigm." *Kentucky Romance Quarterly* 32 (1985):227-43.

Lee, A.C. *The Decameron: Its Sources and Analogues.* New York: Haskell House, 1966.

Legenda aurea: sept siècles de diffusion. Actes du colloque international sur la Legenda aurea: texte latin et branches vernaculaires à l'Université du Quebec à Montréal, 11-12 mai 1983. Edited by Brenda Dunn-Lardeau. Montreal: Bellarmin, 1986.

Liebers, Andrea. *"Eine Frau war dieser Mann": Die Geschichte der Hildegund von Schönau.* Zürich: eFeF Verlag, 1989.

Loubier, Jean. *Das Ideal der männlichen Schönheit bei den altfranzösischen Dichtern des XII. und XIII. Jahrhunderts.* Halle: Kaemmerer, 1890.

Lucas, Valerie R. "Hic Mulier: The Female Transvestite in Early Modern England." *Renaissance and Reformation/Renaissance et Reforme* 12 (1988):65-84.

Lyons, John D. *A Theater of Disguise: Studies in French Baroque Drama* (1630-1660). Columbia, S.C.: French Literature Publications, 1978.

Marshall, Rosalind K. *Virgins and Viragos.* London: Collins, 1983.

Masque et déguisements dans la littérature médiévale. Edited by Marie-Louise Ollier. Montreal: Vrin, 1988.

Meyer, Otto Richard. "Das Quellen-Verhältnis der 'Borten.'" *Zeitschrift für deutsches Altertum* 59 (1922):36-46.

Munari, Franco. *Ovid im Mittelalter.* Zürich: Artemis, 1960.

Nauerth, Claudia, and Rüdiger Warns. *Thekla: Ihre Bilder in der frühchristlichen Kunst.* Wiesbaden: Harrassowitz, 1981.

Oppel, Hans D. "Die exemplarischen Mirakel des Engelhard von Langheim." Ph.D. diss., University of Würzburg, 1976.

Ott, Norbert. *Rechtspraxis und Heilsgeschichte.* Munich: Artemis, 1983.

Pardoe, Rosemary, and Darroll Pardoe. *The Female Pope: The Mystery of Pope Joan.* Wellingborough, Northamptonshire: Aquarian, 1988.

Paris, G. "Le Cycle de la Gageure." *Romania* 32 (1903):481-551.

Patlagean, Evelyne. "L'Histoire de la femme déguisée en moine et l'évolution de la sainteté féminine à Byzance." *Studi Medievali* 17 (1976):597-623.

Paton, Lucy A. "The Story of Grisandole: A Study of the Legend of Merlin." *PMLA* 22 (1907):234-76.

Pavlovskis, Zoja. "The Life of St. Pelagia the Harlot: Hagiographic Adaptation of Pagan Romance." *Classical Folio* 30 (1976):138-49.

Pearcy, Roy J. "Relations between the D and A Versions of *Bérenger au long cul.*" *Romance Notes* 14 (1972):173-78.

Perret, Michèle. "Travesties et Transsexuelles: Yde, Silence, Grisandole, Blanchandine." *Romance Notes* 25 (1985):328-40.

Peyronnet, Georges. "Gerson, Charles VII et Jeanne d'Arc: La Propagande au service de la guerre." *Revue d'Histoire Ecclesiastique* 84 (1989):339-70.

Pfeiffer, Ernst. "Die Pilgerfahrt der heiligen Hildegund von Schönau." *Cistercienser-Chronik* 47 (1935):198-200.

Pinzino, Jane Marie. "Devil or Angel? Fifteenth-Century Verdicts on Joan of Arc." Diss., University of Pennsylvania, 1996.

Price, David. "When Women Would Rule: Reversal of Gender Hierarchy in Sixteenth-Century German Drama." *Daphnis* 20 (1991):147-66

Rackin, Phyllis. "Androgyny, Mimesis, and the Marriage of the Boy Heroine on the English Renaissance Stage." *PMLA* 102 (1987):29-41.

Raknem, Ingvald. *Joan of Arc in History, Legend and Literature.* Oslo: Universitetsforgaget, 1971.

Radermacher, Ludwig. *Hippolytus und Thekla: Studien zur Geschichte von Legende und Kultus. Sitzungsbericht der kaiserlichen Akademie der Wissenschaft in Wien. Philosophisch-historische Klasse,* 182. Vienna: Hölder, 1916.

Raemond, Florimond de. *L'Anti Christ et L'Anti-Papesse* Paris: L'Angelier, 1599.

——————. *Erreur populaire de la Papess Jane.* Bordeaux: Millanges, 1587.

Rehermann, Ernst Heinrich. *Das Predigtexempel bei protestantischen Theologen des 16. und 17. Jahrhunderts.* Göttingen: Schwarz, 1977.

Reichl, Anton. *Die Beziehungen zwischen Schernbergs "Spiel von Frau Jutten" und dem niederdeutschen Theophilus.* Arnau: Gymnasialprogramm, 1890.

ReImagining Women: Representations of Women in Culture. Edited by Shirley Neuman and Glennis Stephenson. Toronto: University of Toronto Press, 1993.

Reinhold, Joachim. *Floire et Blancheflor: étude de littérature comparée.* Paris: Larose, 1906.

Rice, Eugene F., Jr. *Saint Jerome in the Renaissance.* Baltimore: Johns Hopkins University Press, 1985.

Riley, Hugh M. *Christian Initiation.* Washington, D.C.: Catholic University Press, 1974.

Röhricht, Reinhold. *Die Deutschen im heiligen Lande.* Innsbruck: Verlag der Wagner'schen Universitäts-Buchhandlung, 1894.

Royidis, Emmanuel. *Pope Joan: A Historical Study.* Translated by Charles Hastings Collette. London: Redway, 1886.

Rudwin, Maximilian Josef. *Der Teufel in den deutschen geistlichen Spielen des Mittelalters und der Reformationszeit.* Göttingen: Vandenhoeck und Ruprecht, 1915.

Rychner, Jean. *Contribution à l'étude des fabliaux.* Neuchâtel: Faculté des Lettres, 1960.

Salmonson, Jessica Amanda. *The Encyclopedia of Amazons: Women Warriors from Antiquity to the Modern Era.* New York: Paragon, 1991.

Schaab, Meinrad. *Die Zisterzienserabtei Schönau im Odenwald.* Heidelberg: Winter, 1963.

Schanze, Friederich. "Der Graf von Rom." *Die deutsche Literatur des Mittelalters: Verfasserlexikon,* 3:209-12.

Schleiner, Winfried. "Male Cross-Dressing and Transvestism in Renaissance Romances." *Sixteenth Century Journal* 19 (1988):605-19.

Schröder, Edward. "Goethe's *Faust* und *Das Spiel von Frau Jutten.*" *Deutsche Vierteljahrsschrift für Literaturgeschichte* (1891):333-39.

Schröder, Walter Johannes. *Spielmannsepik.* Stuttgart: Metzler, 1962.

Schurer, Gustav, and Joseph M. Ritz. *Sankt Kümmernis und Volto Santo: Studien und Bilder.* Düsseldorf: Schwann, [1934].

Seeking the Woman in Late Medieval and Renaissance Writings: Essays in Feminist Contextual Criticism. Edited by Sheila Fisher and Janet E. Halley. Knoxville: University of Tennessee, 1989.

Séminaire d'Histoire des Textes (Paris). *Pelagie la Pénitente: metamorphoses d'une légende.* Paris: Etudes Augustiniennes, 1981-84.

Sinclair, Keith V. *Tristan de Nanteuil: Thematic Infrastructure and Literary Creation.* Tübingen: Niemeyer, 1983.

Shank, Michael H. "A Female University Student in Late Medieval Kraków." *Signs* 12 (1987):373-80.

Söder, Rosa. *Die apokryphen Apostelgeschichten und die romanhafte Literatur der Antike.* Stuttgart, 1932; reprint, Stuttgart: Kohlhammer, 1969.

Specht, Henrik. "The Beautiful, the Handsome, and the Ugly: Some Aspects of the Art of Character Portrayal in Medieval Literature." *Studia Neophilologica* 56 (1984):129-46.

The Spirit of the Court: Selected Proceedings of the Fourth Congress of the International Courtly Literature Society. Edited by Glyn S. Burgess and Robert A. Taylor. Cambridge: Brewer, 1985.

Stallybrass, Peter, and Allon White. *The Politics and Poetics of Transgression.* London: Methuen, 1986.

Stiefel, A.L. "Ritter Beringer und seine Quelle." *Zeitschrift für deutsches Altertum* 39 (1895):426-29.

Tavard, George H. *Women in the Christian Tradition.* Notre Dame: University of Notre Dame Press, [1972].

Thompson, Stith. *Motif-Index of Folklore-Literature.* Bloomington: Indiana University Press, 1955.

Thurston, Herbert. "The Story of St. Hildegund: Maiden and Monk." *The Month* 127 (1916):145-56.

Tinsley, Barbara Sher. "Pope Joan Polemic in Early Modern France: The Use and Disabuse of Myth." *Sixteenth Century Journal* 18 (1987):381-97.

Usener, Hermann. "Legenden der heiligen Pelagia." In *Vorträge und Aufsätze*. Leipzig: Teubner, 1907.

Vries, Jan de. *Die Märchen von klugen Rätsellösern: Eine vergleichende Untersuchung*. FF Communications 73. Helsinki: Suomalainen Tiedeakatemia, 1928.

Waitz, Georg. "Über kleine Chroniken des dreizehnten Jahrhunderts." *Neues Archiv der Gesellschaft für ältere deutsche Geschichtskunde* 3 (1878):49-76.

Warner, Marina. *Alone of All Her Sex: The Myth and Cult of the Virgin Mary*. New York: Knopf, 1976.

—————. *Joan of Arc: The Image of Female Heroism*. London: Weidenfeld and Nicolson, 1981.

Wayman, Dorothy G. "The Chancellor and Jeanne d'Arc." *Franciscan Studies* 17 (1957):273-305.

Weiland, Ludwig. "Die Chronik des Predigermönches Johannes von Mailly." *Archiv der Gesellschaft für ältere deutsche Geschichte* 12 (1874):469-73.

Wheelwright, Julie. *Amazons and Military Maids: Women Who Dressed as Men in the Pursuit of Life, Liberty, and Happiness*. London: Pandora, 1989.

Williams-Krapp, Werner. "Euphrosyne." In *Die deutsche Literatur des Mittelalters: Verfasserlexikon*. Edited by Kurt Ruh et al., vol. 2:641-42.Berlin: de Gruyter, 1977– .

Women in the Middle Ages and the Renaissance. Edited by Mary Beth Rose. Syracuse: Syracuse University Press, 1986.

Wood, Charles T. "The Doctor's Dilemma: Sin, Salvation and the Menstrual Cycle in Medieval Thought." *Speculum* 56 (1981):710-727.

—————. *Joan of Arc and Richard III: Sex, Saints, and Government in the Middle Ages*. New York: Oxford University Press, 1988.

Worstbrock, F.J. "Hildegund von Schönau." In *Die deutsche Literatur des Mittelalters: Verfasserlexikon*, 4:4-8.

Zeidler, Julius. "Der Prosaroman *Ysaye le Triste*." *Zeitschrift für romanische Philologie* 25 (1901):175-214, 472-88, 641-68.

Die Zisterzienser: Ordensleben zwischen Ideal und Wirklichkeit. Katalog zur Ausstellung des Landschaftsverbandes Rheinland, Rheinisches Museumsamt, Brauweiler. Edited by K. Elm, P. Joerissen, and H. J. Roth. Cologne: Rheinland-Verlag, 1981.

Zobeltitz, Fedor von. "Die Päpstin Johanna: ein Beitrag zur Kuriositätenlitteratur." *Zeitschrift für Bücherfreunde* 2 (1898):279-90 and 437-39.

Zwierzina, Konrad. "Der Pelagiatypus der fabulosen Märtyrerlegende." *Nachrichten von der Gesellschaft der Wissenschaften zu Göttingen*. Philologisch-historische Klasse. Berlin: Weidmann, 1928.

INDEX